THE
BIG
HEIST

ALSO BY ANTHONY M. DESTEFANO

The King of the Godfathers

Mob Killer

THE BIG HEIST

The Real Story of the Lufthansa Heist, the Mafia, and Murder

ANTHONY M. DESTEFANO

CITADEL PRESS
Kensington Publishing Corp.
www.kensingtonbooks.com

CITADEL PRESS BOOKS are published by

Kensington Publishing Corp.
119 West 40th Street
New York, NY 10018

All Kensington titles, imprints, and distributed lines are available at special quantity discounts for bulk purchases for sales promotions, premiums, fundraising, educational, or institutional use.

Special book excerpts or customized printings can also be created to fit specific needs. For details, write or phone the office of the Kensington sales manager: Kensington Publishing Corp., 119 West 40th Street, New York, NY 10018, attn: Sales Department; phone 1-800-221-2647.

CITADEL PRESS and the Citadel logo are Reg. U.S. Pat. & TM Off.

ISBN-13: 978-0-8065-3830-3
ISBN-10: 0-8065-3830-9

First Citadel hardcover printing: July 2017

10 9 8 7 6 5 4 3 2 1

Printed in the United States of America

Library of Congress CIP data is available.

First electronic edition: July 2017

ISBN-13: 978-0-8065-3831-0
ISBN-10: 0-8065-3831-7

CONTENTS

INTRODUCTION

THERE IS NOTHING GOOD HAPPENING AT 3:00 A.M. when someone cries out for help in a desolate cargo area at John F. Kennedy International Airport. Rolf Rebmann, a security guard at Building 261 which happened to be the Lufthansa Airlines cargo terminal, heard the scream and despite his unease went over to ask of a man standing by a black Ford van whether he needed assistance.

"Can I help you?" Rebmann asked.

"No," the man replied. His voice sounded like the cold of the December night.

His next reaction wasn't to say thank you but rather to pull out a snub-nosed .38 caliber handgun, stick it in Rebmann's face and order the startled airport worker to get in the back of the van. Do as you are told. Fast.

Shaking with fear as he was hustled into the back of the van, Rebmann noticed another man lying facedown in the vehicle, someone with a bloody face and whose cry earlier had alerted the security guard to trouble. Whatever he made as a salary wasn't enough for the unarmed Rebmann to try any heroics. Certainly not in the darkness of a cold night. Not any night. He did what he was told and thus became a reluctant witness to a crime that he and the rest of America would never forget.

Of all the Mafia heists, rip-offs, scores, and plunders, none has been more iconic a part of American popular culture than the brazen robbery done by a group of New York gangsters on December 11, 1978, at John F. Kennedy International Airport. In the very early hours, as most of the city slept, a crew of thieves and killers, who were armed with inside knowledge of the airport security system, beat, threatened, and otherwise terrorized workers at the Lufthansa airline cargo terminal. When it was all over, the criminals disappeared before the sun came up with over $5 million in U.S. currency and nearly $1 million in jewels. The loot, which in 2016 would have had an equivalent value, taking into account inflation, of nearly $22 million, has never been recovered.

True, more valuable cargoes have been stolen over the years than what was taken from the high-value room at the Lufthansa terminal that morning. In August 1963, a gang of at least seventeen held up a British Royal Mail train in Buckinghamshire and made off with 2.6 million pounds sterling, the equivalent at the time of $7.4 million. Securities, bearer bonds, and stock certificates sent through the airlines and with a value of tens of millions of dollars were purloined years before the Lufthansa theft. One thief named Robert Cudak admitted to Congressional investigators that while working at JFK as a cargo handler he and his accomplices notched up $100 million in stolen jewels, cash, and securities, usually through stealth and a little ingenuity.

But it really didn't matter which case set the world record for an armed robbery. Happening as it did in the media and Mafia capital of the world, the 1978 Lufthansa heist became an obsessively covered news event and earned the reputation as being one of the biggest rip-offs ever, certainly in the United States. One pundit believed that the success of the armed thieves made people in New York feel good that finally somebody could do something nasty and get away with it.

"If they pull it off, I say hats off," one denizen of Frankie & Johnnie's Steakhouse told columnist Pete Hamill the day after the crime.

Cops got a pretty good early line on who ripped off Lufthansa after they discovered the black van used by the gang in the getaway from the airport. The van was supposed to be taken to a junkyard for destruction. But as the old adage says: If anything can go wrong it will. The hapless man who was supposed to take care of the vehicle never did so and would eventually pay for his screw-up with his life.

Fingerprints and shoe prints lifted from the vehicle put police and the FBI on the trail of a number of suspects, and it seemed like there would be a break in the case. Informants came up with some of the same names. But after months of work, investigators would convict only one man—lowly Lufthansa cargo employee Louis Werner—for his role in the crime. The bigger Mafia fish would elude justice, particularly after a number of mob associates who took part in the robbery—as well as some of their lady friends—wound up dead or missing.

The growing body count added to the dark allure of the Lufthansa caper, and over the years the story spawned a number of books, notably Nicholas Pileggi's *Wiseguy*, which was turned into the hit film *GoodFellas*. The film made mob associate Henry Hill (whose character was played by actor Ray Liotta) a household name. Hill was the central figure in both the book and movie, which showed Mafia life in all its glamour, gore, and futility. Hill grew up in Brooklyn and was one of an army of poor kids, all of whom aspired to grow up to become a gangster. Lucky for Hill, he became connected to the Lucchese crime family crew of Paul Vario and his associate Jimmy Burke, whose characters in *GoodFellas* were played by Paul Sorvino and Robert DeNiro, respectively. A complex man who mixed homicidal terror with smoothness and courtesy as he served his Mafia bosses, it was Burke who put together the crew of men who pulled off the Lufthansa raid, although Hill himself actually wasn't around to directly participate.

Other books followed, including one co-authored by Hill, who died in 2012. But Hill's book, and the others that retold the story of the heist essentially ended their narratives in the early 1980s. That is when Hill was ensconced in the federal witness protection program, living a life with new identities for himself, his wife Karen, and

their two children, away from New York. The books from that period fleshed out details of the heist and spun theories about where
the loot may have wound up. At that point the Lufthansa saga became firmly part of Mafia legend and lore. It remained a crime that
eluded justice, and with the passage of time seemed destined to stay
that way.

Then in early 2014, an entire generation of Millennials who
weren't even born when the Lufthansa robbery occurred were introduced to the case when an elderly, irascible, down-on-his-luck gangster named Vincent Asaro was indicted by a Brooklyn federal grand
jury. The charges against Asaro, whose son, father, grandfather, and
uncle were also part of the mob, were varied and numerous. But the
biggest and most sensational accusation seemed to come out of left
field: Asaro played an active role in the JFK robbery and helped
divvy up the loot, giving some of it to a powerful Bonanno crime
family member named Joseph Massino.

For Mafia aficionados, the 2014 Asaro indictment was an astonishing blast from the past and promised to finally solve the mystery
of what happened to the $6 million airport haul. The case also held
out the promise that—at last—a major player would finally be held
accountable, even though Burke and everyone else who took part
was long dead. Federal prosecutors, some of whom also weren't
even born when the heist occurred, painted Asaro as a major, un-
publicized member of Burke's team of thieves. He was also portrayed as a brutal killer, accused in the indictment of strangling with
a dog chain a Queens trucker and hijacker named Paul Katz. Prosecutors dressed up the case by indicting a few of Asaro's alleged
compatriots in the Bonanno family, notably reputed street boss
Thomas DiFiore, but only for some garden variety crimes not connected to the Lufthansa case. They were secondary characters and
soon would plead out to lesser charges and be gone from the case.

The FBI had as its main witness against Asaro his own cousin
and confidante, Gaspare Valenti, a wannabe gangster who never
made it to the mob big leagues and turned to the government for
help when he was broke and disillusioned with what the Mafia had

become. On paper, the case against Asaro seemed strong, particularly with the fact that for over three years he was secretly tape recorded by Valenti. The tapes showed, federal prosecutors argued, that Asaro, as well as Valenti, took part in the heist with Burke and his gang of bandits

Rehashing as it did the events depicted in *GoodFellas*, Asaro's trial in the fall of 2015 was a reprise of Mafia history from a time when the Five Families of the mob wielded great power and influence. All of the gangsters seemed to have money, and they flouted their lawless lives with no shame. But by the time Asaro faced the jury, the clout of organized crime had greatly diminished in the Big Apple. Cooperating witnesses turned up all over the place, showing how greatly diminished the Mafia creed of silence—*omertà*—had become. Asaro's own Bonanno crime family had been decimated by FBI investigations led by some of the very federal prosecutors who were trying to send him away to prison for what was left of his life. They were confident in the strength of their case and that the sensational crime would finally have its day in court, solving years of mystery.

But while federal prosecutors win convictions in over 90 percent of their cases, you can never tell with a jury. Despite the testimony of Valenti and mob turncoats like former Bonanno underboss Salvatore Vitale and Peter Zuccaro, the six men and six women whose job it was to weigh Asaro's fate were unconvinced. On November 12, 2015, right after the lunch break, the jury unanimously acquitted Asaro of the charges against him, and he walked out of the Brooklyn courtroom a free man, stunned, smiling, and striding with his arm around both his two women attorneys who were young enough to be his granddaughters and whose lives he had sometimes made miserable during the trial. Of course in victory Asaro treated them like his best friends.

The Big Heist is the book that will be the definitive and I think final story about the crime. Purists may say that the cash haul was only $5 million, but, let us face it, the jewelry also taken was of no use to the mob unless converted to cash—hence the $6 million total.

The Asaro trial laid out details and allegations that had never emerged before in previous renditions of the story. These details are presented here thanks to the voluminous trial record. In addition, confidential sources have provided information that showed how corrupted law enforcement had become in some places, notably Queens and Brooklyn. What also makes *The Big Heist* different from previous books on the subject is that it takes a longer historical look at the way New York City had become an open city for the Mafia in the years before the JFK crime. The Five Families lorded over a number of industries—the garment district, the docks, construction, carting, as well as the airports. The mob exercised that control by coercion, ownership over businesses, and union corruption. Such power allowed two crime families in particular, the Bonanno and Lucchese families, to hold sway over JFK, turning the airport into a veritable cash register as mob crews ripped off cargo almost at will.

Knowing how powerful the Mafia was back in the day is an important part in understanding how the Lufthansa score was able to take place. But that is only part of the story. For decades, law enforcement was behind the eight ball when it came to mob investigations, a state of affairs that created an atmosphere where gangsters had a certain invincibility. Under the leadership of its late director J. Edgar Hoover, the FBI refused to go after the Mafia in any concerted way. When in the early 1970s the FBI was finally building cases they seemed to be piecemeal and half-hearted efforts. Veteran FBI agents remembered that the agency's New York office didn't even have open investigations into the likes of Gambino boss Paul Castellano or even his underboss Aniello Dellacroce. The situation wasn't much better for the law enforcement with the other Five Families. Bureau files on the Mafia were filled with outdated intelligence and gossip. They would have been better off just reading the newspapers.

The situation was often as bad with the NYPD, something Henry Hill and Jimmy Burke knew well. Cops and more seasoned detectives whose job it was to go after the Mafia were instead cozying up to gangsters. During the course of researching this book, I came across disturbing and previously tightly held law-enforcement information about allegations that some NYPD investigators working in the Queens District Attorney's Office were feeding information to the mob. Among the allegations were that detectives even may have assisted in hiding evidence of Paul Katz's demise.

Police corruption was systematic and gave gambling and drug operations a lot of room to maneuver. This was particularly true in the late 1960s and early to mid-1970s, the very period when Henry Hill and his mentor Jimmy Burke were in their prime and running their rackets. In turn, Hill and Burke and their band of killers and thieves paid tribute, quite literally, to Mafia bosses like Paul Vario, whose character Paul Cicero in *Goodfellas* was played by actor Paul Sorvino. Vario and his bosses like Carmine Tramunti (the successor to Thomas Lucchese) were able to consolidate their power with the knowledge that they had co-opted law enforcement to a degree. Scores of NYPD officers were often observed frequenting Vario's Brooklyn junkyard, and it was a fair bet that they weren't all there to find replacements for lost hubcaps.

I was just a neophyte crime reporter in New York City when the heist happened. While I had then recently completed a groundbreaking series for *Women's Wear Daily* about the Mafia in the garment business, I really wasn't on top of all the things happening in the mob. But covering the mob on Seventh Avenue soon gave me a solid grounding in the Five Families and I was able to absorb what writers like Pileggi were doing in setting the bar for crime reporting. The challenge in writing *The Big Heist* was how to extend the story beyond the previous telling of the tale. With Hill's death, we are left only with his accounts as told to Pileggi and Dan Simone, the latter who penned *The Lufthansa Heist: Behind The Six-Million-Dollar Cash Haul That Shook the World* with Hill. But with Hill having gone through bouts of drug and alcohol abuse, a researcher has to be careful about his recollection of events. There is also the nagging suspicion that Hill in later years may have embellished events or had been confused. Burke and his notorious crew are all dead, and any account of the heist that tries to recreate the words, actions, and motives of that gang have to be viewed with some skepticism since anyone who was a direct participant is no longer available.

Thankfully, the passage of time created new opportunities and new sources of information to bring to life the story of the heist and deadly events that surrounded it. Since the early 1980s, when many of the earlier accounts of the heist were written, the federal government went on a concerted rampage against the Mafia, building cases and creating a body of evidence through wiretaps, photographs, and informants that has exposed the inner workings of the mob in a way that we never had before. The investigation of the Bonanno family, capped with Massino's conviction and his decision in 2004 to become the first official boss of a New York crime family to cooperate with prosecutors, gave investigators new sources of information about the likes of Asaro and helped build the case against him.

But it was Valenti's decision to turn on Asaro that gave federal investigators ammunition to finally put together the 2014 Lufthansa indictment. Whether or not you agree with Valenti's mercenary reasons for turning on his cousin, the secret tapes he made showed there was some circumstantial evidence to support the idea that Asaro had a role in Lufthansa. Testifying for the government, Valenti fleshed out through his trial testimony the allegations that Asaro was involved in the heist. Much of what Valenti recalled on the witness stand rang true, at least so far as it was consistent with Hill's own accounts and previous testimony in the Werner case.

Asaro had never before been *publicly* linked to Lufthansa: he certainly didn't show up in Hill's published accounts, although he did surface in a few references in *Wiseguy*. As spelled out in Pileggi's seminal account, Asaro hung out in Burke's mob club, ran a junkyard, and allegedly, as the Bonanno family liaison at JFK, was due a cut of the proceeds (but who, in the book, was said never to have received anything). Until the 2014 indictment, Asaro was not in any way part of the popular and public story line that had developed over the years since the 1978 robbery. In his testimony, Valenti puts himself right on the scene when the heist occurred and contended that Asaro was near the airport in a vehicle with Burke and helped hide the loot. These were all new allegations, at least for the public. Yet in the end, while Valenti sounded convincing, he didn't carry the day for the government. It remains a fair question for the hardened skeptic as to how truly involved Asaro was and even if he was, did he play an important part in the conspiracy?

The Big Heist will explore what went wrong with the case against Asaro and how he was able to win an acquittal. Federal prosecutors, once confident they had a strong case against Asaro, were stunned in defeat. Critics, including some very experienced attorneys and investigators, believed the case was over-tried, with too much evidence that proved too confusing for the jury. Others think the jurors viewed an aging Asaro as a scapegoat who was being prosecuted for a crime many had all but forgotten.

The Big Heist is divided into three sections, covering decades of New York mob history. The first section, chapters 1 through 6, portrays the Mafia world Asaro was a part of in the years leading up to the heist. It was a world in which the Five Families were at or near the pinnacle of their power in New York City, policing themselves with untold murders as they squeezed various industries through extortion, thefts, and scams. Chapters 7 through 12 reveal how the heist was spawned from the financial desperation of Werner, a hapless man who found a willing accomplice in Burke and his band of thieves. As a career criminal, Burke was the expert mechanic of crime who could figure out how to carry out the heist. But his failing was in his reliance on bone-headed accomplices who pushed him into an orgy of killing to prevent federal investigators from implicating him in the crime. Chapters 13 through 22 deal with Valenti's betrayal of Asaro at the Lufthansa trial, a prosecution that resulted in the stunning acquittal.

Asaro's trial took place over a ten-day period in the fall of 2015. The extensive trial record developed in the case plays an important part in the preparation of this book. I also had the benefit of the trial records of the Werner case thanks to the National Archives. There were also numerous interviews with investigators and access to previously undisclosed law-enforcement files. Asaro's case provides the framework for the retelling of the Lufthansa story in a way that helps the reader to understand what it was like in the world of La Cosa Nostra in the days before and after December 1978. It is also a coda to the evolving story of the Mafia in New York City, still an important part of our social history even in the face of its diminished power.

July 2016
New York, N.Y.

CHAPTER ONE
THE MESSAGE FROM THE BONES

BRADLEY ADAMS WAS SOMEONE who was not squeamish when confronted with the dead. As a forensic anthropologist, he was around human remains all of the time. The pieces could be as large as a thigh bone or as small as a fingernail. Adams's subjects usually never died peacefully.

As a child visiting his grandparents' funeral home in Kansas, Adams had to go through the embalming area to get to the garage when he stayed with them on school vacations. Sometimes he would see the deceased on the preparation table, although he was spared seeing the corpses having embalming fluid pumped into their body cavities. Their internal organs would have been sliced open with a trocar, a blade designed to cut a person' s internal organs so that the fluid could be more readily absorbed by the lifeless tissue. He didn't have to witness that procedure either.

No, dead people didn't seem to bother Bradley Adams. As a college man he took to specializing in archeology and worked on prehistoric sites in the United States and Central America. He then became more interested in the forensic aspect of science, spending time in graduate school at a body farm in Tennessee. It was a place where, in the interests of science, corpses were placed all over the grounds in various states of burial—or no burial at all. The bodies were consigned to this natural state so that scientists could study the decomposition of human bodies in assorted situations. Students like

Brad Adams would sometimes have to stick their hands—gloved of course—into the decaying flesh to understand what was happening to our mortal remains. At first he thought the putrefaction might make him vomit or pass out. But, no, Brad Adams discovered he wasn't bothered by it. It was something you got used to.

There aren't many jobs for forensic anthropologists. It is a rather rarified field with most of the positions in big cities or at major universities. However, Adams was good enough at what he did that he got a job with the Office of the Chief Medical Examiner in New York City as the resident forensic anthropologist and was something of a legend, the go-to guy whenever cops needed help when a body or human remains were found. He knew his stuff and was often loaned out to study cases all over the world.

Prior to joining the OCME, as the office is known, Adams worked with the U.S. military in Hawaii, the headquarters of the command that was responsible for finding and identifying the remains of U.S. servicemen killed in various conflicts. He spent time in Vietnam to sort through the graves of U.S. servicemen killed in the war. Adams even did the same in North Korea, where he was kept in a guarded compound after the Communist government there allowed American experts in to examine what were believed to be the graves of Americans killed in the Korean War. The North Koreans did relax things enough that Adams and his colleagues were able to go on guided tours during weekends.

In New York City, the cases Brad Adams was called to deal with weren't as politically charged as the wartime stuff. If the NYPD or other law enforcement agencies telephoned it was a safe bet that Adams would be going to what could be a crime scene to examine the remains of some unfortunate. It could be a railroad siding, a ditch, a sewer, a sandy beach, the inside of an apartment, even a drainage pipe in a cemetery: Brad Adams had been to just about any place imaginable where a dead body or bones might wind up.

On June 18, 2013, the request for assistance to Brad Adams came from the Manhattan office of the Federal Bureau of Investigation. Agents were preparing to dig in the basement of an attached home in Ozone Park, a section of the Borough of Queens. They had a tip—a pretty good one from a trustworthy source—that the remains of a murder victim might be under the concrete floor. If they found something, Adams would be needed to do a quick examination to determine if the finds were human and then take them back to his lab for further analysis. To keep Adam's mind open and to avoid saying anything suggestive that might later taint the investigation, the agents didn't tell him very much about the victim.

It wasn't uncommon for cops to come across bones, only to discover they were not human. In fact, in Brooklyn once under the basement floor of an old mob social club police uncovered some bones after an informant swore that many bodies had been buried there. They found bones all right, but they turned out to be those of a horse. Fragments of chickens sometimes littered city parks in the aftermath of Santeria or other religious rituals. After years of study Adams could quickly tell if the bones he was looking at were those of a person. He had co-authored a forensic textbook on the subject, complete with photographs comparing human bones with those of animals ranging from birds to water buffalo. Alligators it turned out had shoulder blades very similar to those of a man, Adams noted.

Adams had actually been alerted by the FBI about the dig a day earlier, June 17. It was then that the agency's evidence response team showed up with jackhammers, pick axes, shovels and other tools to begin digging in the basement floor of 81-48 102nd Road. To cover all their bases, the agents also did some digging in the backyard. The bureau's informant had said the body was toward the rear of the cellar, under some relatively fresh cement by a door. That was enough for the agents to get a search warrant from a federal judge. The residents really had no say in the matter. Agents unlocked the garage door, which was at the end of an inclined driveway and started to work inside. News media crews eventually showed up and took photographs of the agents, who had set up a blue tent at the house to shield their work from prying eyes as they started to go about their business

The cellar area didn't look at all sinister. The main room was well lit and cluttered with boxes of household items, children's games, and laundry baskets. Agents moved the stuff aside and with jackhammers broke through the concrete rather easily. But the agents had only dug down about six inches when they were suddenly and unexpectedly confronted with a problem. They hit a small water pipe and the resulting flood caused everybody to stop digging and rush to repair the leak. It took the rest of the day to fix the pipe, and the digging was put off until the next morning, when Adams returned with the rest of the team.

Agent Michael Byrnes was leading the FBI team that day, and as the jackhammer broke through the concrete and other agents pulled away pieces of the floor, it seemed clear that the spot where the digging was going on had some distinctive characteristics that indicated someone had been there before them. Unlike other portions of the floor, this particular spot didn't have reinforcing metal mesh in the concrete. The soil also seemed to have been disturbed in the past.

The agents resumed digging, carefully using trowels to scrape away layers of the sandy soil. They used small paint brushes if they had to. Going down about six inches at a time, the agents sorted through the various rock, pebbles, and bits of broken cement. The work was tedious and each scraping that wasn't productive brought them closer to a dead end. They repeated the process through a number of half-foot increments, going down around two to three feet.

Then they saw it. Lying in the soil was an unmistakable piece of bone, around two inches long. It was stained brown, had no odor and had no flesh adhering to it. It was clearly bone. Based on his expertise, Adams didn't need much of the bone fragment to tell if it was human, although in some cases really small pieces would require microscopic analysis to distinguish them from another species. But Adams was pretty certain that what was sticking up in the earth came from a human hand, a fact borne out when further careful brushing away of the soil revealed other parts arranged roughly as a hand would be if the fingers were splayed. The additional hand pieces were also stained brown, an indication that they had been in the ground for several years. Adams believed the bones had to have been there for at least five years and likely more.

The agents kept digging and brushing. Very soon their efforts were rewarded with more bones: a human vertebra, a piece of a skull, a part of the coccyx or tailbone, the hyoid bone which normally lies behind the tongue and just above the Adam's apple. A tooth was also uncovered, as were two ribs. There was also some mummified flesh and bits of clothing. Clearly, Adams and the agents were staring into a grave. Or what had been a grave.

There was no complete set of remains so it was obvious that the remainder of the corpse had at some time in the past been removed and taken somewhere else. In cases where a grave is disturbed, unless the diggers are very careful, smaller bones get churned in the process and can migrate deeper into the ground or get overlooked. This is particularly true if those making the removal are working in haste, which is what had happened at 102nd Road. For mobsters, the act of disinterring the remains of a murder victim is unnerving, especially to people who didn't expect to have to perform such a grisly task to later conceal the crime. As a result, bones are sometimes left behind. The result was that Adams and the FBI agents found the evidence they were looking for. Just to make sure nothing was overlooked, Kristin Hartnett, another member of the medical examiner's team, supervised the screening of the soil on another portion of the property.

Adams took what was found and returned to the medical examiner's laboratory on First Avenue in Manhattan, in a building adjacent to Bellevue Hospital. It was there that the bones would be sent to a laboratory to extract DNA evidence to see if the remains could be identified. Actually, based on what the FBI informant said, the agents had a pretty good idea that the bones were those of Paul Katz, a small-time hijacker and fence for stolen property who disappeared in December 1969. The FBI source had said Katz had been strangled and dumped in the basement hole because James "Jimmy the Gent" Burke, an infamous homicidal mob associate, believed, based on tips from law enforcement, that the trucker might have been an informant. Given that Katz and Burke had committed some crimes together, Burke was not about to be thrown to the wolves by the ill-fated hijacker. Burke struck first. But, since he died in 1996 while serving a state prison sentence for the murder of another associate who had crossed him, Burke had escaped justice for the Katz killing.

It was up to Frances Rue, a specialist at the medical examiner's office, to do the actual analysis of the DNA testing, which began about ten days after the bones were discovered. The bones taken by Adams should be enough to allow lab experts to extract DNA material for comparison with samples provided by Katz's surviving children, a son Lawrence and a daughter Ilsa. Teeth can be of some usefulness for DNA analysis but generally forensic experts like to deal with bones and hair samples that contain the roots. DNA identification is based on the reality that each human being gets half of the genetic makeup from the father and half from the mother. Experts think maternal DNA gives more possibilities for identification, but the paternal side is also adequate.

Since the agents had kept much of the information about Katz, and his possible killers, from Adams so as not to bias his finding, he really didn't know the backstory to the body parts found under the floor in Ozone Park. But while he didn't know about Burke and the other suspects in the killing, Adams was really that day not only doing the work of a forensic expert but also acting as the archeologist, the kind of job he originally studied for. However, this time his subject wasn't an ancient civilization like that of the Maya but rather New York City's Mafia past. What Adams found wouldn't wind up in a museum but instead would become important evidence in an historic trial that would rock New York City and dredge up the ghosts of one of its spectacular twentieth-century crimes.

CHAPTER TWO
"THE FEDS ARE ALL OVER . . ."

WITH NEWS OF THE FBI DIG all over the radio, television, and newspapers, it didn't take long for the curious to come by the house at 102nd Road and gawk at the blue tent set up in the driveway. Agents took the soil from the dig and sifted it through screens and, in fact, found some other pieces of bone that had been overlooked in the burial pit. The tent shielded that activity from the public and news photographers. The word was that the FBI was looking for a victim of a mob hit, a "hood." To the good citizens of Queens, long used to searches for mob victims in the area, the identity of the deceased was a source of speculation. A quick check of real estate records showed the home was owned by Burke's daughter Catherine, who leased it to an elderly woman Burke had known growing up in an orphanage after being born with the name "Jimmy Conway."

Gasper Valenti knew the house on 102nd Road well. His father had helped construct it as part of a series of attached and unpretentious two-story brick homes that took up most of that section of the block. Valenti was a local guy who always had dreams of becoming a gangster. It was the career path of preference for young men in that neighborhood who harbored romantic notions of what being a wise guy could mean. With idols like the old John Gotti, the "Teflon Don," to look up to, there seemed to be prestige, money, power, status in the mob.

But as life would have it, and try as he might, Valenti couldn't break into the ranks of the made Mafia men. A nondescript man with thinning hair, Valenti didn't have a fearsome nature. He committed small crimes such as peddling pornography and bigger ones such as thefts from trucks. He rubbed shoulders with the likes of Burke and his gang of misfits who everybody knew over the years had killed whenever it seemed convenient for self-preservation, particularly over the big theft of loot in December 1978 from the secured cargo area of Lufthansa Airlines at John F. Kennedy International. It was a crime everybody knew was a job Burke had put together but for which neither he nor any of the big fish were ever caught. Bodies were rumored to be planted under the floor of Burke's Brooklyn social club and were found scattered around the five boroughs.

Valenti had left for Las Vegas in 1990 after stealing $20,000 and tried to reinvent himself there, getting a job at a casino and doing a bit of thievery. He came back around 2005, made amends with his old New York mob friends and tried making it again as a low-level criminal. God knows he needed something. When he returned from Las Vegas, he had just the suit he was wearing and a new baby daughter in tow. Murder was something Valenti didn't do although he falsely bragged while in Las Vegas about taking part in killings back in New York. He didn't have that lust for blood that just might have given him mob membership. Instead, he worked his niche as a mob associate, earning money here and there but never getting ahead of the game. He was constantly borrowing from one loan shark to pay off another. The mob had no retirement plan for lowly associates like Valenti, or for that matter even the higher-ranked men who found themselves stretched to even raise cash to pay for lawyers.

So, by the time the sun had risen on June 17, 2013, and agents began digging in the basement on 102nd Road, Gaspare Valenti had already decided years ago that mob life wasn't the path forward in his life. But he didn't tell that to his cousin Vincent, with whom he had a few falling outs over the years but who seemed to forgive him. If truth be told, Vincent Asaro wasn't much better off financially than Valenti. Asaro may have been a captain in the once-vaunted Bonanno crime family, but that was no guarantee that he would find himself living above the poverty level.

Asaro was what was known in the mob as a "brokester," a made member who was constantly scratching around for money, a situation made worse by the fact that the old Mafia rackets just weren't making anybody rich. People who owed him cash—it could be as little as $50—might pay him when they got around to it. Or in some cases they didn't pay him at all. He just didn't have the muscle to scare anybody and was bitter about all the dough he threw away gambling.

"We did it ourselves. It's a curse of this fucking gambling," Asaro would complain to his cousin. In his waning years Asaro found himself living off the beneficence of friends and loans, along with whatever Social Security gave him.

"What's broke? I'm in so much trouble I took $2,500 from a broad," Asaro once complained with some embarrassment. Gone were the days when he could toss around hundred dollar bills with ease and throw more away at Aqueduct Race Track.

The morning of June 17, Valenti had arranged for Asaro to meet him at the Esquire Diner, a neighborhood place on Woodhaven Boulevard, which everybody—be they mobsters or regular folks— would go for coffee or dinner. Valenti had waited outside the diner and watched his cousin drive up in a black Mercedes shortly after 10:00 A.M. Asaro might be broke but he was able to drive a nice car, which was registered to a woman he knew. Valenti got into the passenger seat, and the car entered the parking lot of the diner. He had already hinted in an earlier telephone call to Asaro that he needed to talk with him about a problem.

"What happened?" Asaro asked as he drove.

"The feds are all over Liberty Avenue," answered Valenti.

Liberty Avenue wasn't an exact description of where Adams and the FBI team were working. But it was very close, Liberty being right around the corner from 102nd Road where the dig site was. The avenue skirted the north border of the old Bayside Cemetery, and FBI cars and vans were all around the spot. Asaro asked for more precise information.

"By—you know—" Valenti didn't get to finish because Asaro mentioned the name of an old Bonanno family associate who actually happened to live near the location.

Asaro asked why the FBI was there.

Valenti said he didn't know but saw all of the law-enforcement activity because he had visited his doctor who had an office there. This was a lie of course. Valenti knew very well when and why the FBI had showed up at the house because he had been secretly working with the agents for a year. He was a mob mole. A turncoat. A rat. It was because of him that the agents were at the house in the first place. They had primed him to bring up the news about the dig with Asaro. Since he was wearing a recording device, the agents hoped that Asaro would react and say something incriminating.

Hearing about FBI activity, Asaro's first thought was that the agents were looking to make an arrest. The Bonanno crime family had been easy pickings in recent years and arrests of family members were commonplace—never a total surprise but unpredictable in terms of timing. Since the old boss Joe Massino was picked up in January 2003 at his home on 84th Street in Howard Beach, members and associates of the family seemed to have bull's eyes on their backs. Agents had arrested over eighty people linked to the *borgata* and added some Gambino crime family members, notably Charles Carneglia, another mob killer who, like Asaro, was broke and drifting in his old age.

Asaro thought the FBI was looking for an old friend named "John" and asked Valenti if that was the case. Valenti's response as the car drove the short distance in the parking lot would prove disconcerting.

"I'm talking about Liberty Avenue where . . ." said Valenti. His voice trailed off as the car slowed to a stop. Asaro put the transmission into park. They were still in the diner parking lot. "You know what I mean?" Valenti continued, with a slight touch of inquisition in his voice.

There was something in that last remark, the inflection of Valenti's voice, that apparently made Asaro suddenly aware that maybe his cousin knew something he didn't. Perhaps Valenti was fishing around for him to say something, something incriminating. Asaro's mental antenna, likely tuned by his own sense of paranoia from years on the street, led him to want to end the conversation. Perhaps he was being taped. There was no good that could come from this talk. He sighed, a reaction that seemed pregnant with disbelief and disappointment. Asaro wanted to get away from his cousin. The guy sounded like he was fishing for something. It sounded like he was a rat.

"No, I don't know what you mean," Asaro finally answered. Then, he told Valenti to go away.

"All right, let me go, go ahead, go," commanded Asaro.

Valenti wanted to know where he should go and what should he do. Asaro didn't want to say anything but managed to answer in one word: "Nothing."

Sensing Asaro's discomfort, Valenti left the car but not before asking his cousin to keep in touch.

"Don't call me," Asaro demanded of Valenti. It would be the last words he would ever say to his old lifelong friend. As later events would bear out, any sudden suspicion Asaro may have had about why Valenti was quizzing him about the FBI dig location was well placed.

The entire meeting between the two men may have taken about four minutes, and Valenti walked away down Woodhaven Boulevard, under the watchful eyes of federal agents. At that point the agents knew that Valenti's role as an informant was over. With his conversation with Gaspare Valenti still playing out in his mind, Vincent Asaro drove away and was spotted leaving his car and getting into the passenger side of a different vehicle on Liberty Avenue. The car drove east to the town of Inwood on Long Island where Vincent's son Jerome had an auto-body shop.

Vincent only stayed about ten minutes at Inwood, and it wasn't clear what he may have said to his son. It is possible he told him about the FBI dig and Valenti's suspicious, inquisitive behavior. He drove back to Liberty Avenue and got back into the Mercedes. Perhaps Vincent was preoccupied thinking about his earlier conversation with cousin Gaspare and the suspicion that his cousin was setting him up. In any case, Vincent was so distracted that he backed up the Mercedes—which he didn't own—straight into a metal pillar. It wasn't turning out to be a very good day.

With no money, no job, and no prospects in the gangster life he aspired to, Gaspare Valenti had come to a realization that his only way to a better existence was to volunteer to give the FBI what it wanted. The best career path for many aging wise guys, particularly in the Howard Beach area, was to become an informant. The big historic prosecutions of recent years had resulted in convictions of Massino, his underboss Sal Vitale, as well as scores of other family captains and soldiers. The once powerful *borgata* had become a loose group of scared mobsters who were afraid to even meet with each other at their favorite Italian restaurants, lest they violate the terms of their probation, something that the FBI routinely tried to haunt them with.

So, in September 2008, as the newspaper headlines chronicled more indictments of the Bonanno family, Gaspare Valenti looked up the telephone number for the local New York-area FBI office and placed a call. It was that simple, although he almost was disconnected when he phoned in that first time. His first meeting with special agent Adam Mininni was on September 23 at a hotel near JFK Airport and was really just a meet-and-greet session where Mininni took a copy of Valenti's driver's license and some other details and then started checking into his background.

Valenti did indeed have a criminal background, and his claims that he knew information about the Bonanno crime family and his cousin Vincent Asaro sent a quiver through the FBI. The next meeting with Valenti on September 29, saw some law-enforcement heavyweights in attendance: Assistant U.S. Attorney Greg Andres, who had made many cases against the Bonanno family, notably Joseph Massino, as well as Nora Conley, the supervisor of the FBI's Bonanno squad. To represent Valenti's interests he had attorney Scott Fenstermaker sit in on the interviews.

During that meeting and others that followed, Valenti acknowledged the crimes he committed and those in which he claimed Asaro was involved. He would eventually plead guilty to crimes of robbery and racketeering in a sealed federal courtroom and then was set loose, under FBI supervision, to live a secret life as a cooperating witness. As part of his cooperation deal with the FBI, Valenti got the financial help he needed to support his family. He received a stipend. His rent was paid for, as were his utilities and medical insurance. He received over $178,000 in living expenses from the government. When necessary, security details were provided. It was a comfortable deal and was what a lot of turncoats got when they decided to turn their backs on Mafia life.

Because he had easy access to Asaro, Valenti assured the agents he would be willing to wear a wire and make recordings to back up the things he would tell them. Valenti was busy with the tape recordings. From November 2008 through June 17, 2013, he recorded over 100 hours of his conversations with an additional 200 hours of telephone conversations. He began taping Asaro in earnest in October 2010. In his extensive debriefings, Valenti told the agents about the Paul Katz murder and he put Asaro right in the middle of it. Within days of Katz's disappearance, Asaro asked Valenti to have one of the houses on 102nd Road available for a "meeting." Then, Valenti told the agents, Asaro and the infamous Jimmy Burke arrived a few days later with the body of Katz. As Valenti told the FBI, Asaro related how he and Burke had strangled the unfortunate Katz with a dog chain, although a close examination of what Valenti would say in court raised a question about that scenario. Katz's sin, according to Valenti, was that he was cooperating with the cops.

Burke and Asaro dug the hole in the basement floor and dumped in Katz's body, remembered Valenti. Burke never served a day in prison for Lufthansa and is believed to have carried out many murders, mostly in the aftermath of the Lufthansa robbery, that crippled the FBI's ability to make a case. However, in April 1979, Burke was picked up for a federal parole violation and would essentially stay in prison for the rest of his life, following convictions for killing a fellow drug dealer and playing a role in fixing basketball games at Boston College during the late 1970s. Concerned that Katz's body would be discovered in the basement of what was his daughter Catherine's property, Burke wanted the remains moved. Valenti said Asaro asked him and his own son Jerome Asaro to dig up the bones and move them. Katz's body had disintegrated by then, leaving behind bones, a skull, and bits of clothing in the pit, Valenti told the FBI. He and Jerome Asaro took out the remains the best they could and cemented over the hole.

As the FBI dug up the basement on 102nd Road, what the agents discovered soon started to corroborate what Valenti had told them. In fact, he had done more talk. After meeting Asaro at the diner, Valenti went with the agents to the basement of the house on 102nd Road and among the board games, toys, and laundry bins pointed to the place where the grave was. Then the agents started to dig.

At that point whatever they would find was the icing on the cake because investigators had already believed they had enough recordings to implicate Asaro in a host of other crimes. But having a murder to add to the indictment is always nice. The cement they broke through with the jackhammer had shown signs of being of a different age and constitution than the cement found in the other parts of the cellar floor. That was evidence that new cement had been laid down at some point after the original construction.

Most important were the bones found in the cellar soil. Brad Adams could tell they were those of a man because even something as small as a hand bone could be measured and compared to statistics that could indicate with some certainty the sex of the deceased. The race of the victim or the age couldn't be determined from such small samples in the grave. But, again, using the finger bones and the jaw, an approximate height of the person could be estimated: somewhere between five feet one inch to five feet ten inches.

Paul Katz had been about five feet eight inches when he lived. But estimating the height of the deceased was not a way to determine with certainty the identity. Back at the New York City Medical Examiner's Office, the bones and teeth collected by Adams were sent to the DNA lab for further work. Bones can be extremely useful for DNA analysis because they may contain genetic material that has survived the passage of time. Since the FBI already had information that the bones were those of Katz, the agents were able to track down two of his children, Lawrence and Ilsa, as well as the dead man's sister Deborah and get DNA samples for comparison with the remains. For living people, the process was as simple as taking a swab from inside the cheek or collecting a few hairs.

Tests on the bones found in the burial pit came up with a very close match with the samples taken from the Katz children. It was almost a perfect match. Frances Rue, from the medical examiner's office, would later remark that she was 99.9 percent certain that the remains were those of Paul Katz. No, it was actually better than that. Rue was confident that the probability was more than a 99.9 percent certainty that the corpse which had rotted in the grave had been Katz. Gaspare Valenti had a good memory, at least about what he knew about the body in the basement floor. For the FBI that also meant that he was a reliable source of information.

Paul Katz had disappeared on December 9, 1969, at the age of twenty-eight after telling his wife Delores and their young children he was going, with some apprehension, to a meeting with a fellow hijacker named Joe Allegro. If he didn't come back in fifteen minutes, his wife should call the police, said Katz. Wherever he went and whatever he did that day ended badly for Katz, and the DNA finding was clear evidence that Valenti had good information and was reliable—certainly about the demise of Katz and his burial. The condition of the bones also seemed to bear out what Valenti had said about the body being disinterred and taken away. Brad Adams and the FBI team found more hand bones farther down in the burial pit. To investigators this was a good indication that when the decomposed body was lifted out of the grave and taken away, the hands simply separated away from the arm bones and were left behind.

So, Valenti was right about the burial and the fact that the mystery remains were those of Katz. But was his recollection about

Asaro and his allegation about the cousin's involvement in the Katz murder something that could be corroborated? If the agents were hoping that Asaro would say something clearly incriminating to his cousin on tape about Katz's fate, they would be disappointed. But they were in no rush to build a case. Time and the racketeering laws were on their side.

CHAPTER THREE
A GOODFELLA'S LAMENT

VINCENT ASARO HAD OVER HALF A CENTURY of a life of crime under his belt when he finally left Gaspare Valenti at the Esquire Diner that June 17 day as the FBI was digging for the bones of Paul Katz. It wasn't the only life he knew. Asaro had his own fencing business in Howard Beach, so he had a source of legitimate income and by some accounts did a very good job of building fences. But as any gangster knows, life in the Mob is defined by what you do on the street with all of the other *amigo nostri*, the term Mafia members use to refer to each other.

The goal of the Mafia was to make money, and Asaro knew that from the time he was a teenager. His father was Jerome Asaro, a somewhat handsome Italian man with a distinctive aquiline nose, a trait that he passed down to his son and a grandson also named Jerome. The family lived for a time at 1484 Sutter Avenue in the area of South Ozone Park. Around the corner, on Drew Street, was the home of Gaspare Valenti and his family. The houses were within a low-lying area of Brooklyn known as "The Hole," so called because its sunken street level made it prone to flooding and the buildings were small and forgotten. It looked like a meteor hit it, was how mob associate Peter Zuccaro described the area.

Today, although some development has made improvements, The Hole still has chicken coops, and tomato plants are known to grow by the side of the road. Drainage sewers are nonexistent in some places, and thick sheets of ice form in the streets during the coldest winters. The area gained its own brand of notoriety when in 2004 some FBI agents doing another dig in a vacant lot on Ruby Street unearthed the remains of Dominick Trinchera and Philip Giaccone, two Bonanno crime family captains who were killed in a power struggle back in May 1981. It was another mob burial that Brad Adams was called in by the FBI to work on.

We know Jerome Asaro settled on Sutter Avenue because an old article from the *Long Island Star* newspaper reported that as his home when he was arrested in December 1949, at a time when his son Vincent was about fourteen years old. It seems that Jerome was suspected by police to be working in a policy place in the Ridgewood section of Brooklyn that was printing what were said to be Italian lottery slips. Policy operations are illegal lotteries, historically popular in immigrant communities. According to police, the gang once a week received payoff numbers cabled from people in Italy and did $5 million a year in business. Jerome Asaro was thirty-seven years old at the time of his arrest with five other men and according to the newspaper was held on $1,000 bail. Detectives from the NYPD Confidential Squad seized printing plates and six cars, which the group allegedly used in its operation. Jerome Asaro was arrested in a car as he and three other men waited for runners to come and bring them receipts, said police.

It is unclear what happened to Jerome Asaro in the Italian lottery case. But he didn't stay under the radar very long. Three years later he was again arrested on charges he set fire twice in one day to his women's clothing store at 14-23 101st Avenue in Ozone Park. Officials told the *Long Island Star* that Asaro was believed to have set fire to the premises to collect on a $5,000 insurance policy, which was just about to lapse. The fires, which were on the ground floor of a forty-five-family apartment building didn't do much damage, and Asaro denied any wrongdoing. His daughter was quoted in the newspapers as saying business had been bad in the eleven months the store was open and that she had not been paid in that time. The disposition of that case has been lost to history, but it did lead to photos of Jerome and his daughter being in the newspapers.

At some point—it is not clear exactly when—Jerome Asaro's criminal propensities earned him the distinction of induction into what was originally known as the Bonanno crime family. He also had another business, a junkyard in East New York, which seemed to work out better than the clothing store. Jerome did a good job of staying out of public light until January 1970 when he and thirteen other men were charged as part of a Nassau County grand jury investigation with organized-crime activity. The district attorney for the county, William Cahn, had discovered that the Mob was using his county as a focal point for its activity and fired up a grand jury probe that seemed to be focused on gambling. There were some interesting names indicted along with Jerome Asaro, who at that point had an address in the city of Long Beach and was traveling in some very good company Mafia-wise. Charged was Salvatore "Sally The Shiek" Musacchio, at one time a former underboss of the old Mafia family run by olive oil king Joseph Profaci; Sebastian "Buster" Aloi, a captain in the Colombo crime family; Pasquale "Paddy Mack" Macchiarole, a reputed soldier in the Colombo borgata; Salvatore Ferrugia, a Bonanno soldier known by the moniker "Sally Fruits" and who a decade later would be appointed temporary caretaker of the Bonanno family by the Mafia commission as the crime clan suffered through the incarceration of official boss Philip Rastelli.

There was also another man, younger than the others at age thirty-two, who was charged with possession of gambling records. He was identified as Henry Hill and lived in Island Park, a community near the water in Nassau County. Not much else was widely known about Hill at that time. Later, that would change dramatically with his involvement with the Burke gang and the Lufthansa heist.

Jerome Asaro reached the rank of soldier in what newspapers called the Sciacca crime family, which was just another name for the Bonanno family. It was Paul Sciacca, with the Commission's approval, who took over the crime family after family patriarch Joseph Bonanno was forced to leave New York in the late 1960s following a war among its members and disgust with his imperious, high-handed manner of leadership. But while law enforcement was paying attention to the problems created by Bonanno, as well as the other crime families, Jerome Asaro remained relatively low key. His name didn't appear in any of the congressional or Department of Justice lists circulated about Mafia members at the time, but he was clearly considered a member of the mob.

Jerome's son Vincent didn't do much in his early years to separate himself from his father's life of crime. Beginning in 1957 at the age of twenty-one, Vincent Asaro started getting arrested for all sorts of crimes: rape, burglary, bank robbery, kidnapping, felonious assault, and weapons possession. Records show that a lot of those cases were dismissed. But in 1960 a petty larceny arrest and a charge of unlawful entry led to convictions for what were relatively minor offenses. Asaro added to his record in 1967 with a conviction for assault in the third degree, again a relatively minor crime.

Vincent started to have more serious trouble when he reached age forty-four. Then, a 1970 federal arrest led to a conviction for theft from interstate commerce and a sentence of five years' probation, the time for which had not expired when he got arrested for burglary of a post office. The burglary arrest led in 1972 to a federal conviction and six months in prison, to be served on weekends.

Vincent's federal convictions didn't keep him off the street, and he gravitated to the well-known mob bar called Robert's Lounge at 114-45 Lefferts Boulevard in South Ozone Park. The saloon was run by Jimmy Burke and became the place where Burke held court and planned his own crimes with a crew of mob associates—a group of killers, hijackers, cigarette smugglers, credit card scammers, overall thieves, and assorted outlaws that included Henry Hill, Tommy DeSimone, Angelo Sepe, Robert McMahon, and many others. The bar was not far—about fifteen minutes—from John F. Kennedy Airport, a favorite target for their thievery.

Robert's Lounge also had a dark reputation. As Hill would later recount in a memorable scene to writer Nick Pileggi in *Wiseguy*, one night DeSimone, an out-of-control, sadistic murderer, started picking on a young man named "Spider," the club waiter. DeSimone wanted Spider to dance and shot at his feet, wounding him. Vincent Asaro, who happened to be in the club that night, took the injured Spider to a doctor for first aid. But that didn't stop things with DeSimone.

"One night we are playing cards in the cellar—Tommy, Jimmy, me, Anthony Stabile, Angelo Sepe, when Spider walks in," recalled Hill. "All of a sudden Tommy wants him to dance. 'Do a dance,' Tommy says. For some reason Spider tells Tommy to go fuck himself."

The others started teasing DeSimone around the card table and finally an increasingly angry DeSimone, baited by his friends' taunts, pulls out a handgun and shoots Spider in the chest three times, killing him, remembered Hill. It was a brutal scene immortalized in *GoodFellas,* and from that moment on Hill decided DeSimone was a psychopath.

After a moment of stunned silence, an angry Burke chastised DeSimone about the mess he had made and ordered him to dig a hole right in the basement of the club and bury Spider's body, said Hill. Many years later police would dig in the basement of Robert's Lounge in search of remains of Spider and other victims Hill told them were buried there but found nothing, save for some animal bones.

Yet, there may have been good reason why the FBI digs found nothing because the agents just might have been too late in getting to the scene. In 1983, detectives debriefed a mob associate who reported that around 1980 he was told to dig up a body in a basement at the request of Paul Vario. The corpse, the informant told the cops, was in the ground about ten years and was in a good state of preservation with skin intact. But once the body was lifted from the ground, the skin came off and it was all he could do to get the remains out and away in the nick of time before federal agents arrived with a warrant to do the digging, the informant said. The associate didn't appear to identify the exact location, but the detectives believed he indicated, based on the sandy soil conditions, it was Robert's Lounge.

The murders that followed in the wake of Burke and his crew didn't seem to deter Vincent or his cousin Gaspare, who by 1968 were hanging out at Robert's Lounge with regularity. It was a dive that drew the mob crowd of wannabe gangsters and those who would eventually make it into the ranks of made men. An NYPD intelligence document from 1971 and based on a source said to be "reliable and confidential" said the lounge was a hangout for "the top men connected with gambling, loansharking and hijacking." Raised in an orphanage, Burke eventually as a young man became a bricklayer but gravitated to crime, working as a bookmaker and dabbling in loansharking, things he became very adept at. He also developed a reputation for beating recalcitrant debtors but later hit upon the idea of forgiving all or part of what was owed in exchange for information about cargo shipments and truck deliveries—prime targets for hijacking.

Burke was known as "The Gent" because of his smooth style and charisma. Back in the 1930s Jimmy Cagney starred in a film known as *Jimmy the Gent* in which he played a city guy involved in the "missing heir" racket, a business of finding unknown or missing heirs to valuable estates. In Burke's case, the ironic twist was that he got involved with many things to make money—usually stolen— and the people with whom he was involved would often go missing permanently.

In the Mafia life, Burke was with Paul Vario, a Brooklyn Mafioso from the Flatlands section. The relationship meant that Burke had the protection of Vario and access to his network of crooked cops and shady businessmen. In return, Burke passed along a share of the proceeds of his crimes to Vario and kept him informed of any big scores or problems that needed to be worked out. Burke was an earner for the mob, and other Mafiosi would try to work with him and in such cases things would have to be worked out with Vario. When he needed to, Vario could also turn to Burke and his associates at Robert's Lounge to put together hit teams to kill rival hijackers or those suspected of being informants.

A born and bred Brooklyn guy, Vario didn't like to stray too far from his home borough. It was a short trip from his junkyard in south Brooklyn and his own bar known as Geffken's at 9508 Flatlands Avenue to Burke's lounge in a three-story brick building on Lefferts. Vario, a big, burly man, was blooded to the Lucchese crime family and in the days after the death of family namesake Thomas Lucchese in 1967 of natural causes, the family was led by Carmine Tramunti.

Known as "Mr. Gribbs," Tramunti was a Neopolitan-born gangster and drug dealer who earned his reputation as a strong arm for the likes of labor racketeer John "Johnny Dio" Dioguardi. Fleshy faced and often photographed with a scowl on his visage, Tramunti didn't have the polish or prestige of Lucchese, who was of a different generation of older Mafiosi. But investigators were certain Tramunti was following in the footsteps of Lucchese by having some political district leaders of both the Republican and Democratic parties under his control, as well as at least one judge. Those were connections that would prove useful over the years. He also had the muscle and blessing of the Commission to take over the family. Both Tramunti and Vario had one common connection in business: they had legitimate floral shops. But if Vario steered clear of Big City night life, Tramunti was considered by police to be a major hidden investor for the Mob in bars and restaurants all over town. He also invested in heroin, something that would lead to his undoing.

While he was linked to a different crime family than that of Vario and Burke, Vincent Asaro and his father had no problems circulating among those in the Lucchese circles. Mafia men weren't barred from hanging out with other wise guys from different families. It was just that any business deals had to be worked out by the higher-ups in the borgatas. In Vincent's case his immediate boss wasn't his father but rather his uncle Mickey Zaffarano, a captain in the Bonanno family and the king of the Times Square peep shows and porn industry. The Asaros had an interest in a junkyard near Fountain Avenue in East New York, not far from Burke's lounge, and when junk cars had to be disposed of Burke only had to reach out to the Asaros.

In June 2013, the likes of Jimmy Burke, Paul Vario, and just about everybody else who frequented Robert's Lounge back in the day were gone. Jerome Asaro had succumbed to a heart ailment. Burke and Vario had already died in prison and DeSimone and Sepe either disappeared or were found murdered. Zaffarano was also long gone, having dropped dead of a heart attack during an FBI raid in Times Square. The Bonanno family itself had been carpet bombed by numerous federal prosecutions, with many of the old timers dead, in prison, or, like Joseph Massino, cooperating with the FBI. Only a few of the old men like Vincent were among the last dinosaurs still standing.

Vincent Asaro and cousin Gaspare Valenti were still around on the street and their worlds were very circumscribed. Gaspare wasn't his own man, secretly working for the government and trying to stay afloat financially. Vincent acted and sounded like a busted valise, a shell of what he once was. If there had been big money in the mob, it had flown out of his hands as fast as he got it. His jewelry had been hocked for cash years earlier. He couldn't go to old social clubs run by the wise guys because he couldn't pay his dues. So he stayed home

"I don't come out early no more," said Asaro. "Where am I going? I got no place to go."

Asaro wasn't a hermit. He still took lunch at the Esquire and would meet other aging Mafiosi at places like the Tuscany Deli in Lindenwood where he could sit outside as he bemoaned his misfortune. He still liked to fish and once in a while reeled in a nice flounder or fluke, which he cooked himself, perhaps with a side of orzo.

Without much money, Asaro had to be content with growing old, something he couldn't do gracefully. He felt detached from the Mafia life, marginalized and adrift. He didn't know what was going on among the families. When on Thanksgiving Day in 2011, Salvatore Montagna, the Brooklyn ironworker who took over the Bonanno family, was killed in Canada, Asaro didn't have a clue about that or just about anything else.

"I don't even know what is going on in Ozone Park," he told Valenti after news of Montagna's murder hit the newspapers.

Part of the reason Asaro was so out of the loop in the Mafia was that his *amigos* in the life didn't know what to make of him or maybe were just too uncomfortable around him. Talking over coffee one day at a diner on Long Island, Anthony Urso, a gangster who for a time ran the street business of the Bonanno family, minced no words when asked about Asaro.

"He's a fucking lunatic," said Urso.

At least in the 1990s Asaro was a guy right in the middle of things in his role as a crime family captain. When then-Bonanno boss Joseph Massino was released from prison about 1992 following a federal labor racketeering arrest, his consiglieri Anthony Spero and underboss Salvatore Vitale called a meeting of all the captains at a spot in Queens. Former boss Philip Rastelli had died in 1991 after spending years fighting various indictments and spending most of his time in jail. Massino wasn't in attendance because he was on supervised release from prison and if he was spotted at the meeting by the FBI in such company, the government would send him right back to a cell.

The meeting was a big one. All of the big captains were present: Louis "Ha Ha" Attanasio, Anthony "Tony Green" Urso, Joe "Desi" DeSimone, Gerlando "George From Canada" Sciascia, and Louis Restivo, the only one of the group with a college education. Vincent Asaro rounded out the group. Spero told all of the captains that Massino wanted them to step down and await reappointment by Massino after he finished his supervised release period. Massino likely did that so he could see how each of the captains reacted and how they behaved during this transition period. Asaro and the others complied—they had no real choice in the matter. After Massino finished up his supervision period, he began meeting with the Bonanno captains, usually in small groups.

Vincent Asaro remained in the good graces of Joe Massino until sometime in the mid-1990s when things started to go sour, according to intelligence developed by the FBI. Being a captain in the Mafia usually works out to be a good position for those who have it. But Massino would later tell his FBI handlers that Asaro started to abuse the men under him and allegedly steal their money. Massino also is said to have noticed Vincent's volatility, which included everything from fighting to cursing a blue streak in public. Such conduct was enough to have Massino demote Asaro to the rank of soldier, taking his men away from him.

The later years had not been kind to Asaro, and when 2014 rolled around things suddenly got much worse for the rapidly aging man. The morning of January 23, FBI agents fanned out from their headquarters building in lower Manhattan and in the early hours knocked on the doors of five men to unceremoniously arrest them for assorted crimes. Pulled out of his girlfriend Michele's home in Ozone Park was Vincent. Given a few minutes by Special Agent Adam Mininni and the rest of the raid team to freshen up, Asaro was taken from the house in a heavy dark sweat suit and athletic shoes. He took with him a pair of tinted sunglasses. The agents took his cell phone to analyze later.

Asaro was taken from Queens to the FBI offices at 26 Federal Plaza where he went through the ritual of having his mugshot taken and was fingerprinted. Then, he and the other four men arrested that day—Thomas DiFiore, Jack Bonventre, John Ragano, and Vincent's son Jerome—were led out of the building for the perp walk so that news photographers could have a field day. Vincent, handcuffed in the front, was led out by Robert Ypelaar and other agents, each of whom firmly held him by his arms. Cold and old, Vincent appeared gaunt and worried. His mind raced back to the days at Robert's Lounge and all of those conversations he had with Gaspare, especially the last one on June 17, 2013, as Paul Katz's bones were being dusted in the basement and he was no doubt aware that he might be in deep trouble.

The news release put out that day hit New York like a bombshell: "Bonnano Family Captain Vincent Asaro Indicted for Participation in The 1978 $5 Million Robbery at JFK Airport and The Murder of Paul Katz Who Disappeared in 1969." Although five men had been charged, only Vincent faced the most sensational allegations about participation in the Lufthansa heist. He and his son were also charged in connection with the murder of Katz. If proven, those charges guaranteed a life sentence for Vincent.

For Steve Carbone, the retired FBI agent who investigated the Lufthansa case in 1979, his reaction was mixed. He knew of the renewed interest in the case and actually had been debriefed by the new team of agents.

"I knew there were a lot of stones unturned," Carbone said later. But with Asaro being thrown in the mix, Carbone said he felt a slight sting and a hurt feeling that "maybe I had failed."

For a generation unfamiliar with Lufthansa, Brooklyn U.S. Attorney Loretta Lynch laid out for the media the old story that had become part of the folklore of American crime.

"Asaro helped pull off the 1978 Lufthansa robbery—still the largest robbery in New York history," said Lynch in a statement. "Neither age nor time dimmed Asaro's ruthless ways, as he continued to order violence to carry out mob business in recent months."

Lynch's latter remarks referred to the other charges in the indictment, easily overlooked given the sensational nature of the Lufthansa charges, that Asaro had been involved in various extortions and armed robberies, as well as a solicitation to have a suspected informant murdered before he could testify at the trial of another Bonanno crime family member for fraud. But those counts in the indictment almost seemed like afterthoughts, given what had surfaced about the Lufthansa robbery, the size of which the government slightly underestimated with its loss figure of $5 million.

"Asaro himself was in on one of the most notorious heists—the Lufthansa robbery in 1978," New York FBI assistant director-in-charge George Venizelos told the media. "It may be decades later, but the FBI's determination to investigate and bring wiseguys to justice will never waver."

After leaving the FBI building, Asaro and the other four were taken to Brooklyn federal district court for the first of what would be many court appearances. Vincent was represented by Gerald McMahon, an experienced criminal defense attorney from Manhattan who in recent months had won some impressive victories in mob cases against federal prosecutors in Brooklyn, including one in which Massino himself had been the star witness. A thick-chested Irishman with a pile of white hair, McMahon wasn't easily intimidated in court and was known to lock horns with judges when he thought he had to for his client's sake.

Arrayed against McMahon were assistant U.S. Attorneys Nicole M. Argentieri and Alicyn L. Cooley. Argentieri had been a veteran of a number of mob prosecutions and had risen over the past two years to become head of her office's organized crime unit. She was familiar

with McMahon's litigation skills, having lost to him with the acquittal in 2012 of reputed Genovese crime captain Anthony Romanello. Cooley was a relatively new prosecutor, having joined the
office in 2013. Physically, both women were a contrast: Argentieri
was dark haired and dark eyed while Cooley was a blonde.

During the arraignment before Magistrate Judge Marilyn D. Go,
the afternoon of the arrests started out with Vincent Asaro, his son
Jerome, and Ragano pleading not guilty, while Bonventre and Di-
Fiore were to appear in court the next day. McMahon told Go that
Vincent had received a copy of the indictment and Vincent answered "Yes," when the magistrate asked him if he understood the
charges.

Not surprisingly, Argentieri and Cooley presented to the court a
detention memorandum which spelled out why the Asaros and the
other defendants should be held without bail. The fifty-three-page
document recounted all of the alleged connections between the defendants and the Bonanno crime family, their criminal histories, and
described why each was dangerous and should be kept in jail. In the
case of Vincent, the prosecutors said that while he had been demoted as a captain, he had been reinstated to his old rank sometime
in late 2012 or early 2013 and in fact was on a committee running
the crime family.

The government had three major cooperating witnesses against
Asaro labeled CW-1, CW-2, CW-3. It didn't take long for Asaro to
figure out, based on the descriptions of each witness in footnotes to
the memorandum, who the witnesses against him were. CW-1 was his
cousin Gaspare Valenti; CW-2 was his former boss Joseph Massino;
CW-3 was former Bonanno underboss Salvatore Vitale. Massino had
told investigators about Vincent's erratic career in the crime family,
including his loansharking and habitual gambling. Vitale had related how Vincent had been demoted and now reported to his son
Jerome, who had risen to the rank of captain as his father's star lost
its luster in the mob.

But the real damaging information in the indictment, as spelled out
in the memorandum, had been provided by Valenti. Over the years of
tape recordings, according to the memorandum, Valenti had impli-

cated Vincent in many crimes, including the murder of Katz and old shakedowns in the pornography industry. But the most compelling charges involved Asaro's involvement in the Lufthansa case, and for that Valenti's tapes seemed damning.

As spelled out by Argentieri and Cooley, Gaspare had said that he, his cousin Vincent, James Burke, and others associated with the Lucchese family all had meetings to plan the heist at the Lufthansa secure cargo facility. Burke's involvement and that of Henry Hill and the rest of the crew had been well known. But the government papers revealed publicly for the first time the alleged involvement of Asaro and Valenti in the notorious crime. This was information that had never appeared in the previous published accounts of Hill and others of the robbery. In addition, Valenti had also claimed that Massino himself was kept apprised of the crime, even though at that point he was only a captain in the crime family—although admittedly a very powerful one who was an emissary for Rastelli.

The prosecutors also revealed that one of the recordings Valenti had made of his cousin captured him bemoaning the way Burke had kept all of the money from the heist and didn't spread it around.

"We never got our right money, what we were supposed to get," Asaro said on February 11, 2011. "We got fucked all around. Got fucked all around, that fucking Jimmy kept everything."

At this stage of the case, any argument by McMahon or the other defense attorneys to try and convince the court to grant bail would have been a waste of time. That would have to be tried later. Magistrate Go ordered Asaro and his son, as well as Thomas DiFiore and the others, to be held without bail. McMahon made a point of saying that Asaro had a triple bypass operation ten months earlier and had to be sure he got his medications while he was being held in the federal Metropolitan Detention Center. All three men were then taken out of court and off to jail.

Outside the courthouse, McMahon had a field day playing into the *GoodFellas* hype that had surrounded the case. As he spoke, McMahon referenced the film and indicated he thought the indictment was nothing more than an extended screenplay.

"Literally and truly this is the sequel to *GoodFellas*," McMahon told the gaggle of reporters assembled on Cadman Plaza East. "Marty needs a screenplay; Loretta said she would help him out."

Those references were to *GoodFellas* director Martin Scorsese and Brooklyn U.S. Attorney Loretta Lynch. McMahon said he appreciated the hype created by the indictment but stressed the government sometimes sends up smoke without a lot of fire. Vincent Asaro, he said, wanted to fight.

"Vincent Asaro said categorically, 'We're going to trial,'" said McMahon, promising another big court battle—at least if his client came up with some money.

CHAPTER FOUR
"SUPER THIEF"

BEFORE IT BECAME JOHN F. KENNEDY International Airport, gateway to the United States and a favorite target of the Mafia, the area of southeast Queens was a popular and fashionable golf course situated on Jamaica Bay. With large expanses of land surrounding it, Idlewild Golf Course was looked upon as the ideal place to site a large airport befitting the city's status as a major international city. There were about 200 summer homes spread out amid the creeks and wetlands, and the course was a favorite of popular golf tournaments. Mayor Fiorello LaGuardia had sparred with the City Council on what to name the new aerodrome that occupied a massive chunk of land on the border between Brooklyn and Queens. LaGuardia favored New York International Airport, while many in the council liked the name Idlewild, which is said to have been of Indian origin.

With the start of hostilities in World War Two, the airfield when it was first constructed was used by the Army and Navy to defend New York City. There was even a proposal to name the location the Colin Kelly Airport in honor of a pilot who died sinking Japanese ships in the Pacific. The location was unusual at the time for the siting of such an airport because it was much farther distant from the core metropolitan area than normal. The existing airport in the area of Whitestone was about a six-mile cab ride from Manhattan. The new Queens airport, popularly known as Idlewild Airport when it finally opened in July 1948, was a good fifteen miles from Times Square as the crow flies. But proponents of the project, having no clue how much road-traffic congestion would grow over the decades, said it would only be a mere twenty-five-minute drive from the center of Manhattan.

While the original plan was for the airport to encompass 1,110 acres, its size during construction grew to nearly five times that to nearly 5,000 acres. Idlewild or New York International attracted many of the major air carriers of the day and was the entry to the United States and New York City for hundreds of thousands of passengers each year, a number that swelled to 56.8 million passengers by 2015. By 1963, it was renamed John F. Kennedy International Airport in honor of the assassinated thirty-fifth president. To locals it became known as JFK. In the 1970s, cargo operations had increased so much that it was said to be the busiest commercial cargo airport in the world.

More cargo traffic meant more opportunity for the Mafia. As cargo operations increased at JFK, the mob didn't waste time. There was Mafia control of labor unions for sure. But the big money maker for the wise guys was in the unbridled theft of cargo of all sorts: everything from stock certificates to jewelry to cash, valuable metals, and more. While under the control of the bi-state Port Authority of New York and New Jersey, the agency's small police force was taxed to the limit by airport thievery, which is to say that it couldn't cope.

Long before Jimmy Burke's crew made its name in the 1978 Lufthansa robbery, there was Robert Cudak, who earned the moniker "super thief" for a life of crime. Born in Baltimore in 1941, Cudak moved to New York City where his youth was notable for the number of times he was arrested for all kinds of larceny, from car theft to burglary. After spending over seven years in the New York State prison system, Cudak was finally released in early 1966 and shortly thereafter noticed a newspaper ad for Northwest Airlines seeking men to work on its cargo ramp at JFK. He was fingerprinted and then, in a stark case showing how porous and meaningless the system of employee background checks was at the time, bluffed his way around his prison stint during the job interview.

"On the application and during the questioning, I stated that I had been in the armed services, had recently been discharged, and that my wallet had been stolen and therefore I could not provide driver's license, discharge papers, or other identification," Cudak recalled.

Lack of identification was no problem, and Northwest hired Cudak to work as a ramp man for all flights during the course of a fifteen-hour work day. Poor background checking wasn't the only problem with security at the airport. About three days after he started working, Cudak noticed that procedures were lax around the high-value boxes used to transport valuable cargo and began stealing again—first taking small items and then working with partners to pulling off bigger and bigger thefts, which eventually totaled $100 million. Stocks, bonds, jewelry, cash, furs. Anything that wasn't nailed down, Cudak and his fellow thieves took. They ripped open mail sacks to steal from them and eventually began taking entire bags of registered mail, including one certified package that contained radioactive material. They occasionally came across classified Pentagon documents that had been sent through the mails, although the military assured everyone the secrets weren't that big.

Cudak found that security at all the airports was poor, with JFK and O'Hare in Chicago among the worst. In Atlanta there didn't seem to be any security at all. The only exception was Los Angeles, which seemed a hard place to steal from.

"At most airports, a person who put on a pair of coveralls and wore a plastic helmet or ear mufflers such as airport personnel use was not questioned and could move about the airport without restriction," remembered Cudak.

Henry Hill knew what Congress was learning about JFK security—or about the lack of it—because in his own way he had tested JFK security about a year before Cudak had taken his job at the airport. Hill's first entrée to the airport was through Robert "French" McMahon, so named because he worked for Air France as a cargo foreman. McMahon was a cocky guy who walked with a swagger and told cops he was to the manor born, supposedly a descendant of a wealthy business family from Pennsylvania, something no investigator was ever able to verify.

Even if he did come from a privileged background, McMahon liked to live close to the edge. Investigators who monitored the airport would see him at local bars known to attract thieves, notably the Owl and the Riviera, both of which were close to JFK. He also started hanging out at Robert's Lounge, which is where he solidified his relationship with Hill. At the lounge, McMahon would bring Hill and Burke stolen things they could unload for a nice profit.

"Once he came across a small 24-by-48-inch box of silk dresses which Jimmy unloaded at the garment center for eighteen thousand dollars and which French got a piece," remembered Hill. "Frenchy always got a piece of everything he brought us or pointed us toward."

It was in early 1967 that McMahon tipped off Hill and Burke to the fact that shipments of cash from Europe would be coming into Air France's new strong room for valuables where the money would be kept before it was to be taken to New York banks. Hill recalled that his group, which included Thomas DeSimone, thought about holding up the facility. But security measures made that risky, so the crew figured out a way of compromising and distracting a cargo supervisor who possessed a key to the safe room with a prostitute at a motel outside the airport. The ruse was a classic variation of the old "panel room" tactic practiced in the nineteenth century by hookers in Manhattan where they distracted a client long enough so that an accomplice would open up a wall panel and steal the man's wallet. In this case, Hill and McMahon got a prostitute to take the supervisor to a steam room at the motel long enough so that Hill could take the key, get a copy made at a locksmith and then return the original before the prostitute had finished with the clueless man.

It was over the weekend of April 10-11, 1967, that Hill, DeSimone, and McMahon pulled off the theft. Hill said that with McMahon's assistance he walked to the secure valuables room, opened its steel door with the duplicate key and put seven white bags loaded with cash into a suitcase he had brought for the job and then walked out the door. DeSimone was waiting outside in a rented car with bogus license plates, and the duo drove away unmolested. It was that easy.

That Monday, the newspapers reported the theft as $420,000 missing from the Air France cargo building. Investigators were stumped. The theft occurred even with a security guard on duty, up to twenty people working in the area, and no sign of forced entry into the secure room. According to Pileggi's later account of the theft as told to him by Hill, the actual amount of the loss was $480,000, and the money was spread around a number of Mafia bosses, including Colombo crime captain Sebastian "Buster" Aloi and Paul Vario, Burke's mentor. Both men got about $50,000 each in tribute while Hill, Burke, and DeSimone took shares as well.

Investigators also learned that Hill took credit for another airport theft around 1969 involving cash stolen from Alitalia Airlines by two black associates. The problem with that money was that it consisted of consecutively numbered currency, which would be easier to trace, so Hill said he sold it at a discount to Paul Vario. Then a year later Hill and hijacker Joe Allegro robbed a concession store at JFK and netted $60,000. For Hill, the airport seemed like easy pickings and a place where he could get away with any crime he put his mind to without being caught.

Cudak wasn't as lucky as Hill and DeSimone, and eventually postal investigators arrested him. But even when he was freed on bail, Cudak continued his thievery until he pleaded guilty in November 1970 in Brooklyn federal court and received a seven-year prison sentence. In the hopes of getting leniency and parole, Cudak decided to tell his story to a U.S. Senate investigating committee in 1971, revealing the extent of the crimes just one group of thieves could carry out at the airports. In New York, according to Cudak, a group of Mafia members and associates became the people who could fence the stolen property all over the metropolitan area.

Cudak wasn't a member of the mob; not with that surname he wasn't. But he relied on a number of Mafiosi who either fenced the stolen merchandise themselves or were plugged into a network of associates who were experts in moving the products. When dealing with over $100 million in stolen airport cargo, those involved had to know what they were doing and be well connected in the Mafia. According to what Cudak told the Senate committee in his testimony, the men through whom he fenced included Anthony "Tony" Boiardo, Albert DeAngelis, and Greg Scarpa.

The three men were not household names, and the senators who questioned Cudak didn't go into detail about their criminal histories. But to police they each had a certain mob pedigree that was unmistakable. Boiardo was son of the legendary New Jersey gangster Richie "The Boot" Boiardo. Anthony Boiardo, known as "Tony Boy," became in his own right a member of the Genovese crime family. DeAngelis, who ran a jewelry business on Canal Street in Manhattan, also was tied to the Teamsters. Scarpa was a powerful member of the Colombo crime family who in fits and starts had been providing information over the years to the FBI. The most notable bit of cooperation by Scarpa involved leads that led to the solving of the disappearance and murders of three civil rights workers in Mississippi in the 1960s.

Cudak identified others fences who either worked under Scarpa or were as one senator said part of "syndicated crime." Among them was Cosmo "Gus" Cangiano, a Colombo crime family member, who decided to appear before the Senate committee and testify in a half-hearted effort to defend himself. Appearing without a lawyer, Cangiano listened as a committee investigator read excerpts of Cudak's testimony about airport crime and once answered, "It's true, and I respectfully stand on the Fifth Amendment." Cangiano invoked the Fifth Amendment numerous times, even when asked if he knew an associate found murdered in the trunk of a car at JFK in October 1969.

The cargo rip-offs credited to Cudak and his associates were substantial and in total over the years dwarfed anything the Burke crew would later gain from the Lufthansa heist a decade later. But for the customers who suffered the losses, it appeared that they only reported to the authorities a fraction of the true losses. In other words, airport robberies and theft were likely much greater than anyone imagined. This was illustrated by an analysis done by investigators with the U.S. Post Office who looked at a sample of ten percent of the robberies of registered mail Cudak had identified. The survey found that the amounts of claims filed with postal authorities didn't represent the true value of the losses since victims had originally undervalued their cargo to reduce the fees they had to pay for registered mail. In some cases, victims didn't file any claims with postal authorities because they had commercial insurance.

Cudak's revelations put into stark relief the size of the mob take of airport cargo, particularly jewels, cash, and securities. The latter were as good as cash because they were often bearer instruments, which could easily be converted to cash. Although the Port Authority police had jurisdiction over the three major airports—JFK, Newark, and LaGuardia—many in law enforcement and government had for years been questioning the agency's ability, as well as that of private security firms, to handle the problem in the face of an increasingly serious escalation in cargo thefts.

But the mob infiltration of the airports and the cargo industry didn't just involve rip-offs of highly valuable items. After months of investigation and several days of the public hearings, the New York State Commission of Investigation, a body set up in the aftermath of the infamous Apalachin meeting of top mobsters in 1957, found that the Mafia had been able to infiltrate the New York airport trucking industry, particularly at JFK. There was also evidence of mounting cargo thefts, despite industry claims to the contrary, and reports of protection rackets and loansharking at the airport.

In terms of the Mafia, what appeared to be happening at the airport was similar to what New York City had seen in other industries that relied on trucking, notably the garment industry in Manhattan. Mafia figures owned and operated a number of garment trucking companies, and police had numerous reports about the way the truckers had formed a cartel, with the industry carved up among themselves. In addition, gangsters along Seventh Avenue loaned money at usurious rates, influenced the garment unions, and had interests in dress manufacturing companies. Trucking was a key link in the garment production cycle because manufacturers needed to have their products shipped to contracting factories, which produced the finished products, and then taken over the road to retail outlets. Control of trucking often meant control of the price of shipping goods, and, if needed, the mob could hold out the threat of a delay in shipments to exact an advantage over the manufacturers.

At JFK, state investigators found evidence that the top Teamster union official, Harry Davidoff, had been threatening at least two airlines, Northwest Airlines and National Airlines, not to switch their trucking business to another company. Both airlines, according to testimony before the state commission, had wanted to switch to a newer and more reliable trucking company but were warned off by Davidoff.

"The gist of the conversation was that if National persisted, National would find it very difficult to handle any of their trucking requirements in the New York area," Alvin C. Schweizer, an official of an airline industry group, told the commission in testimony. The same call was made by Davidoff to Northwest, said Schweizer. Both airlines decided not to switch, he added.

Davidoff, said Schweizer, had enormous power as a union official with Teamsters Local 295, a union that would be dogged by allegations of organized crime for years to come. The local was also found to have ties to noted labor racketeer John "Johnny Dio" Dioguardi. However, despite the revelations and allegations against him in the state probe, Davidoff remained a powerful figure in the union for decades and had his own connections to some of those involved in the 1978 Lufthansa heist.

The Commission of Investigation findings underscored how the mob influence at the airport had extended beyond control of gangs of thieves like that involving Robert Cudak. It was also apparent that the airline cargo industry was downplaying the losses it suffered from cargo theft and hadn't been able to quell mounting losses. At JFK alone, state police determined that in 1968, a time when Cudak and his associates were stealing tens of millions of dollars of high-value cargo with abandon, there were 128 thefts involving $2 million in cargo reported. This was obviously a low-ball figure, but in the prior year the losses amounted to a measly $877,000, again an outrageously minimal amount given what Cudak later revealed he was stealing from JFK and elsewhere.

With the nation finally waking up to the Mafia infiltration at the airport, a push began to ramp up cargo security by pushing aside the Port Authority police and replacing them with something seen as more capable of dealing with the mob. For that, Governor Nelson Rockefeller started pressing to have the Waterfront Commission—a bi-state organization set up by New York and New Jersey in 1953— take over policing the cargo and trucking operations at JFK, La-Guardia, and Newark airports. The commission had been set up to combat Mafia and racketeering activity on the docks of both states. The mob not only controlled labor unions but also bled stevedores dry with loansharking and gambling. The seamy life on the docks was fodder for director Elia Kazan's 1954 film *On the Waterfront*, which was inspired in part by the efforts of a Brooklyn priest to combat the mob, as well as testimony before the commission.

The Waterfront Commission didn't push itself to the forefront on the airport cargo issue: Rockefeller's staff believed it was better suited for the job than the hodge-podge of Port Authority cops and private security. In 1968, the commission did its own investigation and found that the underworld (i.e., Mafia) was encroaching into the growing cargo business at JFK and that things were reaching a "dangerous situation." But opposition to the Rockefeller plan came from the airline industry and others, including the Queens District Attorney Thomas Mackell, who admitted he took financial support from the International Longshoremen's Association, the powerful dock union that for years police said had been under the influence of racketeers like Anthony "Tough Tony" Anastasio, a Gambino crime family member and brother of the murdered crime boss Albert Anastasia. Mackell defended the kind of help he got on his campaign from the union, saying "it is not an unusual thing."

There was some legitimate concern that while the Waterfront Commission had done a good job in combatting some racketeering activity and labor abuse on the docks, it didn't have the experience dealing with air cargo. Industry officials believed that putting the commission into the airports would lead to congestion, confusion, and delay in moving cargo. Relatively small numbers of ships enter New York harbor, compared to the thousands of daily aircraft arrivals and departures at JFK and Newark, noted the critics.

But with cargo losses appearing to grow, support continued to increase for the Waterfront Commission taking an expanded role. Even *The New York Times* editorialized in favor of the move. By 1971, the legislatures of both New York and New Jersey had enacted measures to turn over cargo security to the commission, which would install its own police force at JFK, LaGuardia, and Newark. Any such expansion of the commission power required a congressional resolution and one was submitted by New York Senator Jacob Javits in early 1971.

However, political headwinds increased. Criticism rose against the Waterfront Commission itself. Although the commission was credited with ending some mob influence on the docks such as murders, loansharking, and kickbacks, critics said it hadn't rid the waterfront of all Mafia activity or stopped the cargo pilfering from the docks. Some said the commission really wasn't equipped to run serious investigations into Mafia associates.

Nonetheless, Rockefeller continued to push for the plan to have the commission's policing jurisdiction extended, telling a Senate subcommittee in 1972 that "racketeers have seized control of the air freight industry at these airports by infiltration of unions and the truckmen's association." Hogwash, said Leo Seybold the vice president of an air-transport group, who told the subcommittee that "organized crime has not infiltrated employees of the airline industry" and that the air-cargo theft rate at the New York area airports was not rising but declining. Seybold made these claims even though career criminals like Robert Cudak had already revealed the massive thefts of valuable property from the airports.

By 1973, several airlines such as Eastern and United, had filed lawsuits to block New Jersey legislation aimed at expanding the commission's powers, saying it was unconstitutional. The airlines lost in court. However, as time went on, the Rockefeller plan to expand the Waterfront Commission's role in battling airport cargo theft by the Mafia lost support. Despite backing by both New York and New Jersey, the measure couldn't get key action in Congress. Bickering continued over whether cargo theft was as high as the $10 million estimated by the commission or as low as the $700,000 reported by the airlines.

For Jimmy Burke and his crew at Robert's Lounge, whatever the true extent of the losses really didn't matter since to them it was all found money, which they picked up every day.

CHAPTER FIVE
"WE WILL GET YOU"

FOR THE CREW AT ROBERT'S LOUNGE it didn't really matter who had control over the air cargo security at JFK—be it the Waterfront Commission, the Port Authority police, or Joe Blow private security. The kind of thievery they routinely practiced allowed them to simply wait for the cargo to leave the airport, without having to venture past security guards. Burke had surrounded himself with a group of toughs and psychopaths who became experts at watching the way truck traffic moved in and around the airport. Like stealthy cats, they pounced and robbed lucrative cargo at the barrel of a gun.

A truck driver named Toivo Edward Aroksaar found out first-hand what Thomas DeSimone's way of doing business was like one day in 1973. Aroksaar had worked for several years at JFK, starting as a cargo handler with Lufthansa and then taking a new job at Austrian Airlines as a cargo representative who dealt directly with customers. After Austrian Airlines went out of business, Aroksaar took a job with an air-freight company and after a layoff took a temporary job driving a truck to pick up goods at the airport and then take them to other places in the city.

June 21, 1973, was actually Aroksaar's first day as a trucker. It was a sunny first day of summer. It would be a time he would never forget. His destination was Bush Terminal in Brooklyn with a truckload of women's apparel. Not experienced as a driver, Aroksaar asked for directions from his boss and decided to go north from the airport on the Van Wyck Expressway to the Long Island Expressway where he could then go west to the terminal.

The drive was uneventful until Aroksaar took the exit ramp onto the expressway at about 1:00 P.M. and noticed a late-model Plymouth station wagon slow down and stop. Aroksaar stopped his truck to avoid a collision and saw two men get out of the stopped car.

"I thought it was a funny place to let out hitchhikers," Aroksaar remembered thinking. Then he saw the guns. With no place to go— he couldn't back up or turn around—Aroksaar stayed still and sat in the truck cab.

"There was nothing to do, so I stayed in the truck and was hijacked," said Aroksaar.

One of the men who approached the truck was DeSimone, who opened the passenger door to the cab and told Aroksaar to do exactly what he was told to do, which was to follow the car. If he didn't, DeSimone told Aroksaar he would blow his brains out. He was holding a .38-caliber handgun.

With DeSimone sitting in the passenger seat, Aroksaar followed the Plymouth to the Junction Boulevard exit to a spot on the road near the old Alexander's Department Store. With the truck stopped, DeSimone told the truck driver to get into the Plymouth and lie face down on the seat. After a ride through the streets of Queens, the Plymouth stopped at a garage and a shirt was put over Aroksaar's head. He was told to lie down on the back area of the station wagon.

DeSimone then did something that was a standard tactic of the Robert's Lounge crime crew. He reached into Aroksaar's pocket, took out his wallet, and gave him a $50 bill as a payment to buy his silence. Since he had rifled through his victim's wallet, DeSimone knew the man's personal information.

"I'm going to take your name and address, so if you squeal, we will get you," said DeSimone.

After terrorizing Aroksaar, DeSimone and his accomplice asked the truck driver if he was hungry and wanted anything to eat. A sandwich was brought to him, and Aroksaar ate it. He had missed his lunch hour a long time ago. It was about 4:00 P.M. that DeSimone finally let Aroksaar crawl out of the Plymouth after it had been driven to the Knapp Street exit on the Belt Parkway.

"Get out. Don't turn around. If you do, we'll kill you," said DeSimone, who had emphasized the message by putting a gun to the base of Aroksaar's skull.

Once freed, Aroksaar got to a telephone and called the NYPD and then his boss.

When the cops and the FBI, which had a task force dealing with hijacking, questioned Aroksaar they showed him a few photographs of potential suspects. He picked out DeSimone as the hijacker without any trouble.

DeSimone was known to police because he had been implicated in a number of heists and police had long suspected the crew at Robert's Lounge of being involved. Hijacking had turned into big business in the city, and Burke's gang was among the group of usual suspects police and the FBI—which had been targeting the crime— always considered.

"By 1970 Jimmy owned hijacking at Kennedy Airport," Henry Hill later remembered. "It was Jimmy who decided what and when shipments and trucks were worth taking. It was Jimmy who picked the crew for each job."

Hill occasionally went out on hijackings with DeSimone but usually just helped to fence the loads of stolen property. The strong-arm holdup of Mr. Aroksaar was more of an exception. Usually, truck drivers would give up their shipments by prearrangement. Drivers used to hang out at Robert's Lounge, and to work off their bar bills or gambling debts would sometimes tip Burke and his crew to upcoming shipments.

The tactic for a "give up" was simple, recalled Hill. A driver would stop for a cup of coffee and leave the key in the ignition. When he came out he found the truck and the cargo gone. The driver would report the loss and according to Hill it would be labor racketeer and Lucchese family member Johnny Dioguardi who would protect the driver if his boss tried to fire him.

Burke had honed the tactic of taking a driver's license and other identification from an uncooperative driver to create fear that he would be tracked down if he cooperated with the cops. He would also, Hill recalled, slip the driver $50—just as DeSimone had done with Aroksaar—to help buy his silence.

"There was never one driver who made it to court to testify against him," said Hill. "There were quite a few dead ones who tried."

Well, not quite.

Although he was forced to take the $50 the day he was hijacked, Aroksaar immediately decided that he wanted to help police and the FBI make a case against DeSimone. The trucker not only identified DeSimone from a photograph but took the witness stand in January 1975 to testify for the federal government in the case against him in the 1973 hijacking.

Defending DeSimone was Michael Coiro, a flamboyant Queens attorney who loved the gangsters he represented and at this point had secretly crossed the line in illegally helping mobsters as a true associate of organized crime. Coiro's dark deeds wouldn't be disclosed for a few years in the future. But before DeSimone's trial was supposed to start, the attorney already showed a cavalier attitude toward the court.

Brooklyn federal judge John Bartels had set November 25, 1974, as a trial date for DeSimone. But with the judge and federal prosecutor in court, potential jurors waiting and with a half dozen witnesses ready—not to mention DeSimone—Coiro was a no-show. It seems that the brash attorney had another trial going in Queens state court and couldn't be bothered to show up. Bartels was fuming and called Coiro on the carpet, telling him a lot of money had been wasted in getting things ready. The judge slapped Coiro with a fine, which the attorney appealed to no avail.

In court, the prosecutor told the jury that there was no question DeSimone had hijacked the truck and that trucker Aroksaar had identified him to the police and FBI. DeSimone also made a very clear threat to the driver, said the prosecutor: "I know your address now. I know who you are. If you identify me, you and your family are going to be dead."

Coiro's defense was rather weak. The attorney told the jury that maybe Aroksaar, after being questioned on-and-off by cops for ten months, wanted to "see things a certain way." He suggested that Aroksaar had been coached on how to testify. Aroksaar was the government's main witness against DeSimone and gave straightforward testimony, identifying to the jury DeSimone as the armed hijacker and referring to him numerous times in his testimony.

The jury convicted DeSimone and on April 11, 1975, Bartels sentenced him to a total of ten years in prison. He would spend his time at the federal prison in Lewisburg, Pennsylvania, a place familiar to many of the Robert's Lounge crew.

Although DeSimone was out of action, the crew at Robert's Lounge didn't seem to miss any opportunities. Henry Hill had earlier taken an interest in a bar on Queens Boulevard known as The Suite after its original owner, who was a compulsive gambler, invited him in as a silent partner. The establishment was right across the street from the Queens Criminal Court Building on Queens Boulevard, a public facility that Burke and his crew seemed to be able to avoid because of secret connections they allegedly had in the local prosecutor's office. As Hill remembered it, the place was seen by Paul Vario as a good spot to have as a clean club where no crimes were planned or committed. To keep it that way, Vario ordered all the gangsters and associates in his crew to stay away from The Suite so it wouldn't draw suspicion.

But over time, The Suite became a meeting place for many in the Vario-Burke orbit, including Vario himself. Before he went to prison, DeSimone made the place one of his stops, as did a mob associate out of Brooklyn named Angelo Sepe and a peculiar wig salesman from the neighborhood named Marty Krugman. This trio would later come together in crucial ways for the Lufthansa heist. But that was still years away.

While Hill had been making money with all sorts of crooked deals—hijacking, gambling, credit-card scams with Parnell "Stacks" Edwards and other hustles—Burke remained the top dog of the group. One incident involving a load of stolen furs showed just how much Burke could control things. The truck driver who was supposed to take the $250,000 shipment of furs from Newark Airport to

Manhattan's fur district, drove instead to a warehouse in lower Manhattan where a group of mob associates took the load out of the truck. The driver then was taken to a location in Yonkers where he falsely reported that his truck had been hijacked by several armed men, a typical "give up" heist which was another time-tested method of the Robert's Lounge group.

Meanwhile, the furs were placed in large plastic garbage bags and taken to a home on Staten Island. It was at the house, according to the FBI, that Burke showed up and for a nice discounted price purchased 75 percent of the stolen shipment, or as many as 400 furs. With the help of DeSimone, who was still a free man at the time, Burke took away the furs and brought them back to Brooklyn where he had a number of places, including his own home, to use to sell all kinds of swag for a nice profit, spreading some it around to Vario. The small amount of furs that Burke didn't buy—about 25 percent—was sold on consignment to a couple of the other thieves.

One place Henry Hill remembered as an outlet where Burke fenced his goods was the Bamboo Lounge, a place he described as a "high class rug joint" on Rockaway Parkway in Queens, right near JFK. It was run by a mob associate known as Sonny Bamboo but whose real name was Angelo McConaugh. Rug joints were night-clubs that by gangster standards were supposed to be higher class but were really furnished in tacky style, complete with potted plants. But the real use Burke had for the Bamboo Lounge was as a bazaar for stolen property, or as Hill would later say, "a supermarket for airport swag." Criminals and legitimate customers, from insurance adjusters to union delegates and discount-store owners, came by for bargains, according to Hill.

"It was like an open market," said Hill. "There was a long list of items in demand, and you could get premiums if you grabbed the right cargo."

Burke, Hill, and the rest of the Robert's Lounge group had a great deal of success hijacking trucks. Dresses, furs, lobsters, cigarettes, coffee, televisions, watches, jewelry were always in demand, and Burke's boys always found a way to get them to an army of eager buyers. But Burke was a bit of a rube when it came to dealing with stolen securities, which could prove lucrative as Robert Cudak and his clique had found at JFK. Hill and Burke did get involved in securities thefts but for a quick buck sold them for pennies on the dollar to Wall Street crooks who used them as fake collateral for big bank loans. Hill and Burke would later kick themselves for the way they so easily lost out on making millions of dollars.

CHAPTER SIX
TALES OF THE GOLD BUG

PAUL VARIO COULD BE FOUND at two places in south Brooklyn with regularity. One was Geffken's, the old German bar on Flatlands Avenue. The other was a sprawling junkyard on Avenue D in Canarsie where a trailer was Vario's favorite place of business. The southern part of the borough, particularly the Old Mill section, was the spot where Vario grew up and where he always felt comfortable.

Geffken's had been in the family of Evelyn and Henry Geffken for as long as anyone could remember. The family had immigrated from Germany and settled on a piece of Flatlands Avenue, which contained a house and a bar in separate buildings. Vario and his crowd of mob associates adopted Geffken's as a favorite watering hole sometime in the 1960s. On warm days Vario would sit outside and play chess. When he had marital problems and was separated from his wife, Vario took to living for a time in an apartment next to the establishment. Then when the Geffken family decided to sell the property for good in 1971 for $40,000, the buyer turned out to be a son of one of Vario's friends, Peter Abinanti.

Vario liked antique cars, so the junkyard was a place where he could also feel at home. Among his favorite old vehicles was a 1957 red-and-white Chevrolet, which he drove only on Sundays and never very far. If the prized vehicle needed spare parts, Vario just had to look through the piles of scraps he had outside the yard trailer. The junkyard was the place where Vario held court and could talk with people about anything, feeling secure enough that he wouldn't be the object of snooping cops, in part because a lot of local officers would come by the trailer and pay their respects, take some illegal gratuities for favors given and maybe get a good deal on hubcaps. Vario also didn't like using the telephone, the better to avoid wiretaps.

As a grown man, Vario, although he only finished two years of high school, took to reading: medical and legal publications were his favorites. He would tell young associates to go to college and become a professional at something. In quiet moments, he listened to opera recordings. This intellectual side of Vario was in sharp contrast to the way he had grown up in Brooklyn. For a while he seemed destined for a life in the penitentiary, particularly in 1937 when a sixteen-year-old girl from Howard Beach named Frances said a twenty-one-year-old Vario and his friends sexually assaulted her after she had left a church function.

The charges against Vario and his friends were serious and were widely reported in the local newspapers, notably the allegation that friends of Vario had threatened to "bump off" a witness, who was a friend of the victim, if she testified truthfully about the attack. The witness, identified in an article about the trial in the *Leader-Observer* newspaper in Queens as Millie Handelman, said that she had been sitting in a car with Frances when two men approached and chased her away, saying they only wanted the sixteen-year-old victim. Handelman named Vario as one of the young men in the attack but couldn't identity his co-defendant Anthony Romano. Handelman had to be brought to court with police protection because, she testified, Vario and his friend had threatened to "bump her off."

Rape victim Frances (newspapers of the time had no qualms about identifying her by her full name) did identify Vario and Romano as her attackers but said she passed out and wasn't aware of being attacked by three others. Vario and Romano were convicted of the rape and sentenced to a term of ten to twenty years in Sing Sing prison. Vario tried asking for a new trial but was rebuffed. A decade or more in prison was a pretty stiff ordeal for a young man, but under the laws and practices in place at the time Vario was

paroled twice but returned to prison twice for various parole violations, according to a biographic report of him prepared by a New
York State Senate investigative committee. It wasn't clear what
Vario's new offenses were, but he had additional arrests in his life
for burglary and dealing in stolen property. Vario finally earned a
discharge from his state parole in 1962, the committee said.

As a true gangster, Vario didn't toe the legal line very long. After a
major Long Island gambler known as Jake Colombo died, it was Vario
who took over his operation in what was the Cedarhurst-Inwood sections, according to state investigators. Vario had moved in the mid-
1960s to Island Park, a beachfront community in Nassau County, so
the gambling activity was easy for him to keep tabs on. He later expanded his operations in Brooklyn and began making serious money.

In 1965, officials on Long Island arrested Vario and eight other
men on charges they ran a multi-million-dollar gambling ring and
attempted to bribe a police officer who was taking money for the
purported protection of the gamblers but in reality was working for
ten months as a confidential undercover operative for the Suffolk
County police commissioner. The officer, Sgt. Everett Hoelzer, had
reported that a year earlier he was approached to take money to tip off
the ring to wiretaps and investigations. To keep the investigation
hush-hush, Hoelzer would meet commissioner John J. Barry in se-
cluded places and pass along coded notes. Vario was identified in
news accounts as being from Island Park and with an occupation as
a florist, a reference to his Fountainebleu shop.

Not to be outdone, Nassau County officials also targeted Vario's
gambling operations and in June 1966 arrested him and seventeen
others on charges they ran a $30 million a year bookmaking opera-
tion. Vario, whom newspapers described as the "Czar" of the ring,
wasn't the only mobster charged in the case. Also indicted was
Stephen DePasquale of Atlantic Beach, who was described by police as a soldier in the Lucchese family.

Local gambling arrests went with the territory for Vario, and the
legal problems were part of the cost of doing business. Each arrest
burnished his reputation as a major up-and-coming player in the
Lucchese family and made him a better target for law enforcement.

Since gambling rings generate lots of cash, the Internal Revenue Service gets involved to track the money and find out who didn't report that income. There was also the quirky law that required those involved in gambling to purchase a federal stamp, and in February 1966, Vario and several other men were charged in Brooklyn federal court with not having procured the $50 stamp.

Meanwhile, local authorities in Brooklyn were also becoming increasingly interested in Vario's activities, in part because of corruption being uncovered among police after revelations by detective Frank Serpico led to the creation of the Knapp Commission in 1969. About two years later, William McCarthy, the first deputy commissioner of the NYPD, was so disgusted with the corruption problem among plainclothes police in Brooklyn that he decided to revamp the entire unit. Plainclothes cops were those who wore the regular silver shields and worked on gambling and other street-vice crimes. They became notorious for corruption. After the reorganization, one of the new plainclothes units noticed what one official said was "organized crime activity" at Geffken's Bar, notably through the comings and goings of Vario and his crew.

McCarthy's interest was piqued, and he approached Charles J. Hynes, then a senior attorney in the rackets bureau of Brooklyn District Attorney Eugene Gold, to consider a joint investigation into Geffken's and the gangsters who frequented it. With the revelations about systemic police corruption on everyone's mind, Gold agreed but insisted that his office work with a new police anti-corruption unit. But McCarthy assured Gold that the newly revamped plainclothes squad could be trusted and the prosecutor agreed to go along and assigned Hynes to take the case.

There were some immediate problems for investigators looking to probe Vario, not the least of which was the fact that Geffken's was on a largely residential block and traditional surveillance by police would have been easily noticed. To become unobtrusive, police set up a Christmas-tree business diagonally across the street from the bar and staffed it with plainclothes detectives. Since they were in the neighborhood, the detectives were able to take coffee and lunch breaks at Geffken's and blend in with the crowd of regulars, some of which were members of Vario's criminal crew.

The detectives' lunch hours were productive. They spotted Vario inside Geffken's, usually talking secretively with associates at a table in the rear of the bar. The cops also tuned their ears to conversations on a pay phone inside the building which clearly seemed to be related to sports betting. The next move by Hynes and the police was text-book investigative work: They got a judicial warrant for a wiretap on the Geffken's telephone and soon learned that many of the calls were being made to another telephone at the junkyard that Vario owned in Canarsie. A second wiretap authorization was granted by the court and the junkyard telephone was also tapped, revealing more conversations about sports betting.

Vario's Bargain Auto Parts Inc., at 5702 Avenue D, was about more than old cars and junkyard dogs. Associates like Jimmy Burke and Henry Hill could stop by to pay homage to the Lucchese capo. They weren't alone in doing so. Soon, investigators realized that Vario was seeing a great many Mafiosi at the trailer he used as an office. To get a better record of what was going on, Hynes and other investigators set up an observation post across from Bargain Auto inside space given to them by Nazareth High School and started logging in visits by some high-ranked mobsters to Vario's yard. But pictures and telephone taps could only help so much in building a criminal case.

"While our wiretap was productive in gathering information about illegal sports betting, loansharking, etc., we were unable to determine the purpose of the visits to the junkyard of the wise guys from the other [crime] families," Hynes remembered years later. "We needed to install an electronic listening device in the trailer on the junkyard property."

Planting a bugging device in the trailer wouldn't turn out to be an easy task. While Vario left the trailer on most days around 7:00 P.M., a night watchman showed up at that time and stayed until 7:00 A.M. To make access more difficult, the junkyard was surrounded by a fence topped with razor wire and patrolled by a German shepherd and Doberman pinscher. In order to get around such roadblocks, investigators benefited from human nature and a prosecutor named Henry Sobel who had worked for years as a licensed dog trainer.

Detectives noticed that the watchman took a dinner break every night around 9:00 P.M. at a nearby bar and with his sandwich drank a shot of vodka and a beer to wash things down. That dinner took a good 90 minutes, more than enough time for technicians to sneak into the trailer and plant a bugging device in the ceiling, just above Vario's desk. The big "if" was whether Sobel could neutralize the two dogs, which he did with steaks spiked with animal tranquilizer. The bug worked for months as an unsuspecting Vario held court with his myriad associates.

One of those visiting Vario was a twenty-five-year-old Doug LeVien Jr. During his visits to the trailer, LeVien, who was a detective working for Gold's office, posed as a cop on the make who was looking to tip off Vario to confidential investigative information—for a price. LeVien made thirty visits to Vario's trailer and was paid $450 in alleged bribes, money that was vouchered as evidence and would come back to haunt Vario and make his life supremely miserable.

In addition to LeVien's undercover activities, investigators compiled a mountain of tapes from the bug, as well as over 36,000 feet of color movie film and 34,000 still photographs of those who were seen from the observation post entering the junkyard. This kind of surveillance operation was unheard of for city prosecutors and when it came time to take the wraps off things, Gold trooped the news media over to the trailer at Bargain Auto and showed them the bug in the ceiling. The evidence compiled, Gold said, was a window into "a crime story bigger than Apalachin and the Valachi papers combined."

It was October 16, 1972, that over 1,200 police officers fanned out across New York City and surrounding Westchester, Nassau, and Suffolk counties to serve hundreds of subpoenas on Mafia members and associates. In terms of the scope of people being hauled in for questioning, it seemed like Gold was trying to take out the Mafia families. However, pundits noted that it wasn't clear how significant, apart from Vario, Gold's targets were or whether he would be able to make good on his claim that he was involved in "the most massive investigation of organized crime in the history of this country."

In the face of such news from a local prosecutor in New York City, it was fair to wonder how far the FBI had gone in terms of Mafia investigations. The answer was not very far at all. The late FBI director J. Edgar Hoover hadn't taken to investigations of the mob during his tenure. As a result, investigations into La Cosa Nostra were viewed with disfavor. However, with Hoover's death in 1972, the bureau slowly began to change its mindset, and in New York City, FBI special agents started to focus on the local Mafia.

But the problem remained that for a federal bureaucracy, the FBI stayed focused on just showing numbers of cases. So, as former special agent Jules Bonavolanta recalled in his book *The Good Guys,* the agents in New York were making a lot of gambling cases to boost their statistics and not focusing on the real power behind the Five Families.

"Numbers, numbers, numbers—the Bureau was crazy for numbers," recalled Bonavolanta. "How many investigations, how many arrests—more, more, more! It didn't matter if 95 percent of the arrests were shitty or if the punk you had busted the night before was back on the street the next day. As long as the numbers kept piling up, you were golden."

The Mafia bosses weren't targeted to any significant degree. The FBI also in the early 1970s had not attempted to use the new Racketeer Influenced and Corrupt Organizations law—known as RICO—to make cases against the crime families as the agency would later do. Gradually, things changed as new supervisors like James Kossler and Lee Laster revamped the New York City office of the FBI and refocused the agents onto more long-term and substantial cases. But it would be years, until 1980, before those efforts would bear fruit.

Another problem was the ineffectiveness of the federal organized crime Strike Force concept. The strike forces were set up in major metropolitan areas and were supposed to work independently and as adjuncts to the regular U.S. Attorney offices. But a congressional review found that about half of the convictions in Strike Force cases

resulted in no incarceration or else the targets were minor Mafia soldiers who received relatively short prison terms.

So, with the FBI or federal prosecutors not around to steal his
thunder, Gold had the field to himself. Of course when it came to
the Mafia, Gold had a habit of making grandiose investigative gestures in the past. Two years earlier his office had indicted thirty-five
mobsters on charges of criminal contempt. Among those arrested were
some men who were prominent Mafiosi of the day: Aniello Dellacroce
and Anthony Ruggiano of the Gambino family; Benny Aloi of the
Colombo family; and a number of Bonanno family leaders like Philip
Rastelli, Natale Evola, Paul Sciacca, and Frank Mari, even though
he had been missing since 1968. Added to the list of those charged
was Vincent Asaro's father Jerome. The charges eventually petered
out; they were either dropped or led to inconsequential pleas.

Still, the "Gold Bug" case as the investigation was called, brought
trouble for Vario, one of his sons also named Paul, as well as his
crime boss Carmine Tramunti. Vario and his associates like Jimmy
Burke had long had police officers in their pockets, and a handful of
cops were also targeted by Gold. In one case, an NYPD lieutenant
named Meyer Rubenstein was suspended for visiting the junkyard
where at one point he was overheard on a surveillance tape blurting
out in the trailer to one of Vario's associates, "Here's what I want to
tell you. I think your phones are being tapped." Rubenstein was brought
up on administrative charges in October 1972 at which time his attorney disclosed that the cop had "irrationally" blurted out the comment
about the tap.

Some 102 cops were investigated for visiting Vario's junkyard
and were suspected of being paid off for various favors, such as al-
lowing tow-truck drivers to pick up abandoned cars and presumably
bringing them to Bargain Auto Parts. However, only two officers appear to have been indicted as a result of the Gold Bug tapes. Detectives John Cuomo and Ralph Caccia were indicted on charges they
arranged for a dismissal of a case against four women related to one
of Vario's associates. To make matters worse, Caccia was accused
of meeting with Vario and two associates in the trailer, all within

earshot of the bugging device, and asking for a bribe of around $600 for himself and Cuomo.

Having police officers in his pockets was an asset many crooks believed Burke had—and shared with his main mob boss Vario, who had his own arsenal of cops to rely on. When needed, Vario could keep cops away from his people.

"Wiseguys like Paulie [Vario] have been paying off the cops for so many years that they probably sent more cops' kids to college than anybody else. They're like wiseguy scholarships," Hill told Pileggi.

Burke's cop connections were believed to have tipped him off to impending raids and surveillance. In addition, Burke had police connections who could tip him off about informants and people who may have been cooperating with authorities—a security breach that had led to the death in 1969 of Paul Katz after he decided to cooperate with police.

Although New York City had been rocked by numerous revelations about police corruption during the Knapp Commission and witnessed cops getting indicted, in the cases of the Gold Bug it wasn't easy to make a case stick. As for detective Cuomo, the court would eventually dismiss the indictment after it appeared that he didn't know anything about what his fellow officer had done in asking for an alleged bribe. The dispostion of Caccia's case couldn't be found.

Still, Vario didn't need the bad publicity and trouble Gold was causing him, particularly after he had been jailed for nine months in 1970 on contempt charges in what was a continuing war with Nassau District Attorney William Cahn. He also had to face hijacking charges, and the IRS was also beginning to focus on all the money he netted from gambling. On top of everything, Vario's marriage was on the rocks and he was now out of his Deer Park home and living next door to Geffken's Bar.

The day he was arrested, the fifty-eight-year-old Vario led detectives on a car chase through Brooklyn as he tried to elude them without success. While the charges against both Varios stemmed from the Gold Bug surveillance, they actually related to an alleged attempt to corrupt a Nassau County jail guard. The elder Vario was charged with witness tampering while his son Paul was indicted for perjury after he said he couldn't recall meeting a jail guard at Geffken's.

About two weeks after he led detectives on a merry chase through Brooklyn, Paul Vario was again indicted from evidence secured by the Gold Bug. This time the charges involved insurance fraud and grand larceny. Gold also stitched together yet another charge based on the trailer surveillance and the undercover work of detective LeVien. Vario was charged with conspiracy, bribery, and rewarding official misconduct for the several hundred dollars in payments LeVien received while posing as a crooked cop.

While Vario was getting hammered with multiple indictments, his close associates Jimmy Burke and Henry Hill found themselves facing their own serious trouble. It all stemmed from a vacation trip the two made to Tampa, paid for by a union for culinary workers at JFK. Burke and Hill visited a Tampa bar and club with a union friend Casey Rosado who promptly got into a heated argument with a man he said owed him money. The argument became physical and Burke and Hill jumped into the fray, with Burke grabbing John Ciacco, the man arguing with Rosado, and Hill beating him with a revolver. Ciacco was pretty bloodied but in the end agreed to pay his share of what he owed Rosado.

Hill said the whole affray seemed like nothing more than a family dispute. After cleaning up Ciacco, Hill and Burke resumed having a good time for the rest of the trip.

"That was it. Case closed. No big deal," remembered Hill.

It turns out it was a matter of the case being opened. Ciacco had a sister who worked as typist for the FBI in Tampa and when she saw how injured her brother was she told the agents she worked for. The woman told the FBI about Hill and Burke, the gun, the beating, and everything. With so many people having witnessed the fighting, the agents were able to make a case and had the FBI office in New York arrest Hill and Burke for extortion, playing it up as a major organized-crime case. A trial took place in Tampa and on November 3, 1972, Burke and Hill were quickly found guilty. They would get ten-year sentences in a federal prison but were able to stay free while they appealed their convictions.

Burke and Hill, operating out of Robert's Lounge and The Suite, continued to do business as usual. They ran credit-card schemes, sold stolen hijacked truckloads of goods and commiserated with Vario, who at this point was feeling under siege and considered by some a pariah. In fact, law enforcement was feeling good about itself because for the first time in years it seemed like the Mafia was on the ropes. After years of inattention to the Mob, the FBI was making an effort to target Mafiosi and the city district attorneys like Gold, Frank Hogan in Manhattan, and Burton Roberts in the Bronx were putting more people on organized crime cases. Quoting unidentified law-enforcement and underworld sources, the *New York Times* reporter Nicholas Gage penned an article in December 1972 that was headlined "Gambino Believed Seeking Single Mafia Family," about an amazing plan by Gambino crime boss Carlo Gambino to consolidate the Five Families into one group.

"Gambino was said to maintain that growing law enforcement pressure and persistent internal conflicts would destroy the five families here unless they were restructured into a tighter and stronger network," wrote Gage.

Part of the problem for Gambino, according to Gage, was that some of the Mafia families had lost their leaders through death: Thomas Lucchese, Joseph Profaci, and Vito Genovese. The result was that some of the families had become weak and undisciplined, and their members had grown careless. In particular, the Lucchese outfit had not only lost the political connections of its namesake but had become marred by the Gold Bug, which *The Times* said was a low point, especially for Vario, the man considered to be one of the family's important members.

Gambino also believed the crime families had grown too large with too many impulsive younger members. He wanted to expel hundreds of Mafia members who had shown weaknesses that made them a risk to the security or stability of the crime families, wrote Gage. Gambino feared, said Gage, that some mobsters had become soft and vulnerable to law-enforcement pressure which would make them become informants.

The problems Gambino perceived were real, and his predictions were prescient. He had no further to look than the activities of the Lucchese family where Vario, despite his cautious approach to doing business, had been played for a fool by Gold and his staff with the installation of the bugging device. Vario's reliance on men like Burke and Hill was also proving to be misplaced as they in turn associated with impulsive men like Thomas DeSimone and others targeted by the FBI. Burke was also a man with a homicidal streak, and his propensity for violence drew the attention of police and had already landed him and Hill in trouble.

The audacious plan ascribed to Gambino in late 1972 never came to be fulfilled as the five Mafia families went on to endure, with different levels of success. By early 1973, Vario himself had his hands full with problems. His many gambling arrests had finally led the IRS to charge him in mid-1972 with evading taxes on an indeterminate amount of gambling income in 1965 and 1966 while running a numbers operation in Inwood and Atlantic Beach on Long Island. Vario and his associate Steven DePasquale were charged with being "bankers," the men who were responsible for overseeing the computation of all bets and financing the operation.

Federal agents built the case against Vario and DePasquale by sending in undercover agents who ingratiated themselves as numbers runners or other operatives with the numbers operation doing business in the St. Albans area of Queens. The agents testified, as did a number of people who worked for the business. Then, Vario himself took the witness stand and under questioning by his attorney denied what other witnesses had said, particularly about his having taken a paper bag full of gambling cash and putting it in a desk at a social club on Long Island. Vario had to admit on the witness stand that he had pleaded guilty to an earlier charge of gambling conspiracy but said he only did that to go along with a plea bargain worked out by his lawyer. Otherwise, said Vario, he wasn't guilty.

The Brooklyn federal court jury thought otherwise about Vario and convicted him of evading taxes for a two-year period. In April

1973, Vario was sentenced to a total of six years in prison and fined $20,000. For prison, Vario was sent to Lewisburg Penitentiary, considered a high-security prison in Pennsylvania and about two hundred miles from New York City. As it turned out, Lewisburg was a Mafia social club. Doing time in the prison along with Vario were John "Johnny Dio" Dioguardi, a Lucchese family labor racketeer, and Vinny Aloi, a key leader of the Colombo crime family after family boss Joe Colombo had been put in a coma after being shot in 1971. Added to the mix was Henry Hill, who began serving his sentence for the Tampa extortion in 1974. Jimmy Burke had to serve his time in a different prison.

Life in prison for Vario and the other Mafiosi, as well as favored associates like Hill, was different from what the regular inmates experienced. The gangsters had food and liquor smuggled in with the help of pliant guards and cooked in their own rooms in special areas. A memorable scene in *Goodfellas* showed the mobsters cooking Italian dinners, with Dio using a razor blade to thinly slice garlic for the sauce.

"It was wild. There was wine and booze," Hill recalled. "Looking back, I don't think Paulie [Vario] went to the general mess five times in the two and a half years he was there. We had a stove and pots and pans and silverware stacked in the bathroom. We had glasses and an ice-water cooler where we kept the fresh meats and cheeses."

Although he was besieged by numerous investigations, Vario wasn't afraid to put up a legal fight. After he was convicted in the Gold Bug case for giving money to a cop, Vario's attorney Joel Winograd appealed and argued that there was never any proof that undercover cop Doug LeVien had actually been given any cash by Vario. In fact, during the trial LeVien admitted that prosecutors had never tested the cash allegedly given by Vario to his associate Clyde Brooks [serving as an intermediary in the bribe] to see if Vario's fingerprints were on the money. It was an embarrassing lapse in police procedure, and the appellate court used it to reverse Vario's conviction as well as that of Brooks.

The day he learned of the decision overturning the conviction,

Winograd showed up at Geffken's and found Vario, who had been freed from his federal tax prison sentence, hanging out wearing an undershirt and trousers. Vario was one of the older, working-class Mafiosi who didn't find it necessary to impress people by being well dressed. Winograd played coy and told Vario he wanted to have a drink with him so the mobster ordered two whiskeys from the bar.

"What this all about?" asked Vario quizzically of his lawyer.

"I wanted to toast you and celebrate because," and here Winograd paused for dramatic effect, "your conviction was just overturned."

With that, Vario lumbered up out of his chair and embraced Winograd. That night at Geffken's there were drinks all around. The decision effectively meant Vario wouldn't have to face the prospect of another prison term—at least for the foreseeable future.

By mid-1978, Vario, Hill, and Burke where either out of prison, or in Burke's case, completing the rest of the sentence at a half-way facility in Manhattan. Yet the Mafia they were coming back to in 1978 was different than it was when they all went to prison. The Lucchese family had gone through upheaval with the death of its namesake, Thomas Lucchese, in 1967, and his successor Tramunti was taken off the street in 1973 after being convicted in a federal heroin case. Tramunti died in prison in October 1978, and the leadership of the family remained in flux, although Vario was still considered consiglieri. Carlo Gambino, the most respected and powerful of the Five Family bosses had also died in 1976 of natural causes and was succeeded by his cousin Paul Castellano.

In the Bonanno family, which had criminal interests in the airport, upstart Carmine Galante had tried to bully his way to the leadership position with the help of Sicilian gangsters. However, the official boss Philip Rastelli still had considerable backing, particularly from a group led by Massino, a newly made Mafia member who had a hijacking racket that rivaled Burke's operation. For the Genovese family, the acting boss was Frank Tieri, the latest in a line of successors who took over as leader after the murder or incarceration of other candidates like Thomas Eboli and Gerardo Catena. For the Colombo family, considered the weakest of the Five Families, Vincent Aloi had become the boss. Aloi's family had seen its power diminish since namesake Joseph Colombo was paralyzed in a 1971 shooting and died in May 1978.

To ease the transition from prison, Burke would have a legitimate job during the day and at night would have to report back to the facility. The idea was for inmates like Burke to get acclimatized back into civilian life and hopefully lead law-abiding lives. But there was no way a man like Burke, who had grown up scheming, stealing, and killing, would change into anything other than a criminal. Hill also couldn't leave the criminal life, and said that after Lewisburg he got into drug dealing to catch up on the money he couldn't make while he had been in prison. Vario, now sixty-four years old, had to be careful about what he did but knew that there was still money to be made on the street. All three were hungry and eager for a big score—if the opportunity came along.

CHAPTER SEVEN
"I GOT A COUPLE OF MILLION"

THE BIRTH OF THE IDEA for the Lufthansa heist came not from Paul Vario or Jimmy Burke but rather from the desperation and greed of Louis Werner, a man who couldn't be trusted. He had been working for over a decade at the Lufthansa Airlines cargo operation at JFK, and his personal life story read like a low-rent version of Peyton Place. His marriage to Beverly—who was sleeping with his good friend William Fischetti—was on the rocks, and he was spending money like water on a new girlfriend. Plus, Werner gambled and was into his bookie for thousands of dollars. That was a debt that had to be paid. He was also behind in child-support payments.

Entrusted with the oversight of high-value cargo such as cash and jewels, Werner didn't care about such lofty things as his fiduciary duty. If Werner saw an opportunity for thievery, he took it. He was the kind of risky, dishonest airport employee with money pressures who Robert Cudak had told congressional investigators years early could easily be compromised and help make JFK easy pickings for the Mafia.

It was October 8, 1976, when Lufthansa flight 493 from Quito, Ecuador, arrived at JFK with a special sealed bag containing currency. Banks and foreign-exchange operations often sent cash by airline back to New York City and had the money placed in high-value bags that got special handling and were secured by a chain around the bag. This particular shipment from Quito contained the equivalent of $22,000 in currency: Italian lira, Belgian and French francs, Canadian and American dollars, Swedish kronor. The bag was placed in a special high-value room and Lufthansa employees noticed the security chain was still intact. Things seemed to be in order.

The next day, October 9, when the bag was checked, it was discovered that the currency was all gone. Suspicion immediately fell on Werner since it was his job to meet incoming flights, and he knew the contents of the bag from the airline manifest and other documents. He also had lied to his boss when he said there was no valuable cargo on the flight. But without video surveillance evidence or anything more concrete linking him to the theft, Werner wasn't arrested.

Of course, Werner had taken the money and within a few days took it all to Gruenewald who offered to exchange it but keep it buried in his backyard until the heat of the investigation cooled off. But after becoming increasingly paranoid, Werner took the cash back from Gruenewald, paid him $5,000 for his troubles and then asked another friend, Bill Fischetti, to help make the currency exchange. Fischetti was an old gambling and bowling buddy of Werner, both frequented Falcaro's Bowling Alley in the town of Lawrence in Nassau, a popular sports venue run by champion bowler Joe Falcaro who notched over sixty-five perfect games in his career. Fischetti made several trips to Manhattan where he exchanged the foreign currency into dollars.

Werner was never fired from Lufthansa after the disappearance of the Quito shipment of currency. Instead he was assigned to work in the cargo area of the airlines in a large warehouse bearing the number 261. It was one of those events, combining with so many other things, some quite by chance, that would later come together in the big heist. The facility had a valuable-property room, which had been made more physically secure with the building of a cinderblock wall and the installation of alarm systems. Werner had the run of the place. He knew the alarm system, and every day knew what was going in and out of the secure room.

Gruenewald and Werner still kept their friendship alive. In fact,

Werner needed friends because after getting away with the Quito currency caper he felt emboldened about targeting bigger money shipments, maybe even diamonds, something that could make him big money and take care of all of his problems. In 1978, he told Fischetti they could do something big. The best time was in the cold weather, when his heavy winter coat would make it easy for Werner to hide a package of jewels and walk out of the cargo area without being detected.

The Owl Tavern on New York Boulevard [now known as Guy R. Brewer Boulevard] was one of many bars and dives around JFK, the kinds of places airport workers, cargo brokers, and mobsters would frequent. These were joints where connections could be made, big scores dreamed up, and conspiracies of all kinds hatched. Even if you were down on your luck, The Owl was a place any aspiring thief could try and get someone to buy them a drink.

It was early August 1978 that Brian Weremeychik, a Lufthansa worker who was a little short of cash stopped by The Owl. He spotted Gruenewald, who looked like a guy who could spot him a quick loan. Maybe $5 or $10? Gruenewald leaned over and said don't worry about a few bucks—"I got a couple of million more." Weremeychik laughed because he didn't believe him. Gruenewald wasn't kidding, and said he could take it out of Lufthansa, "his place," as he called it, where gold and diamonds were plentiful. Now, Weremeychik knew he wasn't messing around.

"I know you are a little wild. Do you have any friends who are as wild as you?" Gruenewald asked.

A few days later, Weremeychik came back to The Owl with a friend named "J.J." Gruenewald showed up at the bar dressed in his Lufthansa uniform and carrying an attaché case. They all left the bar and drove to a nearby park where Gruenewald showed why he wasn't fooling around. He had a copy of a Lufthansa cargo manifest listing gold and diamonds.

At another bar on nearby Pitkin Avenue in Ozone Park, the group met another of Weremeychik's friends and over more drinks Gruenewald said he wanted to pull off the heist on the approaching Labor

Day weekend. That was too close, said one of the men. The plan was put in abeyance.

A few days later, the group again met, and Columbus Day 1978 was also discussed since Gruenewald believed there would be as much as $6 million in the cargo area. There were a number of planning discussions, and Gruenewald brought along a schematic of the outside and inside of the cargo building. The best time for the rip-off would be on a Sunday night into Monday morning when the night shift was lightly staffed and the Lufthansa people could be easily overcome and handcuffed. The shift supervisor would be forced to neutralize the alarm system, and the valuables room would be looted. Gruenewald said a friend would tell him how to set the system so the secure area could be entered without tripping the alarm. Although Weremeychik didn't know who Gruenewald's friend was, it turned out to be Werner who by now was very knowledgeable about the secure cargo area of Lufthansa and its operation.

It was a risky plan. It required five men and two vans to penetrate a couple of levels of airport security for up to an hour without being detected. Two vans, or one larger vehicle would be needed because there could be as many as 140 boxes of valuables to take away. While the take could be as much as $8 million, one of Weremeychik's friends didn't like the way Gruenewald was rushing things for the holiday. Weremeychik himself had to go to a wedding over the Columbus Day weekend, and the holiday came and went. Nothing happened, and Gruenewald was getting very impatient.

The reason Gruenewald was getting antsy was because Werner, his old friend, was getting pressure from his bookie over a $6,000 debt. The gambling debt was on top of the other obligations eating into his salary of an estimated $15,000 a year. The heist would be child's play, he insisted. The next time Gruenwald saw Weremeychik at The Owl he waved him away. As far as Gruenewald was concerned, Weremeychik and his friends were less than children, and he walked away in disgust. It was just after Thanksgiving Day 1978. The big heist everybody was salivating over as the score of a lifetime was dead in the water.

CHAPTER EIGHT
THE RING

MARTIN "MARTY" KRUGMAN WAS KNOWN to the public in the late 1970s as the tacky men's hairpiece merchant who advertised his "For Men Only" business with late-night television ads. A slight, Eastern European Jewish man with pronounced, bulging eyes—said to be the result of a thyroid-gland disorder—Krugman ran his business in Queens, and because his store was near Henry Hill's club The Suite, he became friendly with the mob associate. Krugman was fascinated with the Mafia life and would listen to stories for hours, either in The Suite or at Burke's Robert's Lounge.

Krugman's association with mobsters was more than just out of curiosity. While he had the wig and hairpiece business, Krugman was also a bookmaker who knew a host of other gamblers and bookmakers. There were plenty of them around Queens. One of them was Frank Menna, a former hairdresser who ran a luncheonette but also sometimes served as an intermediary between Krugman and his bookmaking clients. One of those clients was Louis Werner.

Menna really served as a glorified errand boy or go-between for Krugman. Menna would get a call from Werner about a bet and then would call Krugman to get a betting line and then relay the bet back to Krugman. That relationship lasted until about September 1978 when there was a discrepancy about a bet Werner had placed with Krugman. Menna decided he didn't want to be in the middle of both men and bowed out of the relationship. Werner would make calls to Krugman on his own from that point. If necessary, Menna would act as a courier, ferrying money back and forth between both men.

Just because he no longer worked as a middleman didn't mean that Menna stopped seeing both Werner and Krugman. He sometimes ran into Werner at Falcaro's Bowling Alley, and one November day in 1978 stood out. It was then that Werner started talking about his job at Lufthansa and all the money that passed through his hands in the valuables room. But it didn't sound to Menna like just idle talk.

"He commented on the fact if he had the right people he might be able to do something with it," Menna would recall later.

Menna knew enough to tell Krugman about the tantalizing idea Werner had raised: the theft of what could be millions of dollars' worth of loot from Lufthansa. If there was a moment where the conspiracy behind the Lufthansa heist started, the conversations between Werner, Menna, and Krugman would later seem to investigators to be that crucial point in time. To check things out further, Krugman arranged to have someone meet Werner at an airport diner parking lot and press him for details. For security purposes, either the emissary from Krugman or Werner would drive a distinctive yellow car so that he would be easily identified.

It appeared that Menna met Werner in the parking lot at the diner. But whoever it was reported back enough information that Krugman told Menna he was impressed with what Werner had to say. For his part, Werner thought the heist could happen and told Menna he would take care of him. Smelling trouble somewhere in this plot, Menna said no thanks, he didn't want to be involved.

As Henry Hill would later tell Pileggi, once Krugman connected with Werner he raced to tell Hill about the potential for riches that could be theirs for the taking. It was a ton of cash, maybe some jewelry too, and the money was U.S. currency coming back to the country after being spent in Europe by Americans. The cash was untraceable and didn't require any machinations with foreign exchange. There had already been a plan put together, courtesy of Gruenewald and Werner, about how to pull off the heist. All that was needed was the right bunch of criminals to do it.

At this point Hill was freed from his prison sentence and Burke was living in a special halfway house in Manhattan. Although he had to return to the facility in the evenings, Burke was free to roam around the city as he ostensibly tried to work at a legitimate job. In fact, Burke went back and met his old crew members like Hill at Robert's Lounge where he was told of what Krugman had learned about the potential for a big haul at Lufthansa.

As Hill recalled, Burke was intrigued with the idea and cautiously moved forward, having his people check out the Gruenewald-Werner plan, which focused around a group of at least five men serving as the actual robbers. Although Burke didn't trust Krugman and didn't like him, that didn't prevent the plan from moving forward. The basic plan that Werner and Gruenewald hatched seemed workable, particularly with Werner able to show how the alarm system could be compromised. Burke now took an active role.

"Jimmy started running the Lufthansa heist right out of Robert's," Hill told Pileggi. "He'd go to the halfway house at night and then get picked up by one of the guys who drove him to Robert's. It was Jimmy's office."

We know much of what preceded Burke's involvement in the heist through testimony Menna and Gruenewald would later give in federal court, under oath. Information about what Burke did to finally put together the robbery team that did the heist comes primarily from Hill, either from his debriefings by the FBI or from what he told Pileggi and then later shared with writer Dan Simone in a book he co-authored. In both those books, Hill described what he believed to be the group of robbers. Talking to Pileggi for the seminal mob book *Wiseguy*, Hill said Burke lined up Thomas DeSimone, Joseph Manri, Angelo Sepe, Louis Cafora, and Paolo LiCastri. But Hill also said he later learned that Licastri didn't take part but that Robert McMahon was likely used instead. But years later and no longer a federally protected witness, Hill told in his own book *The Great Lufthansa Heist*, co-authored with Simone, about a slightly expanded lineup of the team: DeSimone, Sepe, McMahon, Manri, and Cafora, with Licastri now also back in the mix.

Hill was not part of the actual robbery team and appears to have been kept out of the intimate planning stages by Burke. Although Hill's version of the composition of the team was largely consistent in the two published accounts, there is a question about whether Licastri was involved as a sixth man. In debriefings with the NYPD, Hill added a seventh name to the list of alleged participants: Danny Rizzo, a Lucchese family associate at the time who was described as a close friend of Burke. In any case, the crew assembled by Burke was a wild bunch of criminals who had one common denominator: they all worked out of Robert's Lounge.

Thomas DeSimone: A man with a homicidal streak who had a sadistic impulse, DeSimone was unpredictable and his characterization by Joe Pesce in *Goodfellas* was pretty close to the mark. Hill recalled that he even killed his own brother over some jewelry the sibling stole and wouldn't return. He was said in later published accounts to have been a relative of Rosario and Frank DeSimone, famous Los Angeles members of the Mafia in the late 1950s and 1960s.

DeSimone was a hijacker whom Burke relied on heavily. He would shoot and kill people with abandon, having murdered Spider Gianco in Robert's Lounge, killed Gambino soldier William "Billy Bats" Bentvena over a slight and then killed his friend and fellow hijacker Ronald "Foxy" Jerothe, who was a friend of John Gotti, then a Gambino associate. DeSimone had been dating Jerothe's sister and assaulted her after a breakup. Fearing retaliation, DeSimone shot and killed Jerothe as the two argued one day in December 1974.

In another example of DeSimone's warped sense of loyalty to Burke, mob associate Peter Zuccaro told investigators how DeSimone once shot at a car in which Burke's daughter Catherine was being driven by her then-boyfriend along Cross Bay Boulevard in Howard Beach. It seems that DeSimone didn't want any man near Burke's daughter and took some shots at the boyfriend, but didn't hit him— nor Catherine—remembered Zuccaro.

DeSimone also had a streak of black humor. According to one mob informant, while DeSimone barbecued food in the backyard of his home in South Ozone Park he would toss a piece of hot dog over into a vacant lot where some of his victims were rumored to have been buried. He explained the food toss by quipping that the buried corpses had to eat too. Funny guy.

Angelo Sepe: A mob associate originally from Bensonhurst, Brooklyn, Sepe had been a fringe player for years. He once had a social club in Brooklyn that he eventually sold to an associate of the Gambino crime family. He did a nine-year federal prison sentence for bank robbery and in January 1978 was arrested on drug charges, but the case was thrown out. Sepe lived in South Ozone Park, a neighborhood not far from JFK. Sepe didn't mix well with Hill, and convinced Burke to keep him away from the actual execution of the heist.

Robert "Frenchy" McMahon: McMahon got his nickname because of the fact that he worked in the cargo operation of Air France at JFK. It was because of McMahon's job with the airline that Hill said he had the necessary entrée to steal over $420,000 in cash in 1967 from the airline's valuable cargo area, a haul that made for nice tribute payments to some mobsters and solidified McMahon's stature with Burke. McMahon not only frequented Robert's Lounge but also The Owl and other watering holes near JFK.

Joseph "Buddha" Manri: Like McMahon, Manri had a job in the cargo operation of Air France at JFK. According to Hill, Manri had checked out the plan for the robbery presented by Werner and thought it was a good one. His nickname was a reference to his big stomach. Manri was also known to police as "Joseph Manri Manriguez."

Louis Cafora: Another associate of Burke who owned some parking lots in Brooklyn. Cafora's usefulness to Burke was as an avenue for laundering money.

Paolo Licastri: A Sicilian immigrant, Licastri was reputed to have been linked to the infamous Pizza Connection drug operation but was never charged. He had ties to the Bonanno and Gambino crime families.

If Henry Hill was right, those were the men involved along with Burke in the big heist. There are, of course, two names missing from the public versions of the group of robbers Burke had assembled: Vincent Asaro and his cousin Gaspare Valenti. Their names would publicly surface as being linked to the heist some thirty-five years later.

But while Hill's public statements on the heist excluded Asaro and his cousin, he had actually claimed to law enforcement as far back as 1983 that Asaro was involved. According to NYPD records, an informant, who was clearly identified by the description cops used as being Hill, stated that Asaro was involved in the planning stage of the heist with Burke, along with Paul Vario who stayed in contact with the crew. Hill also alleged that it was Asaro, along with Burke and a member of Vario's family who "waited outside," the documents stated, although there was no specific description of what was meant by the term "outside." So the previously secret Hill materials came up with the added names of Asaro, Burke, and a kin of Vario. Interestingly, Hill never made mention of Valenti being involved in the heist or anything else.

CHAPTER NINE
"My God, You Lost Millions!"

John Curtin had been a Brink's armored-car guard for about twenty-three years. His job was to sign for shipments that went onto his truck, and he worked about three days a week making pickups in the cargo area at JFK. One of those days was usually a Friday, which is the day of the week December 8, 1978, happened to be when Curtin made his rounds. After an earlier stop at a different airline, Curtin and his guard Frank Crowley made a scheduled pickup call at the Lufthansa Airlines cargo area in building 261. It was around noon.

Stopping by the cargo area, Curtin picked up some paperwork from a Lufthansa clerk. The documents were given to Crowley who waited in the cargo area to take custody of the shipment while Curtin and another guard on the truck drove back to Seaboard Airlines to pick up a couple of items. Curtin quickly got back to Lufthansa and noticed that Crowley was still sitting around without any cargo. The odd thing was that Crowley was continually being told he would be taken care of but never was.

The shipment Curtin was to pick up was said on the paperwork to be $4 million in U.S. currency. But when Louis Werner, the Lufthansa supervisor, finally showed up he told Curtin the amount was actually $5 million. Werner seemed a bit officious, Curtin would later remember, and started talking about problems with another security outfit where there was some money missing from a shipment. Because of that problem, Werner said Lufthansa wouldn't let shipments of cash leave until a big boss verified that nothing had been improperly taken. This would take a little bit of time until a security man could come, said Werner.

Hit with an unexpected delay, Curtin called his office and told his dispatcher what had happened. Curtin told Werner he really couldn't wait around and that he had to leave to take care of another shipment. Brinks would have another truck come by Monday to pick up the Lufthansa shipment, explained Curtin. That was fine with Werner, who took the paperwork back. The $5 million cash shipment, along with a few other valuables, would have to stay in the secured room through the weekend—just like Louis Werner knew they would.

Kerry Whalen was a twenty-three-year-old college man from Queens who seemed to have some good luck when he got a job working in the cargo area of Lufthansa at JFK. Whalen's job often led to overtime hours and good pay, which helped him pay the bills and his college tuition expenses. The night of December 10, an inbound Lufthansa flight was delayed for about twelve hours, and there was plenty of overtime available for cargo people who wanted to stay around and meet the delayed aircraft. Whalen took the overtime, which had been approved until midnight. Another supervisor asked him to keep working until 7:00 A.M. Monday.

"That would be a fifteen-hour day, some of it at double time," Whalen later remembered in his own book, *Inside the Lufthansa HEI$T: The FBI Lied.* "I agreed to stay on as long as possible because the overtime would pay off the Spring tuition bill."

After taking care of a $500,000 shipment of caviar for another airline, Whalen recalled driving back to the Lufthansa cargo building at around 3:30 A.M. and noticing as he approached the building a dark van near the ramp into the structure. Among the things that seemed odd to Whalen, he remembered, was the fact that the van had no lettering on the outside and that it lacked any Port Authority placards. Well, he thought, it might be some cleaning worker or fellows who serviced the soda machines. He made a U-turn and parked in front of the van, exited his car and then began walking toward

Building 261, warily looking at the two men seated in the strange vehicle. Both men were visible to Whalen, the passenger more so, and he saw that they were both Caucasian. One seemed close to thirty years old and was about five feet ten inches tall. The driver, seemed about twenty-two years old, with dark hair and complexion, perhaps five feet six inches in height.

Whalen remembered the man in the passenger seat mumbling the words "get in the truck" at which point he knew he was in trouble and started running to the entrance to the cargo building, screaming "Help!" Whalen got the first door open and had run a few steps toward the second inner door when the passenger who had been seated in the van started to pistol whip him, forcing him to the concrete floor. What Whalen recalled next was looking at the barrel of a pistol in front of his eye and seeing in his moment of terror two bullets which were inside the revolver.

"I was so sure I would die that my body went completely limp causing me to urinate into my long johns," wrote Whalen.

While Whalen may have thought that his co-workers inside the cargo building were oblivious to his plight, they were facing their own moment of horror at the hands of some other armed assailants.

Senior Lufthansa cargo agent John Murray was working the midnight to 7:00 A.M. shift and normally would take his lunch break at 3:00 A.M. But since there was little work to do Murray let his co-worker go to lunch and decided to catnap at his desk at about 3:08 A.M. He had hardly closed his eyes when he sensed something going on behind him.

"I turned around and I saw four people," Murray remembered later. "Three of them with guns and the fourth disappeared on the other side of the office."

Murray was about to get up out of his chair when the armed group rushed up to him and pushed him back into his seat, telling him, "Don't move, don't do anything stupid."

Asked where the rest of the employees were, Murray told the gunmen they were in the lunchroom. Two of the men left while the other two robbers roughed up Murray, first putting him on the floor, then placing him back in the chair and handcuffing him. Then they grabbed Murray by his arms and took him to the lunchroom, telling him to keep his head down and not to look at anybody.

Inside the lunchroom, Murray noticed some of his fellow employees on the floor. He was then told to lay down on the floor. Sensing or knowing Murray was a key man in the cargo building, the gunmen asked him to call the other supervisor. The robbers already knew, thanks to the inside information provided by Werner, that someone like the Lufthansa supervisor knew the protocol for opening the doors to the secure valuables room without tripping the alarms. The thieves needed Murray to call the supervisor back upstairs where everyone was so he could be forced to open the alarmed room. One of the armed men told Murray to make the call and to be convincing or else they would blow his head off.

Murray's mouth was dry from fear and he asked for a drink of water. One of the men gave him something to drink. Able to relax, Murray called the supervisor, a man named Rudy, and gave him a false story about a call coming in from Germany that he had to take.

Tricked by the call, Rudy came upstairs and was jumped by two of the robbers. One of the attackers took Rudy's wallet and glanced through it telling him they now knew where he lived and threatened him with a shotgun before taking him away. Murray couldn't see where Rudy went but it turned out he was taken by the robbers to the valuables room where he was forced to help the thieves open the locked doors in the right sequence so as not to trigger the alarms. Because of Werner's information, the group knew that the two doors could never both be opened at the same time. If they were, a silent alarm would alert Port Authority police who would show up in force. The robbers told the frightened cargo workers, who had been herded into the lunchroom, to stay down if they heard any gunshots.

Twenty minutes passed. The two robbers guarding the workers asked some of them for their car keys. One of the gunmen tried to calm Murray and the others, again offering some water. It was then that Rudy was brought back and the entire group of Lufthansa employees were tied up with rope and handcuffs.

In those twenty minutes, with Rudy's coerced assistance, the Lufthansa heist crew had taken forty boxes of U.S. currency, each about sixteen inches long and containing $125,000, for a total of $5 million. DeSimone unceremoniously opened the first box by smashing it with his foot and reaching into it to pull out cash, exclaiming, "This is it!" The boxes of cash were thrown into the dark van, which at that point had been driven into the cargo building. There was some jewelry too, worth about $850,000, that was taken. Burke knew what to do with the jewels: Paul Vario had a small stash of precious stones in his Long Island home, and there were plenty of fences for hot stuff in the diamond businesses along Canal Street in Chinatown. The robbers knew where to drive, thanks to Werner's floor plan.

Whalen had also been brought into the room and he was definitely the worse for wear. His face was bloodied from the beating he received. With Whalen and the other Lufthansa cargo workers all shackled, the robbers left. Murray waited about ten minutes and managed to untie the rope that had bound him. Murray then made his way to a telephone and called the police.

Port Authority cops reached the Lufthansa cargo terminal at about 4:30 A.M., which would have been about twenty-five minutes to a half hour after Murray made his call for help. The van with the thieves had that much of a head start, and none of the airport guards saw or stopped the van. It is possible that Port Authority officials may have even passed the van and the robbers somewhere along the roads leading to the airport. After getting notified, the Port Authority contacted both the FBI and the 1134th Precinct of the NYPD, which encompassed JFK. Port Authority cops got two markedly different reactions to those calls. The FBI responded immediately. But, according to a later report in *Newsday,* the precinct replied that the local cops were interested just in "bombs, bodies and sex cases" and that the Port Authority could have everything else, or something to that effect.

The fragmented response of law enforcement to the initial report of the biggest armed robbery in American history was something that would haunt the investigation for years to come. While the Port Authority and the FBI responded quickly, the NYPD seemed to have been on the sidelines. Even the precinct commander is said to have learned of the heist while Christmas shopping later on the morning of December 11. Eventually, law enforcement worked out cooperation, with the FBI leading the main investigation. But one local official, newly elected Queens District Attorney John Santucci, was briefly shunted to the side. (Santucci had been appointed district attorney in December 1976 after his predecessor left for a judgeship, and he won the follow-up election for the job in November 1977.)

Some federal officials were concerned that Santucci, a very popular and political prosecutor, had a tendency to showboat, to seek out publicity whenever he could. Less than nine months before the heist, Santucci had castigated the FBI during a news conference for its handling of cargo theft at JFK, saying federal authorities and others in law enforcement had been deceptive in trying to portray the airport as a "Garden of Eden" free of crime.

"We've had difficulty with the FBI," Santucci told reporters during the unveiling of stock- and cargo-hijacking cases involving airport shipments. "What concerns me greatly is that at every meeting we're told that Kennedy Airport is a 'Garden of Eden.' Nobody cooperates in these investigations. If I want to fandango I go to a dance, not to meetings with these law enforcement officials."

Based on recent history and what thieves like Robert Cudak had said a few years earlier to Congress, Santucci wasn't entirely off base with his criticism. True, the FBI had agents working the airport and making some cases. But hijackers and internal thieves like those connected to the mob and Jimmy Burke plagued the airport. Santucci also touched on another problem: labor unions, shipping agents, and airlines that failed to report thefts.

While he was only sworn in as district attorney in January of 1978, Santucci inherited a problem that had been whispered about for years concerning his office. Some in law enforcement believed that in the 1970s Burke had his hooks into Queens cops and others working for the Queens District Attorney's Office. In *Wiseguys,* Hill recounted to Pileggi the claim that Burke had sources of information which could tip him off to investigations. (This particular issue is fleshed out at different points in this book concerning the disappearance of Paul Katz.) Whether those allegations were true or not didn't matter since it cast a pall over Santucci's office and may

have been the unspoken justification for the FBI attempting to keep
the local prosecutor at bay.

But since the airport was within Santucci's jurisdiction, as well as
that of the NYPD, it was difficult to keep him or the police out of
the case. It would take weeks of meetings and bureaucratic arm
wrestling between the FBI, Port Authority, and New York City officials before it was decided that the federal authorities should try to
make the case. Regardless of the turf battles that would develop in
the Lufthansa case, investigators had a good idea within hours of the
discovery of the robbery who pulled off the job. All signs pointed to
Burke and his motley band at Robert's Lounge. But it was one thing
to have gut feelings, even when supported by information from a
confidential informant, about who took part in the heist. It would be
something entirely different to prove it with sufficient evidence, the
kind that would justify an arrest and then take the case before a jury.
As investigators soon found out, it would be a tough road to make a
case.

The day after the robbery, the newspapers in New York had a
field day with the story. The *Daily News* front page focused on the
suspicion that the crime was an inside job, blaring with a headline
"Red Baron Ripped Off: Inside Job Seen in $5M JFK Heist." One of
the suspects was described as having a "Zapata-style" mustache, an
apparent reference to DeSimone. A composite police sketch of two
suspects, including the mustache man, was also included. The article
said lie-detector tests were going to be given to all of the Lufthansa
employees because investigators were convinced the crime was an inside job "possibly ordered by organized crime."

There was initially some confusion on the amount of money
stolen. The first reports told of $3 million. But by December 14, *The
New York Times* reported that officials at Chase Manhattan Bank,
the intended recipient of the money shipped by West German Com-
merzbank, said the shipment might have been as much as $7 million,
a figure that was later knocked down after an audit to $5 million. In-
clusion of the jewelry, as well as some West German marks, would
boost the total to $5.8 million and then even higher to about $6.25
million. Oddly, the shipment's declared value for customs purposes

was about $49,000 in West German marks, a number derived from the weight of the cash shipment of 220 pounds, the *Times* reported. In West Germany, the reaction among bankers was said to be one of anger and distress: "My God, you lost millions," was one exclamation. The loss was substantial, but as one German banker noted to the newspaper the shipment was insured.

The *New York Post* coverage featured the logo of "Great Plane Robbery," a takeoff on the Great Train Robbery moniker given the 1963 heist of the Royal Mail train in Britain. An FBI source was quoted as saying the Lufthansa employees present the night of the crime were all "horribly in fear of their lives." No more so, it seems, than Kerry Whalen whose name was bandied about in many news accounts as having got a good look at two of the suspects. The leak of Whalen's name and the way he was treated by some in law enforcement, notably the FBI and federal prosecutors, would become a long-standing source of resentment for him, which would resurface years later.

As crafty as the robbers were, they made a couple of mistakes, which gave police some early leads. Some of them had removed their ski masks and exposed their faces to the Lufthansa employees, a move that would help police sketch artists. One of the employees also remembered the license plate on the black van, which as it turned out happened to have been stolen about eight hours before the heist. The witness recalled the plate reading "508 HWM."

The 1977 Ford Econoline vehicle, which had been illegally parked in front of 528 E.95th Street in the Canarsie section of Brooklyn had been ticketed two or three times by cops or parking-enforcement agents. But on December 13, 1978, a civilian had noticed the license plate and telephoned police and it was NYPD officer Joseph Rossi, on night duty, who remembered having issued one of those tickets

"I remembered that number," Rossi said later. "I called the station house and my command. They got people over there quickly and it turned out to be the wanted van."

Rossi was one of the first cops on the scene, and detectives arrived and started dusting the vehicle for fingerprints, finding some on the bumper, the door, and mudguard. The prints from the mudguard were considered important because Kerry Whalen had recalled that the man who pistol whipped him had grabbed the car at the point of the mudguard with an ungloved hand during the attack. Inside the van, police also found a leather glove and some pieces of paper. More fingerprints were also taken from the wallet one of the suspects removed from Whalen's pocket. As Whalen remembered, the assailant looked at his name and address, remarking that if there were any problems they knew where to find him.

The recovery of the van and fingerprints were the first big breaks in a case that was fast consuming the investigative efforts of numerous law-enforcement agencies. While the money and jewels were nowhere to be found, it seemed as though Burke's crew had made a number of blunders, not the least of which was the careless leaving of the black van on the Brooklyn street. They also left a number of fingerprints and although this was the era before digital fingerprint analysis was in vogue, the prints could eventually help winnow down the suspects. Catching them would be the challenge.

CHAPTER TEN
THE FRIENDS WHO
HURT YOU

PAUL VARIO'S FAVORITE FAST FOOD was a White Castle hamburger. He could eat bags of the tiny, square patties, known in the business as "sliders," the burgers with the little holes. There weren't a lot of White Castle restaurants in New York City, but Vario could find a few in Queens or in the Bronx.

On one particular day in late 1978, a few weeks before the Lufthansa heist, it wasn't a White Castle that Vario visited but rather a McDonald's on Rockaway Boulevard, not far from JFK. The trip was not for food. An FBI agent named Robert Levinson had contacted the aging mobster through his attorney Joel Winograd and requested a private meeting. The three men sat around a table and Levinson, an agent working organized crime, had something that he said Vario needed to hear.

"We believe your life is in danger," said Levinson.

The FBI often would pick up indications through wiretaps or other means that someone in the mob life might be in danger of being killed. Hits were the way the Mafia policed and protected itself. Sometimes the transgressions were severe enough—like striking or killing a made member—that death was almost a certainty. Other times the reasons were trivial, perhaps nothing more than a perceived slight or sign of disrespect. Each of the Five Families had also gone through periods of warfare, such as the Gallo-Profaci war, which littered the streets of Brooklyn with bodies in the 1960s. The mob life had its risks and everybody in it knew that. Very often the victim was a close friend who had set him up for the kill. There was a saying that only your friend could hurt you and Mafiosi had sometimes gone to their deaths in the company of those who were the people they trusted.

In Vario's case, there were undoubtedly those in the Mafia who believed he had betrayed them by being so indiscrete with the Gold Bug case. Vario didn't open the door for the police and invite them in, but he had been outwitted by the detectives from Gold's office who were able to penetrate the security at the junkyard so ingeniously. As a result, hundreds of Mafiosi and associates had been subpoenaed or otherwise harassed by prosecutors. Some were even arrested and charged based on what the bugging device picked up from conversations in Vario's office.

Levinson's motive in telling Vario that he was in danger was a calculated move. The FBI appeared to be trying to get Vario to switch sides out of fear. It was a classic law-enforcement ploy and sometimes it worked. But not with Vario. He looked at Winograd and then spoke the only words he would say in the brief meeting.

"Thank you very much," said Vario, as he placed his hands on the table and stood up. Both he and Winograd left the restaurant and drove away. Levinson came away empty-handed.

How serious was the threat against Vario? Decades later it was hard to say for certain. Levinson disappeared in 2007 while on a visit to Iran's Kish Island where he was working as a private investigator for some companies. He is believed to still be alive. But for some of those involved in the Vario crew and the Lufthansa heist death came quickly, before they even got hands on their share of the loot.

Parnell Edwards loved hanging around Robert's Lounge. He was a credit-card thief, just like Hill was at times, and found he could move hot cards through Burke's operation at Lefferts Boulevard. Edwards liked being linked to the Mafia, which he called "May-fia" but could never become a made member because he was African-American. For the Lufthansa heist Edwards had a relatively simple task: get rid of the black van.

The job was easy enough, but Edwards didn't see the urgency and thought it better to spend a night with his girlfriend without paying attention to parking regulations. After the Lufthansa robbers left the van in Brooklyn, Edwards parked it on the street where NYPD officer Rossi ticketed it and later identified it as the vehicle being sought after. The cops were able to lift prints from it and naturally had important bits of evidence—all thanks to Edwards's screwup. FBI agents also showed up and collected some heavy wrapping paper that had been on the interior floor of the van and contained footprints of Nike athletic shoes.

On December 18, 1978, police discovered Edwards's body in the bed of his Ozone Park apartment at 109-16 120th Street. He had been shot at least six times in the head and body. Immediate suspicion about who the killer was turned to DeSimone, who had no qualms about slaying anybody, particularly if Burke needed the work done.

The conventional wisdom has been that Edwards was killed because he messed up on the van disposal, something that didn't put him in good stead. But Hill would later tell investigators that Edwards made another terrible gaffe right after the robbery during a Christmas party held at a dress factory Burke had next door to Robert's Lounge. The gathering included Paul Vario, Burke, Hill, DeSimone, Sepe, and others. Edwards shot his mouth off at the party, saying words to the effect that all the "whitey motherfuckers" had made so much money from the airport that they should give him some. Vario was appalled to hear Edwards mouth off in such a way about the heist and turned red with anger, said Hill. Something had to be done.

Vario pulled Burke aside and said that Edwards had to go, and, according to Hill, that command was passed on to DeSimone and Sepe, as well as himself. Within a day of Vario putting out the hit, DeSimone killed Edwards, and Sepe waited outside the apartment, according to Hill. Ironically, DeSimone had actually given Edwards a few hundred dollars at the Christmas party after he had asked for some cash. Burke helped pay for some of the cost of Edwards's funeral, according to Hill.

DeSimone's days were also numbered but for reasons unrelated to Lufthansa. In his short, bloody life, DeSimone had been a volatile man whose uncontrolled rage led him to murder William "Bill Bats" Benventa, a made member of the Gambino crime family. In the Mafia world, that was a serious transgression. DeSimone also didn't improve his stature when he killed James "Foxy" Jerothe, a friend of John Gotti, whose children knew him as "Uncle Foxy."

In early January 1979, Steve Carbone got a call late one night from a fellow agent who had spotted DeSimone's car parked near a grassy area by Burke's home in Howard Beach. Acting quickly, Carbone and his fellow agents placed a radio tracking device under the vehicle and waited to see where the car was driven in the hopes it might turn up a lead. Two days later, the device mysteriously stopped working and the car was nowhere to be found. DeSimone had also dropped out of sight.

As it turned out, investigators learned that DeSimone had turned up at Robert's Lounge one night after the heist and bragged to everyone, "I'm going to get straightened out tonight. They're going to make me a captain." In plain English what DeSimone was saying was that he was going to be inducted into the Mafia and given the rank of captain. Those within earshot of DeSimone when he made that boast were both Valenti and Asaro, who happened to be drinking at the club bar. To Valenti, what DeSimone said sounded odd because people don't get inducted into La Cosa Nostra and then promoted to captain that very same day. The rank of captain, or *caporegime,* is one of the plumb jobs in the Mafia hierarchy and is only doled out when a person has proved his worth to the crime family and is able to lead men. Valenti turned to Asaro and said what DeSimone said sounded strange. "Be quiet," said Asaro. DeSimone then left the club.

On January 14, 1979, just over a month after the heist, DeSimone was reported missing to police by his wife. DeSimone had already been tentatively identified from mugshots by Lufthansa workers as one of the robbers—thanks to the fact that he took off his ski mask. This made him more of a target to become a witness since he was at risk of being sent back to prison after only just having been paroled. But DeSimone's transgressions with the Gambino family were also strong incentives for the mob to do him harm. As Hill would tell Pileggi in *Wiseguy*, DeSimone disappeared after he went to a mob meeting where he was to be inducted into the Mafia. He had a short reprieve from his fate because the so-called initiation ceremony had been postponed a day due to a snowstorm. But the next night DeSimone was escorted to his death by mobster Bruno Facciolo and an associate of Vario, according to what Hill told investigators.

DeSimone's body was never found, and a stunned Burke was told of his friend's death over the telephone during a visit he and Hill had made to Fort Lauderdale to put together a drug deal—something that would come back to haunt them. Burke had actually made numerous telephone calls to find out if DeSimone had been initiated but got nowhere. Finally, just like in the scene portrayed in *GoodfFellas*, Burke made one final call, learned that DeSimone was dead, and started to cry.

Returning to New York, Burke visited Asaro at his fence company in Queens. Still upset, Burke started to cry and said "They killed Tommy, they killed Tommy," apparently without being specific about to whom he was referring. Years later, some authors theorized that Gotti killed DeSimone for revenge. But FBI officials who later investigated and convicted the Dapper Don discounted that idea. In an interview years later, Carbone believed the sudden cessation of the tracking device affixed to DeSimone's car was an indication that the vehicle was taken to a junkyard and crushed following his murder. The more likely scenario about the demise of DeSimone was that the Lucchese family, with Vario's assistance, took the murder contract as a favor to the Gambino family, which at that point was led by Castellano.

Edwards's murder was likely a punishment killing because of his stupidity. But the disappearance of DeSimone was the beginning of a line of sudden misfortunes that befell those connected to Lufthansa: murders and disappearances that steadily started to whittle down the people who were alive as targets of the growing federal investigation and possible weak links capable of cooperating with the FBI.

Burke never liked Martin Krugman. Although the odd-looking wig salesman and part-time bookmaker had made the crucial connection between Werner and Burke's crew, he still wasn't welcomed with open arms around Robert's Lounge. Krugman also was tight fisted, he never paid tribute or protection for his bookmaking activity. Krugman even once threatened to go the district attorney when DeSimone beat up one of his employees.

"Jimmy never trusted Marty after that," Hill told Pileggi.

Yet, Burke had seen the usefulness of Krugman's crucial connection to the inside operation at Lufthansa. After the robbery, Krugman became a pest, hanging around a club Vincent Asaro had opened on Rockaway Boulevard and trying to find out about heist money and anything else, remembered Hill. Burke, according to Hill's recollection to investigators, wanted Krugman killed but then called off the hit. Then, on January 6, 1979, Krugman disappeared. His wife Frances contacted Hill in a frantic state of mind and asked for help in finding her spouse.

In *Wiseguy*, Henry Hill recalled what he did next: "I drove over to Vinnie's fence company, and I saw Jimmy's car parked outside. I walked in and said Fran [Krugman] had just called me. Jimmy was sitting there. Vinnie [Asaro] was sitting next to him. Jimmy said, 'He is gone.' Just like that. I looked at him. I shook my head."

Hill repeated the same story to investigators about Krugman, relating how Burke, during the visit to Asaro's Astro Fence company, had gestured with a cutting motion across his neck to say that the wig salesman was dead. Later, according to Hill, Asaro pointed to a silver lining of sorts in Krugman's death. Krugman and Hill were supposed to split a share of the Lufthansa heist but now Hill would be getting the full share.

Hill said Burke told him to take his wife and visit Fran Krugman and to tell her a story about how her husband was with a girlfriend, knowing full well that Martin the wig merchant was another murder victim. Whatever Hill told Krugman's wife she never believed it. Years later Frances Krugman would have her spouse declared legally dead, even though his body was never found.

The disappearance of Krugman deprived federal investigators of a crucial human connection they needed to solve the case. Perhaps if Krugman had been questioned, he might have folded and thrown himself at the mercy of the FBI to save himself, much as a few others were doing. The case was proving hard to crack and no one could see that better than assistant U.S. Attorney Edward McDonald, into whose lap the Lufthansa case had fallen.

McDonald was a tall, handsome, dark-haired product of a Brooklyn Irish-American family who was on a career fast-track that suited his competitiveness. McDonald continued to live in Brooklyn where he played basketball as a youngster and eventually did well enough to play at Boston College, a fact that would prove to be significant later in the convoluted Lufthansa story. Assigned to the federal strike force in Brooklyn, McDonald worked under the legendary federal prosecutor Thomas Puccio, who would make his name a few years later handling some of the cases against congressmen ensnared in the fabled Abscam bribery investigation, an investigation McDonald would also play a prominent role in. Puccio headed the strike force in Brooklyn, one of several special offices set up by the Department of Justice around the country to handle organized-crime cases. McDonald was his assistant-in-charge.

Although viewed in the early 1970s as a way to focus resources on prosecuting organized-crime cases, the strike force concept of pooling dedicated attorneys to handle those investigations had a rough going in the early days. But by the time Puccio and McDonald were involved in Brooklyn, which eventually would become the largest strike force in the country, the image of effectiveness had been rehabilitated. The Brooklyn strike force in particular had been making Mafia cases and was getting ready to launch a series of major cases on the Five Families when the Lufthansa heist occurred.

While Queens District Attorney John Santucci vied for control of the Lufthansa case, federal authorities took over command, and McDonald was put in charge of the investigation by Puccio. Lufthansa seemed in the beginning like a hijacking case, which was normally not the bailiwick of the strike force. The unit was primed to go after the Five Families of the Mafia, but as it turned out the FBI needed help in getting wiretap authorizations and since McDonald had experience in that specialized area, he remembered being asked by Puccio to help the bureau. Very quickly, the strike force responsibilities spread to the larger aspects of the investigation.

From the very beginning, McDonald and the FBI received intelligence that Burke and his boys were involved in Lufthansa. It really wasn't a secret to anyone on the street, something FBI agent Steve Carbone had picked up quickly from one of his informants.

In the history of the Lufthansa heist, the investigation became an FBI priority because it involved the theft of property and money in interstate commerce. After years of publicity about the problems of theft at JFK, the FBI set up a small satellite office at the airport and at first the agents there were assigned to work on the case. But after a couple of blind turns in the Lufthansa investigation, Neil Welch, the head of the FBI in New York City decided that the case was too big for the airport office and turned it over to the agency's staff working out of Rego Park in Queens. Carbone's hijack squad got the nod and immediately set to work.

Although informants told Carbone and his agents that Burke and his crew were involved, it wasn't going to be easy to make the case. For a start, the Lufthansa employees who were terrorized by the armed robbers couldn't pick out any suspects from various photo arrays showed them, Carbone would recall years later. But he added that there was one exception: Kerry Whalen, the pistol-whipped worker, indicated after looking at a photograph that Angelo Sepe resembled one of the men involved.

Informants also mentioned that Sepe and others were talking about the robbery, including in his car. Agents tailed Sepe and found him driving to the Brooklyn social club of Alphonse "Allie Boy" Persico, the brother of Carmine Persico and for a time the underboss of the Colombo crime family. Some of the informants reported back that Sepe had given some tribute from the heist—about $20,000—to Persico. Armed with bits and pieces of information, Carbone and his technically savvy agents got a warrant and late one night placed a bugging device in Sepe's car outside his house in Mattituck, Long Island. Then everyone, the FBI and McDonald, sat back in the hopes that they would pick up incriminating talk. They would be disappointed.

Sepe had a habit of playing music as he drove, and that created a big problem for the device. Burke and he were overheard talking but the interference from the radio made many of the conversations indecipherable. Surveillance technology would improve by leaps and bounds in the years to come with digital technology. But as Carbone and the others tried to eavesdrop on Sepe, they suffered from the limitations of what now seems primitive technology. To assure good reception from the bug, Carbone's agents had to follow Sepe's vehicle with an FBI car carrying detection equipment in a luggage container mounted on the roof. An FBI spotter plane would also have to be aloft. It was a cumbersome arrangement, and in the end the tapes provided some tantalizing conversations but none were clear or complete enough to get an arrest warrant.

At Lufthansa, suspicion had fallen quickly on Werner, and that information was passed along to McDonald who shifted his focus on the troubled employee. Werner was not a hardened criminal like Burke, DeSimone, or the others. Werner not only had troubles with a divorce and a girlfriend, he couldn't keep quiet about what was going on in his life, and he began telling people close to him that he had been involved in the heist. He had blabbed to his estranged wife, his girlfriend Janet Barbieri, and Bill Fischetti about the crime. He had even offered to give Fischetti money to invest in a cab business. With the FBI hot on the case, it wasn't long before the agents learned of Werner's pattern of indiscretions in talking and tightened the screws on him.

Tickling the wire is a term cops use when they try to use information they believe criminals will react to and talk about over wiretapped phones or in conversations captured by eavesdropping devices. McDonald used that tactic as the Department of Justice approved leaks to the news media that investigators hoped would spark conversations among the Lufthansa robbers. It was hoped that one of the bugs placed in Sepe's car would pick up useful evidence but that didn't turn out to be the case.

In any case, Sepe was arrested on February 17, 1979, on a parole-violation charge. He was nabbed as he drove with Burke. The hope was that Burke might think that Sepe was now a risk to cooperate. The case stemmed from the fact that Sepe allegedly violated his parole in his earlier bank-robbery case by traveling without authorization to Florida. Bail was set at $1 million as a way of keeping Sepe in custody so that he couldn't flee or harm any other potential witness in the case, something McDonald believed he was liable to do. The case against Sepe seemed thin, but McDonald was trying hard to get something on the Lufthansa crew any way he could. The day Sepe was arrested, agents raided his home in Mattituck, Long Island, in the hopes of finding evidence, including some of the heist money. They came up empty. Although a federal grand jury was hearing evidence on Lufthansa, there was just not enough evidence to make a case against Sepe, and on March 24, a federal magistrate dismissed the charges against him.

Sepe wouldn't cooperate with investigators. But McDonald had another avenue with Peter Gruenewald, the Lufthansa cargo employee who several months earlier had actually dreamed up the idea of a big heist and had started sniffing around the bars and dives close to the airport to get help in pulling off such a theft. It was Gruenewald who had tried to work out a plan with him to raid the Lufthansa valuables room. In the end, Gruenewald was cut out and discarded by Werner. McDonald saw Gruenewald as a key witness, and in February 1979 had him picked up by the FBI on a material-witness warrant, a legal process that allowed the government to hold someone who has information about a crime.

Gruenewald was pulled off the street and began to cooperate, telling the FBI how Werner had admitted participating in the robbery and had earlier conspired with him to put together the scheme. To purchase his silence, Gruenewald said Werner had paid him $10,000. McDonald's strategy of working up the food chain to the top, hopefully to ensnare Burke and the others, appeared to be working. The next link was Werner.

The night of February 20, 1979, FBI agents arrested Werner on a federal criminal complaint of taking a $300,000 cut from the robbery proceeds and being part of the conspiracy. But the arrest was not the end of the game. McDonald brought Werner to his office at Cadman Plaza East in Brooklyn and came in the room with the defendant's old friend and confidante Gruenewald. Upon seeing Gruenewald, Werner became red-faced and his chest began to heave, leaving McDonald to think for a moment that he might be on the verge of having a heart attack.

"They know everything," Gruenewald told Werner. "Why should you be the only one punished?"

McDonald was hoping that Werner would see the light and would simply agree to become a government witness himself now that he was faced with the fact that Gruenewald would be giving evidence against him. Gruenewald tried to convince Werner, who if he did cooperate would likely get a light sentence in return for his testimony against the Robert's Lounge crew. But Werner, despite his initial panic upon seeing Gruenewald, wouldn't fold for McDonald. He insisted he didn't know what Gruenewald was talking about and told McDonald to take the case to trial.

On April 6, a Brooklyn federal grand jury indicted Werner for the Lufthansa heist. There was also an added surprise in the indictment. Werner was also charged with the 1976 theft of $22,000 in foreign currency from the Lufthansa cargo building. It was a case in which Werner had initially been the suspect but was never charged. What changed in the intervening two years was that both Gruenewald and Bill Fischetti, who Werner had approached for helping in exchanging the stolen money into U.S. currency, were able to fill in the blanks for investigators. Unable to raise a $1 million bail even with the offer of the posting of property from his family and girlfriend Janet Barbieri, Werner had to cool his heels in jail.

While he was being held in the federal jail, Werner learned some distressing news. His seventeen-year-old daughter Diane had been seriously injured in a car accident in California. The court allowed him to travel to the hospital near the town of El Cajun, with an escort comprised of FBI agents Douglas Corrigan and William Lynch.

Compassionate gestures to accommodate defendants and get them out of jail were not uncommon. Who knows, it might spur some cooperation.

After Werner visited with Diane, he and the agents went to a restaurant. While seated at the table, Corrigan couldn't resist asking Werner a question.

"How do you expect to beat this trial? I am just curious," said Corrigan.

Werner responded with his stock line: he was innocent.

"Do you mean to tell me that you were not involved in this thing at all?" replied Corrigan.

"I didn't say that," answered Werner. He then clammed up.

CHAPTER ELEVEN
"SEE, BIG MOUTH"

THE TRIAL OF *U.S. V. LOUIS WERNER*, the only one at that point to result from the Lufthansa investigation, began in earnest on May 3, 1979, after one day of jury selection. It had only been about a month since the formal indictment, a remarkably speedy start in such a high-profile case. But then the government had collected a fair amount of evidence and both prosecutor Edward McDonald and defense attorney Stephen Laifer were ready. The jury came into the courtroom of Judge Mark Costantino just a few minutes before noon. The Lufthansa heist had been a major news story for months, with every wrinkle in the investigation covered extensively. Jimmy Burke and his murderous crew had become household names. Now, for the first time, the world would hear the inside story of what had happened at Building 261 in the early morning hours of December 11, 1978. It would all come down around the sad sack Werner.

In his opening statement, McDonald told the jurors that Werner was on trial for both the December 1978 Lufthansa robbery and the October 1976 theft of the smaller foreign currency shipment. Stripped of all the legal noise, the charges were simply that Werner played a role in both crimes, said McDonald. When he had his turn to talk to the jurors, Laifer said in his opening that it really was Gruenewald who planned the big $6 million heist with the seedy characters he met at The Owl bar. Bill Fischetti was a miserable character who was fornicating with Werner's wife behind his back and then did so openly. Is that the kind of person Louis Werner would be in league with? Laifer asked the jurors to ponder that question when the testimony started.

By the time he took the witness stand, Gruenewald was living under the protection of the federal government. Before the jury, he wore a light blue three-piece suit, and he spoke with a trace of a German accent. McDonald first started questioning him about the $20,000 in currency taken after it arrived on the flight from Quito in October 1976. This was the theft that investigators believed was the thing that wetted Werner's appetite for more. Gruenewald wasn't involved in the actual pilfering of the cash bag but had been approached by his close friend Werner to help him hide the money and then exchange it for dollars.

For the jury, Gruenewald recalled that right after the currency theft Werner brought him a box filled with the money and asked him to hide it, which he did in a garbage dump. It was the next morning, said Gruenewald, that he retrieved the money and drove to a gas station where he met Werner. Both men put the cash into shopping bags, tore up the box into small pieces and then drove around Long Island to dispose of the pieces at various shopping malls. Then, said Gruenewald, he took the money back to his home in Levittown and buried it temporarily in his backyard.

Gruenewald told the jury he was a reluctant holder of the cash and that he breathed a sigh of relief when Werner took it back. The risk of losing one's job and spending time in prison if his involvement ever came to light was simply not worth the $5,000 he had been paid, said Gruenewald.

It was Bill Fischetti, the man who wound up having sex with Werner's wife, who offered to help. Fischetti agreed to take the stolen cash into Manhattan where he was able to get the various foreign currencies into greenbacks. For his troubles, Fischetti told the jurors that he took a ten percent cut and gave the rest of the money to Werner.

There was also circumstantial evidence that played against Werner, notably the fact that he was the man in charge of personally securing valuable cargo like the currency and never told his supervisor that something as important as the cash had come in on the flight from Quito. But what was more suspicious was the lie Werner had told investigators who questioned him after the loss was discovered. Werner had said he didn't go home the evening of the theft but instead went to Gruenewald's house to collect some money he had been owed. While it was true that Werner had gone to his co-worker's home, it was Gruenewald who explained to investigators that Werner actually showed up with the $22,000.

The stolen currency charges were really just a sideshow for the testimony about the big December 11th heist. McDonald built the case by showing the various links in the conspiracy. Through the testimony of Bill Weremeychik, the jurors heard how Gruenewald had approached him and some friends at The Owl bar with the idea that there were millions of dollars that could be had at the Lufthansa cargo area. Weremeychik said he wasn't really sure about Gruenewald and his big ideas.

"I didn't believe him again, and then maybe a day or two later, he showed me some load manifests declaring valuables on these things, and he said this was all gold and diamonds," said Weremeychik. "Then I knew he wasn't kidding around."

Testifying under a grant of immunity, that he wouldn't be prosecuted for conspiracy if he told the truth, Weremeychik described how Gruenewald explained how the robbers could enter the cargo building, neutralize any guards, round up the night-shift workers, and take a crucial set of keys from the night supervisor. Once down at the valuables room, the crew of thieves would turn off "some kind of switch," said Weremeychik.

"My friend Joe brought up a question, how would we get in?" Weremeychik testified. "He explained to us that after turning off that switch with these guys from the supervisor, there would be like two dials, he referred to them as two clocks. With these keys, they would have to be turned to a certain position, maybe—I don't know—maybe 12 o'clock positions or maybe 3 o'clock position. He would never tell us this."

Gruenewald didn't want to let Weremeychik know all the inside details about the security system at the cargo building as a way of making sure that no one pulled off the robbery without him and Werner. In any case, Weremeychik's group took too much time to figure out what to do and one night at The Owl, Gruenewald basically stopped working with Weremeychik.

"I said, 'How are you doing,' and he said, 'I'm not doing good at all.' He waved his hands in disgust at me," said Weremeychik.

Gruenewald said that Weremeychik couldn't pull off the heist and dismissively told him and the rest of the crew at The Owl that they "are nothing but children."

When Gruenewald was questioned about the heist, he said that he and Werner talked about the idea of a big rip-off from the cargo building as far back as early 1978 and by August of that year had a plan but needed people to help make it happen. Then, Gruenewald essentially backed up Weremeychik's testimony and said he met a fellow named "Brian" at The Owl bar who seemed interested in the robbery.

"After this happened, I told Lou Werner about it. He was aware of it," testified Gruenewald. "The next time I met Brian, I told him that we would go along with it, and he said he has at least four other people which could accomplish this."

"Did you tell this to Lou Werner?" asked McDonald.

"Definitely," Gruenewald answered.

Werner never met with Weremeychik or anyone who was part of this potential robbery crew, explained Gruenewald.

"He wanted to be completely out of the picture," said Gruenewald. "The only thing he wanted from this heist, he would like to have $200,000 in order to be settled for life."

To aid the plan, Werner said he would provide the robbers with information about the alarm and security system, said Gruenewald. McDonald then had him walk over in the courtroom to a mock-up model of the Lufthansa cargo building and had Gruenewald explain how the robbery was to take place according to the plan he had worked on with Weremeychik and his friends. A gang of six would be needed, along with one large van. After the night cargo crew would be corralled and neutralized, the cargo supervisor would be tricked into coming upstairs with the false story about a telephone call he needed to take from Germany. Then, said Gruenewald, the supervisor would be forced to go back down to the valuables room and made to unsecure the alarm system. The plan, as Gruenewald explained to the jury, would have taken about forty-five to fifty minutes to execute if everything went okay.

"What did you expect to be obtaining from the valuables room?" McDonald asked.

"We figured roughly between three and eight million dollars. As high as eight and as low as three because it was shortly before Christmas and everybody ships everything to the United States at that time . . . we expected gold jewelry, plus diamonds, palladium," answered Gruenewald.

It would have been a major heist no matter what was in the cargo room. As it turned out, the plan as explained to the jury was remarkably similar to what actually occurred during the early morning hours of December 11, 1978. The major difference was that neither Gruenewald nor Weremeychik were involved. For while Werner was enthusiastic about the plan, he wasn't happy with the pace of things. Gruenewald said Werner owed his bookie $6,000. Then, in late November 1978, Gruenewald said he dropped the whole idea. After some defense objections to the testimony, Judge Costantino wouldn't let Gruenewald say what led him to forget about the plan.

Despite so much time spent in preparation for the heist, Gruenewald said he was surprised to learn on the morning of December 11 that Lufthansa had been robbed. He immediately thought Werner had been behind it. At the cargo building, Gruenewald said he asked Werner if he did it. Werner answered "no" and then told Gruenewald that he would visit him at his house later that night.

Gruenewald testified that he wasn't certain which night Werner showed up but when he did he admitted that he was involved in the robbery. What Gruenewald remembered Werner saying during their meeting was very incriminating.

"He told me that he couldn't wait any longer due to the debt of $6,000, and this bookie was asking questions about his money," said Gruenewald. "He said he had gotten his own group through a connecting man."

"I asked him how much money, and he said he would get five percent of the heist," continued Gruenewald. "He figured at this time about $250,000, which it later on became $300,000."

Gruenewald was naturally angry. He and his group from The Owl had been promised thirty percent of the haul, and now Gruenewald felt he was double-crossed. Werner promised to give him $25,000, then agreed to $65,000 plus $50,000 if Gruenewald lost his job. Right before Christmas, Werner got a payment of $30,000, of which he paid $5,000 to his co-worker, Gruenewald testified.

Werner had been expecting to get his cut right after the robbery. But according to Gruenewald, Werner said the robbers said they needed to "wash" the cash, an odd explanation since the money was in the form of bills that were untraceable. After a few weeks of delay, Werner got additional payments totaling $80,000 and expected to get a grand total of $220,000 by April 2, Gruenewald explained. Naturally, with his arrest on February 19, Werner got no more cash.

Gruenewald's testimony was important for the government's case because it implicated Werner in the planning of the heist and the division of some of the spoils. Still, there was no link between Werner and anyone close to the Burke crowd. Two other witnesses, Bill Fischetti and Frank Menna, would pull Werner closer to the actual group of robbers.

Although he was afraid that Fischetti would talk to the FBI, Werner never thought that he would be much of a credible witness because he had slept with his wife. The word was that whatever relationship Fischetti had with Beverly Werner she ended up despising him. But gambler Frank Menna didn't have that kind of baggage. He had been Werner's bookmaker for a few years and seemed to be a guy he would trust. What eventually happened was that Fischetti would serve as the intermediary between Werner and another bookmaker named "Martin."

"Did you know what Martin's last name was?" asked McDonald.

"I was under the impression is was Krugman," replied Menna.

Turning to the period in November 1978, McDonald asked if Werner, during a meeting at Falcaro's Bowling Alley, said anything about his job at Lufthansa.

"Well, he commented about the money that passed through his hands and how much money would be laying around the valuables area or the room," said Menna. "He commented on the fact if he had the right people he might be able to do something with it."

Menna went on to explain that the next time he saw Krugman he mentioned Werner's remark about the valuable area to which Krugman said, "Well, if he is for real and he needs help, I might be able to accommodate him."

After learning of Krugman's offer to help, Werner seemed eager to have a meeting, said Menna, adding that a meeting was set up and that everyone came away impressed with what Werner had to say.

In one damaging bit of testimony, Menna said that Werner had offered to give him a share of the robbery proceeds but that he declined because he didn't want to be involved. Menna then recalled for the jury that last time he saw Werner. It was about six weeks after the heist and a distressed Werner had visited him at home and told him about being subpoenaed in the federal probe.

Fischetti's testimony was also damaging for Werner. It seemed both had discussed a robbery plan that Werner and Gruenewald had devised earlier in 1978. Fischetti had been offered by Werner some of the potential cash haul as an investment for his taxi business. But then in the fall of that year, Werner said the earlier idea had been scuttled. Werner said he was planning something bigger that would rock the boat with "the big heist." Not only did Werner talk about the need for the crime to take place with at least five men on a weekend when the cargo facility was lightly staffed, but he confided that he would have to tell the gang about the security in detail so they didn't trip the alarm, Fischetti told the jury.

If Fischetti had hoped to get a cut of the robbery proceeds as an investment in his cab business, he would be disappointed. He and Werner had a falling out over some indiscrete remarks Fischetti had made.

"He said I had a big mouth and I told his wife about it [the plan] and his wife got back to him and I couldn't keep a secret," said Fischetti.

Then, the morning of December 11, after the heist had occurred,

Fischetti said Werner called him at about 9:30 in the morning and said, "See, big mouth," and then hung up the telephone, Fischetti testified.

While Werner had berated Fischetti for being indiscrete, he had done damage of his own. Later in the month, Werner called again and continued to brag about how much money he had made on the heist, enough to pay off his debts and set himself financially for the rest of his life.

"I had to shut him up," recalled Fischetti. "I didn't know the phone conversation was taped or anything like that."

On January 29, as the FBI started tightening the noose, Werner asked to meet Fischetti at a bar near the Long Island railroad station in the town of Merrick. Their conversation was not an amicable one.

"It got pretty heavy," remembered Fischetti. "He starting telling me I better not say anything. If I keep my mouth shut everything will be okay and not to worry . . . If I said anything, probably something could happen to me."

Werner also said his wife Beverly had been opening her mouth and "she may fall from a ten story window," said Fischetti.

Werner then threatened Fischetti by saying, "I will drag your name right through the mud. I will tell everything about you and my wife."

Werner's threats continued into February, testified Fischetti, with the offer of $10,000 if he kept quiet. The sum and substance of Fischetti's testimony put Werner right in the middle of the planning of the heist. It also showed Werner's consciousness of guilt and his futile efforts to obstruct the FBI investigation by threatening witnesses.

McDonald had at least four major witnesses who implicated Werner in the heist—Fischetti, Gruenewald, Menna, and Weremeychik. There was another witness, Werner's girlfriend Janet Barbieri, who had given damaging testimony to the federal grand jury, but when it came time to testify at the trial delivered some theatrics. At one point it seemed she was going to become totally unhinged on the witness stand and maybe even have a heart attack.

The thirty-six-year-old Barbieri had known Werner about two

years and initially had told the federal grand jury that he had told her he had been part of the Lufthansa heist. But on the witness stand, Barbieri collapsed three times and resisted testifying so strongly that McDonald had her arrested as a material witness for the prosecution. Doctors who examined her said Barbieri was suffering from anxiety neurosis. She testified at some point lying on a court spectator bench attended to by a psychiatrist. Her pulse went as high as 110, but one physician said she had not had a heart attack.

McDonald had his hands full with Barbieri who backtracked on her grand jury testimony and said Werner had never told her he was involved in the robbery. At that point, McDonald pulled out her previous grand jury testimony and read portions back to her, including a portion in which she had testified that Werner had reacted to a newspaper article about the heist by saying to her, "You know, I'm involved in this."

In the grand jury, Barbieri testified that she was angry with Werner when he told her about being involved. In fact, when asked if he acknowledged involvement she said at that time he did. But when asked before the trial jury if she had given those answers to the grand jurors, Barbieri waffled.

"I can't say yes and I can't say no," she said.

When defense attorney Stephen Laifer finally got a chance to cross-examine Barbieri, he asked her directly if Werner had anything to do with the robbery and she answered, "No."

"Are you sure of that?" asked Laifer.

"I am positive," replied Barbieri.

The theatrical appearance of Barbieri on the stand was probably a wash in that the jury likely didn't know what to make of her. But her testimony to the grand jury raised a question of whether she had then sculpted her trial testimony to keep Werner out of trouble. If she had a bias it was obviously for Werner.

Still, McDonald had a scored a number of solid points with the jury through the testimony of his other witnesses. In his summation, McDonald reminded the jury how Fischetti had been told so much by Werner after the heist, including the fact that he admitted delaying the armored-car guards so that the big shipment of cash would have to remain in the Lufthansa cargo area over the weekend. Laifer responded in his summation by saying the witnesses had helped make a case that was a "foundation of mud."

Well, the case McDonald made turned out to be rock solid as far as the jury was concerned. On May 16, 1979, after a ten-day trial and less than one day of deliberation by the jury, Werner was convicted of carrying out both the $6 million Lufthansa heist and the foreign-exchange theft in 1976 that netted him $22,000. Werner may have thought he was set for life with the Lufthansa money, but now life as he knew it was over.

The day Werner was convicted, a couple of other members of the robbery team also got their comeuppance from a different kind of jury. On the afternoon of May 16 in the Mill Basin section of Brooklyn a group of teenage boys noticed a two-door 1973 Buick parked by 2085 Schenectady Avenue, close to the intersection with Avenue M. The car wasn't going anywhere and neither were the two men inside on the front seat. Dead with gunshot wounds to the head were Joseph Manri and Robert McMahon.

As Hill would later tell investigators, Manri and McMahon had been lured to the spot in Brooklyn by Paolo Licastri. During a meeting at a motel, Licastri admitted that he killed his two associates, felt bad about doing so but had to do it, according to Hill.

Manri was the man who had met with Werner to talk about the prospect for robbing the Lufthansa terminal. Manri dutifully reported back to Burke that Werner's idea seemed like a good one. McMahon was the Air France cargo supervisor who had participated with DeSimone and Henry Hill in the 1967 theft from McMahon's employer of $430,000, the dry run of sorts for the big Lufthansa heist. McMahon also liked to hang around Robert's Lounge and made himself useful by tipping off Burke's gang about cargo shipments.

In the Mafia, cleaning house by killing off your friends was one way of assuring that they wouldn't fold up and cooperate with law enforcement. Manri seemed particularly vulnerable to turning into a cooperator because he faced going to trial on an unrelated robbery case, and if he decided to become an informant there was no telling what he would say and who he would give up to save his own skin.

In fact, FBI agents had approached Manri's lawyer to dangle the prospect of cooperation. Burke, seeing which way the wind was blowing in the Werner case, must have sensed that he had to take drastic action to protect himself. The result was that Manri and McMahon had outlived their usefulness. Death in the Buick was their reward.

When he was sentenced on June 29, Judge Costantino gave Werner—whom he mistakenly at one point referred to as "Gruenewald"—the opportunity to speak. Werner finally took his last chance to publicly proclaim his innocence.

"I only have to say that I am innocent, your honor," said Werner. "I saw four men come in here who admitted planning the whole robbery and walk out of here with immunity. I don't understand. I don't understand that system."

Costantino made note that Werner knew each of the men and seemed a little incredulous that he proclaimed not to know Fischetti, whom he bowled with. Costantino had heard enough and told Werner that the jury had found him guilty.

McDonald reminded Costantino that the robbery, where Whalen had been pistol whipped, could have turned out to be much worse with a bunch of armed men. Had the alarm not been deactivated properly and had the Port Authority police showed up there could have been a gunfight and a slaughter of some of the Lufthansa workers, emphasized McDonald. Costantino took up McDonald's point and agreed that it was lucky nothing worse happened.

"When they were armed with whatever they had that evening, it is a stroke of luck that someone didn't use bad discretion and get themselves hurt," observed Costantino.

Werner got a maximum of fifteen years in prison with fines totaling $25,000. He also owed the Lufthansa federal credit union money for an outstanding loan although it was doubtful he would be able to pay it back. Using a strange argument, Werner appealed his conviction, in part on the grounds that it was wrong for him to be tried on both the 1976 and 1978 crimes together. He contended that if there had been separate trials that he would have testified in the Lufthansa trial. Such a claim by Werner left the appeals court justices scratching their heads: they couldn't fathom what he meant and why they should give any credence to what he said. On February 28, 1980, the Second Circuit U.S. Court of Appeals unanimously affirmed Werner's conviction.

With no chance of parole for five years, Werner decided to cooperate with McDonald and the FBI. It was his best shot at getting out of prison, and later, in at least two bids to get his sentence reduced, Werner raised the fact that he had helped law enforcement. In a filing with the U.S. Parole Commission, Werner said that if he did get out of prison he would be placed in the witness protection program. He then finally admitted playing a role in the robbery.

"I was not involved in the actual robbery but only gave out the information to the wrong people," Werner said to the commission.

Word finally leaked out that Werner was cooperating, which was hardly a surprise given his predicament. But Werner's connection to the Burke crew was through Martin Krugman and Joe Manri, both of whom were now dead and outside the reach of the law. As a result, Werner didn't have much to offer in terms of choice targets for McDonald. However, Henry Hill just might.

CHAPTER TWELVE
DEAD FELLAS . . .
AND GALS

HENRY HILL DIDN'T RIDE ALONG with Jimmy Burke's gang the night of the Lufthansa heist. While he had sat in on some of Burke's planning sessions, there was a feeling among the crew that he shouldn't be involved in the robbery. Hill had just been released from prison and was being careful about what he got involved in. But not too careful as it turned out. Since leaving Lewisburg prison, Hill was fully involved in moving shipments of drugs, mostly cocaine with some heroin. It was his way to make money fast after years behind bars. Henry always had to do things quickly to make a score since his life was very unpredictable.

Drugs were the fast way to make big money, and if truth be told there were many in the Mafia who were involved. The old myth was that the Commission had banned drug dealing under penalty of death. But while that was taken seriously by some in the Five Families, there were many violators of the edict. However, Paul Vario was one who appeared to toe the line. He had seen how his boss Tramunti, simply by waving his hand, had been implicated in a heroin case and sent to prison, where he would stay. Had Vario known about Hill's drug operation it could have been curtains for the mob associate. But as long as Hill didn't get caught, things were going well.

Then, in 1980, Henry Hill got his comeuppance. A nineteen-year-old Long Island kid, a former high school football player, was arrested by Nassau County police for making multiple sales of Quaaludes. The cops had an airtight case, and the teenager knew it, so he offered to work as an informant for them, wetting the detectives interest with information that he knew of a drug ring run by a mob associate out of Rockville Center. It was a narcotics operation tied into the Lucchese family and Vario through Henry Hill. The detectives used their new find as an informant and over a period of weeks, in cooperation with the NYPD and the Brooklyn District Attorney's Office put Hill under the microscope, tapped his home telephone, and placed him under surveillance for two months.

In April 1980, Hill was busted on the drug charges out in Nassau County, and officials there alerted McDonald about the fact that they had someone in custody who was very close to organized crime. The federal prosecutor sensed that Hill could be a big break in the case, which, since Werner's conviction, had really gone nowhere. Added to the problems was the fact that a number of people involved—Krugman, DeSimone, Manri, McMahon—had wound up dead or missing. Their absence removed potential stepping stones to the real Mafia bosses involved. Hill had been able to move between various mob factions with ease and had been very close to Burke, the man who orchestrated the heist.

Hill knew, based on the wiretap evidence and other materials that he was not going to beat the case. The informant turned out to be Bobby Germaine Junior, the son of Bobby Germaine Senior, an associate of Hill. His only hope to escape jail was to cooperate. Cooperation also seemed more and more with each passing day the only way for him to stay alive. The disappearance of Krugman and DeSimone, and the murders of Manri and McMahon weren't the only victims in the aftermath of Lufthansa. No one who had been close to Burke or did business with him seemed safe. Barely a month after Manri and McMahon were gunned down, Paolo Licastri was found dead in a field in south Brooklyn. Then there was the case of the attractive hairdresser from Long Island.

Theresa Ferrara was a pretty, dark-haired woman who worked in a small beauty salon in the Long Island town of Bellmore. Some said she had aspirations of being an actress and model, although her close friend and niece Maria Sanacore Stewart discounted that story. With her movie-star looks, Theresa could have done more with her life. But in the meantime, she cut hair. Having grown up in Ozone Park, Ferrara gravitated as a young adult back to the neighborhood and rented an apartment in the home of Thomas DeSimone's mother, a situation that gave rise to rumors that she became the mob associate's mistress. If Ferrara was involved with DeSimone, she may have learned something about the heist, and once he disappeared in January 1979 may have gone to the FBI.

Nothing was very clear about Ferrara and the life she led. But the known facts show that on February 10, 1979, about a month after DeSimone had disappeared, Ferrara received a telephone call from a man her niece Maria remembered was either "Kenny" or "Kevin" at the Apple Haircutting Associates salon. Theresa told her niece she had to go next door to a diner to meet someone and that she might be making an easy $10,000. She also said that if she didn't return in ten minutes to come and fetch her. According to news accounts, Ferrara never got to the diner and disappeared.

In May of that year, a headless and limbless torso of a woman washed up at Barnegat Bay on the New Jersey shore, some sixty miles from the south shore of Long Island and Queens. Whoever dismembered the body had tried to shield the victim's identity by severing the head, arms, and legs. But X-rays of the torso revealed skeletal and anatomical features that proved to the medical examiner that the remains were those of Ferrara. The torso also had remnants of underwear of the type the missing woman wore.

Was Ferrara's death tied to the Lufthansa case? No one is certain. She liked the fast night life and the men who were part of it. Mob characters attracted her and if she was the girlfriend of DeSimone as some speculated, well that was the kind of company that could get her killed.

Another woman connected to the Lufthansa crowd disappeared: Joanne Cafora, the wife of Louis Cafora, an old cellmate of James Burke. Joanne had no active tie to the heist. But police suspected that her husband had been laundering some of the Lufthansa loot through some parking-lot businesses he owned in Brooklyn. Not long after the robbery, Cafora and his wife bought a gaudy Cadillac, a fact that Henry Hill said angered Burke who feared any profligate spending would attract the attention of law enforcement. Both Caforas disappeared in March 1979, never to be found.

The Caforas, Thomas DeSimone, Parnell Edwards, Theresa Ferrara, Martin Krugman, Paolo Licastri, Joe Manri, Robert McMahon. The list of those dead or missing showed that the Lufthansa heist seemed to be cursed, much the way the discovery of Tutankhamun's tomb in Egypt in1922 was dogged by its own stories of misfortune surrounding some of those who participated in the expedition. But nothing more underscored the lengths Burke would go to take care of someone he was angered by than what happened to Richard Eaton.

A financial flim-flam artist, reputed arms dealer, and drug dealer, Eaton was a peripheral part of Burke's menagerie of crooks and killers. In December 1978, less than a month after the heist, Hill and Burke purchased a thirty-three-pound load of cocaine. The quality of the drugs was poor for the New York City market, so Burke returned with Hill to Florida and sold what he had to Eaton and two other drug dealers for several hundred thousand dollars. But while Burke got some of his money from the three he was still owed some cash, said to be as much as $250,000, with little immediate chance of getting the balance. On February 17, 1979, as Hill would later remember, Burke told him that he had "wacked the scheming fuck out," referring to Eaton.

On February 18, 1979, an NYPD officer in Brooklyn responded to a radio call telling him to go to the intersection of Drew and Blake Streets in Brooklyn where there was a vacant lot containing a trailer. After cutting the lock with a bolt cutter, the cop found Richard Eaton's frozen body rolled up in a blanket. Eaton's feet were tied, and there was braided rope wrapped loosely around his neck. An autopsy concluded that Eaton had frozen to death. (Eaton's manner of death was echoed in another scene in *GoodFellas*, that of character Frank Carbone found hanging in a refrigerated meat truck.)

It was hard to comprehend that Eaton would roll himself up in a rug and place himself at the mercy of the elements. Years later, Valenti would tell the FBI that he had seen Eaton the night before he was murdered at the nightclub Afters in the presence of Burke, his son Frank, and others. The next morning, Valenti remembered that Jerome Asaro woke him up and said they had to dig a hole to bury Eaton, something that couldn't be done because of the frozen ground. As a result, Valenti said the body was taken by Burke, Asaro, and others to a nearby lot his mother owned in Brooklyn and placed in the trailer.

Hill knew when he heard of the discovery of the body that Burke had killed Eaton, and the murder was just another homicide done as Burke's way of doing business and getting rid of someone he didn't like. So, by April 1980, Hill sensed on a visceral level after his drug arrest in Nassau County that cooperating with the government was the best way to stay alive. Hill made bail on the drug case and met Burke in a Long Island diner to talk about who the informant in the drug case might be. But when Hill was asked by Burke to travel to Florida to kill Junior Germaine, he believed he was being set up to be killed. Hill knew at that point he was going to cooperate, and prosecutor McDonald made it easy for him by having him arrested as a material witness to the Lufthansa heist. However, McDonald remembered later that he didn't have an easy time getting the material witness warrant for Hill. He first approached a Brooklyn federal magistrate who, to his surprise, disapproved the request. Finally, McDonald went to see Judge Mark Costantino, who had handled the earlier Werner trial and he readily approved it with hardly a second glance at the paper work. Hill was then firmly in the government's hands.

McDonald laid it on the line with Hill. He could be prosecuted for the drug case or he could cooperate and help the government break the Lufthansa heist. With a wife and two kids to worry about, and knowing full well what Burke and the mob bosses were capable of doing, Hill made the decision to go over to the government's side. On May 27, 1980, Hill signed an agreement with federal prosecutors to cooperate in the investigation of the Lufthansa case, particularly to help them investigate the roles Burke and Sepe played in the robbery. The government also would be able to use Hill as a witness in connection with any other crimes he knew about—something that would eventually come back to haunt Vario and his friends in the

mob. In exchange, Hill wouldn't be prosecuted for the crimes he revealed, including narcotics trafficking, and he and his family would
be placed in the federal witness protection program. If he screwed
up and lied, Hill could be prosecuted for perjury.

The cooperation agreement Henry Hill signed gave him a new life.
His old days as a wise guy, mob associate—whatever you wanted to
call it—were over. The old life was finished, but by cooperating Hill
was taking his best shot at staying alive.

But if McDonald and the FBI thought Henry Hill would give
them the mother lode of information to prosecute Burke, Sepe, and
any of the other survivors of the heist they would face untold frus-
trations. Burke was arrested in 1979 for parole violations, but that
failed to shake him. Hill knew a great deal about the planning Burke
had done for Lufthansa, but to prove the case McDonald needed
corroboration, and many of those who could give it were dead or as
in the case of Werner had only dealt with people who had been murdered. The result was that Burke was insulated from a conspiracy
charge. Sepe was still alive but the earlier attempt to charge him had
failed miserably.

McDonald soon realized that even with Hill in his pocket the
Lufthansa case was stalled. Some, notably Nassau County District
Attorney Dennis Dillon, thought Hill had been exaggerating his
knowledge of the Lufthansa robbery. McDonald had a lot more on his
plate than Lufthansa. He was commandeering a number of Mafia investigations and getting ready to try one of the Abscam cases against
U.S. Senator Harrison Williams. By 1980, while the FBI was pushing
to keep the heist investigation alive, McDonald viewed it as a case
that was a bottomless pit with little hope of more indictments, especially against Burke.

But then, unexpectedly, Hill provided the prosecutor a gift he had
not expected. Hill had been arrested in the Nassau County drug case,
and one of his co-defendants was a strange woman named Judith
Wicks, described by investigators as a sometimes girlfriend and drug
courier of Hill's. Like Hill, Wicks became a cooperating witness,
and one day in McDonald's office happened to mention a trip Hill
had made with her to Boston. In fact, Hill made a number of trips to

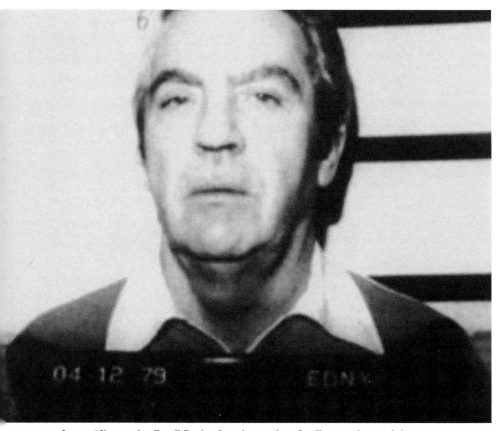

James "Jimmy the Gent" Burke, Lucchese crime family associate and the mastermind of the Lufthansa heist, seen in a federal mug shot.
(Photo courtesy U.S. Attorney's Office, Eastern District of New York)

GOVERNMENT
EXHIBIT
34
14 CR 26 (ARR)

Thomas DeSimone, the crazed killer and associate of James Burke and Henry Hill, who was one of gunmen involved in the Lufthansa heist. DeSimone disappeared in January 1979 and is believed to been killed because he murdered Gambino crime family member William "Billy Bats" Bentvena *(Photo courtesy U.S. Attorney's Office, Eastern District of New York)*

FBI NEW YORK
HENRY HILL

ry Hill, the legendary mob associate, in an undated FBI mug shot. Hill became a government witness
nd gave a great deal of information about the Lufthansa heist, although he was not present at the
ember 11, 1978, robbery. He was a close associate of James Burke, the man who organized the heist.
Hill's life story was the inspiration for the Martin Scorsese film *GoodFellas*. Hill died in 2012.
(Photo courtesy U.S. Attorney's Office, Eastern District of New York)

Parnell "Stacks" Edwards, an associate of James Burke and a credit card swindler,
who botched his job of disposing of the black van used in the Lufthansa heist.
For his screwup, Edwards was shot dead in his apartment a few days after the airport robbery.
(Photo courtesy U.S. Attorney's Office, Eastern District of New York)

This scale model of the Lufthansa cargo terminal and JFK International Airport was used at the 2015 federal trial of Vincent Asaro. The model depicts the terminal, known as Building 261, as it was at the time of the December 11, 1978, heist. *(Photo courtesy U.S. Attorney's Office, Eastern District of New York)*

The area on the Brooklyn–Queens border known as "The Hole" because of its topographically low position. This neighborhood was here Vincent Asaro and his cousin Gaspare Valenti grew up. It is also a place where Mafia families buried the bodies of murder victims. me of the Lufthansa heist crew tried to hide the body of drug dealer Richard Eaton in a trailer in the area. *(Author's collection)*

Surveillance photo showing Lucchese crime family captain Paul Vario (*left*) at his Brooklyn junkyar which had been the target in 1972 of a long-term electronic surveillance operation by Brooklyn Distri Attorney Eugene Gold. Vario is believed to have been the main mobster overseeing James Burke and plan to pull off the Lufthansa heist. Officials believe Vario received some of the proceeds of the heis The man at center in the suit and tie is Vario's defense attorney, Joel Winograd. The man on the right unidentified. *(Photo courtesy Joel Winograd)*

cent Asaro (*center*) walking down an alley that led to a Bonanno family social club on Grand Street in
aspeth, Queens, operated at one time by Sal Vitale. The man Asaro is conversing with is unidentified.
(Photo courtesy U.S. Attorney's Office, Eastern District of New York)

Undated photo showing murder victim Paul Katz with his wife, Dolores. Katz was murdered in 1969 on orders from James Burke after it was learned that Katz was an informant. He was buried under the basement floor of a house in Queens, and some of his remains were found by the FBI in 2013. *(Photo courtesy U.S. Attorneys Office, Eastern District of New York).*

The row house (*second from right*) at 81-48 102nd Street in Ozone Park where the remains of Paul Katz were found by the FBI in 2013. Testimony during the 2015 Lufthansa trial asserted that Katz's body was buried in the basement by James Burke and Vincent Asaro.
(Photo courtesy U.S. Attorney's Office, Eastern District of New York)

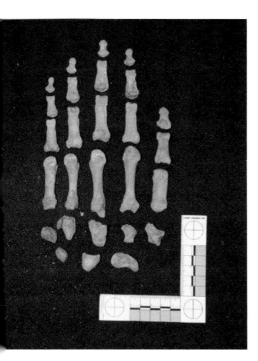

An anatomical array of the hand bones of Paul Katz, murder victim of James Burke, one of the organizers of the Lufthansa heist. During the trial of Vincent Asaro, the 1969 burial of Katz's body in the basement of a house in Queens was described in the testimony of government witness Gaspare Valenti. The bones were retrieved by the FBI in 2013.
(Photo courtesy U.S. Attorney's Office, Eastern District of New York)

Lufthansa cargo worker Peter Gruenewald (*right*) is being led by an FBI agent from FBI offices in Queens, N.Y., in February 1979. Gruenewald would become a government witness and testify against co-worker Louis Werner, the only person convicted of the December 1978 Lufthansa heist.
(Photo courtesy Newsday LLC)

Vincent Asaro with arm around Gambino boss John Gotti outside Gotti's former club on 101st Avenue in Ozone Park. Gotti likely wasn't the boss when this undated photo was taken. *(Photo courtesy U.S. Attorney's Office, Eastern District of New York)*

FBI booking photo of former Bonanno boss Joseph Massino, who became a government witness and was slated to testify against Vincent Asaro but never did. Prosecutors contended that Asaro passed along some of the jewels stolen in the Lufthansa heist to Massino, presumably for the benefit of crime family boss Philip Rastelli. *(Photo courtesy U.S. Attorney's Office, Eastern District of New York)*

ncent Asaro outside
the Maspeth business
of Bonanno crime
boss Joseph Massino.
Photo was taken by
FBI surveillance
team, which included
agent Pat Marshall,
who testified at
Asaro's 2015 trial.
Photo courtesy U.S.
Attorney's Office,
Eastern District of
New York)

GOVERNMENT
EXHIBIT
623d
14 CR 26 (ARR)

GOVERNMENT
EXHIBIT
96a
14 CR 26 (ARR)

Michael Zaffarano, the Bonanno crime
family captain and lord of Times
Square porn shops and theaters in the
1970s. Zaffarano was the immediate
boss of his nephew Vincent Asaro.
(Photo courtesy U.S. Attorney's Office,
Eastern District of New York)

Jerome Asaro, a Bonanno crime family member and son of Vincent Asaro. Jerome, also known as "Jerry," pled guilty to federal charges related to his participation in the disposal of the body of murder victim Paul Katz. *(Photo courtesy U.S. Attorney's Office, Eastern District of New York)*

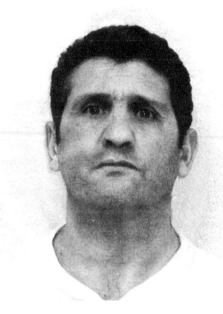

Gaspare Valenti (*left*), seen here with his cousin Vincent Asaro in happier times. Valenti became a government witness against Asaro in the 2015 Lufthansa heist trial. *(Photo courtesy U.S. Attorney's Office, Eastern District of New York)*

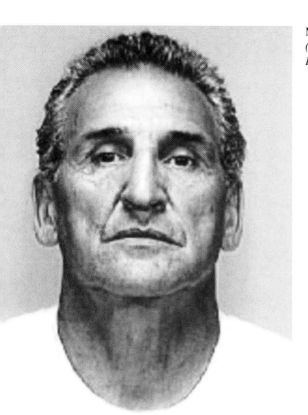

Mug shot of Vincent Asaro.
*(Photo courtesy U.S. Attorney's Office
Eastern District of New York)*

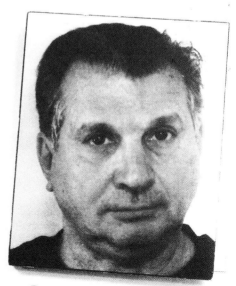

Salvatore Vitale, former underboss of
the Bonanno crime family, in an FBI
mug shot dating from his arrest in 2003.
Vitale became a government witness
and testified at many trials, including
the 2015 trial of Vincent Asaro.
*(Photo courtesy U.S. Attorney's Office,
Eastern District of New York)*

FBI mug shot of Peter "Bud" Zuccaro, a former mob associate who became a government witness and testified at the 2015 trial of Vincent Asaro. *(Photo courtesy U.S. Attorney's Office, Eastern District of New York)*

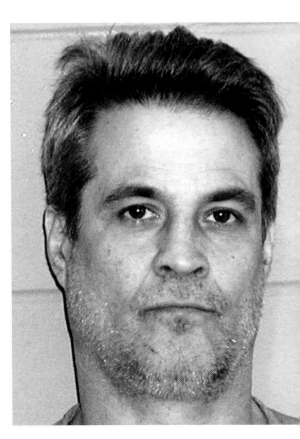

Mug shot of Danny Rizzo, identifie in testimony during the 2015 federa trial of Vincent Asaro as one of the men involved in the Lufthansa heis *(Photo courtesy U.S. Attorney's Off Eastern District of New York)*

Vincent Asaro on November 12, 2015, after his acquittal in Brooklyn federal court on charges related to the 1978 Lufthansa heist and other crimes. On the left is defense attorney Elizabeth Macedonio, and the woman on the right is her co-counsel, Diane Ferrone. *(Photo courtesy Newsday LLC)*

Vincent Asaro (*center, in overcoat*) at a funeral home in Ozone Park, leaving the wake of a friend. *(Photo courtesy U.S. Attorney's Office, Eastern District of New York)*

While Paul Vario was large in life as a mobster, hardly any tangible reminder of him remains after his death. He is buried in a family plot in St. John Cemetery in Queens, but there are so many people in the grave site that his name is at the bottom of the pedestal supporting the tombstone, almost covered by earth and barely recognizable below the name of his brother Salvatore. *(Author's collection)*

Beantown in December 1978 and said that he was there right after the Lufthansa heist. Curious, McDonald asked Wicks what the Boston trip was all about and she demurred, saying he should talk to Hill to find out what the Boston angle was all about. (Wicks was portrayed in *Goodfellas* as the superstitious drug courier character Lois Byrd played by actress Welker White.)

McDonald had Hill brought to his office and during a debriefing session Hill nonchalantly mentioned to the prosecutor that three years earlier he and Burke had fixed some basketball games during the 1978-79 season at Boston College, which as everyone knew happened to be McDonald's alma mater and where he had played on the freshman team. The prosecutor was flabbergasted. Carbone said he almost fell out of his chair when he heard the story.

"The motherfucker almost leaped over the fucking table and tried to grab me, he went berserk" was how a laughing Hill later described McDonald's reaction in a documentary-film interview.

McDonald had a recollection of being more restrained, later recalling that he told Hill that he was "nuts" and had a serious problem.

Actually others had the big problems, including three Boston College basketball players who were ordered to testify to a Brooklyn federal grand jury about the fixing scheme. Among those subpoenaed were the team's starting center Rick Kuhn, who came from Pennsylvania. The investigation revealed how some Pittsburgh area mob associates had linked up Hill and Burke in an effort to get some front money for the scheme and to assure that Hill then went to Boston to recruit Kuhn and any other player who wanted to be part of the conspiracy. Essentially, the fix was aimed at making sure the number of points by which Boston College won or lost a game worked in the betting syndicate's favor. The bets were laid off on unsuspecting bookmakers around the country. To assure that members of the syndicate weren't hassled by bookmakers who had to pay out, Hill said that he mentioned his ties with Paul Vario.

The fix wasn't flawless. When Boston College lost to traditional rival Holy Cross University by only two points, that margin of victory was less then the seven-point spread that gamblers like Burke had expected from the fix. Burke lost $50,000, and at the end of the televised game put his foot through the television at his home in Howard Beach. For a moment, Burke wanted Hill to go up to Boston to give the players some punishment, something that never happened.

With Hill's evidence, as well as that of other witnesses, the grand jury indicted Burke, Kuhn, and several others on racketeering conspiracy and other charges. The trial in 1981 was in its own way a major event and was the first time Hill was publicly unmasked as a cooperating witness. With Hill giving solid testimony, corroborated by others as well as admissions made by Kuhn, a jury convicted Burke and a number of other defendants including Kuhn. Burke was sentenced to twenty years in prison, while Kuhn got a ten-year term, later reduced to just over two years.

"To me and McDonald, this was bigger than Lufthansa," Carbone recalled later about the significance of the college-fixing case. "This was the first sports-bribery racketeering case."

James Burke had finally taken a fall—although not for Lufthansa, and he had Henry Hill to thank for it. Then according to federal investigators, Burke began a relentless campaign to find out where Hill had been sent as a federal witness, which turned out to be Omaha, Nebraska. Somehow, Burke found out where Hill, his wife Karen, and their children were living. In the nick of time, the U.S. Marshals Service, which was responsible for Hill's safety, discovered the security leak and in a matter of hours moved him and his family further out west.

While Hill was safely ensconced in the bosom of the witness protection program, his old associate in crime Angelo Sepe enjoyed no such benefit since he never cooperated. Despite weeks of a concerted effort in early 1979 by federal prosecutors to get Sepe to implicate himself in the heist, he was able to get out from under an arrest, which was the FBI's way of pressuring him. He was then sent back for ten months in prison for violating his parole on a federal bank robbery conviction by associating with Burke. But once that short stint in prison ended, Sepe was seen by those in the mob—suspicion fell mostly on Burke—as a liability. So, on July 18 in an apartment at 8869 20th Avenue in Bensonhurst, Brooklyn, the forty-two-year-old Sepe and his girlfriend Joanne Lombardo were found shot to death. Both had been shot in the head, and cops uncovered drug paraphernalia and a loaded gun in the basement apartment. With Sepe's death, the body count for the Lufthansa people had risen to six. (The two women, Theresa Ferrara and Joanne Lombardo were likely collateral damage.) By late 1984, of the people publicly named by Hill as having participated in the heist, only Burke survived.

Frustrated in the Lufthansa investigation, McDonald and the Brooklyn Strike Force was able to use Hill to make a major case involving JFK's air-freight industry, a business that for decades was viewed by law enforcement as a fiefdom of the mob. The modus operandi of the gangsters was extortion, squeezing the air-freight companies for payments to insure labor peace. A key player in the system was alleged to be Harry Davidoff, vice president of Teamster Local 851 and the founder of Local 295. Davidoff was a powerhouse in the New York City labor scene, and his locals represented clerical workers and truckers at the air-freight companies, which moved much of the cargo coming into and out of JFK.

The key to Davidoff's power was his alleged ties to the Lucchese family, in particular Henry Hill's old mentor and protector Paul Vario. The Lucchese family squeezed the companies the old-fashioned true and tried way done by all labor racketeers: ask for a payoff or else threaten that the unions would enforce onerous terms of the Teamster contract and cause other labor unrest. Once the payments were made, the unions would relax their insistence on strict compliance with the contracts. The shakedowns and other schemes pulled in millions of dollars.

In an investigation known as "KENRAC," an acronym for "Kennedy racketeering," over thirty organized-crime figures were indicted, including Vario, another Lucchese crime family member Frank Manzo and Davidoff. In making the case, McDonald used some of what he had extracted from Hill, although some of his evidence was shaky.

In a trial which was supposed to last about two months, prosecutors promised it would be a window into a lengthy shakedown operation involving the Lucchese family and the unions. Hill, of course, testified, and was called a "rogue, scalawag and a scoundrel" as well as a liar by defense attorneys. But by that time in his life Hill was impervious to the insults. In reality, Hill's testimony was important but largely circumstantial. He wasn't around for the shakedowns, but he told about conversations he had had with Vario's son Lenny.

"He was very excited," Hill told the jury. "He said the airport is ours."

Another conversation Hill said he had overheard involved Paul Vario and Manzo in which they said if there were any problems at the airport involving hirings or firings "you go through Harry." Prosecutors had promised that Hill's testimony would put David-off right in the middle of the conspiracy. While tantalizing, Hill's testimony was hardly the knock-out stuff he had delivered for the prosecution in the Burke trial in the point-shaving case. It seemed, as one appeals court would say, that it "fell far short of living up to its advance billing."

Still, as the case unfolded, the evidence presented by Hill and other witnesses show how Vario and the other members of the Lucchese family, as well as some businessmen, were involved in the complex extortion schemes. Before the case went to the jury, Vario decided at the age of seventy-three to fold up, and he pleaded guilty to running the extortion scheme. He received a sentence of six years in a federal prison.

Vario was not in a good position after the airport extortion case since his six-year sentence came at a time when he was physically ailing. On top of that, Hill had put the screws to him in an earlier case in which the turncoat had actually been the recipient of Vario's help. When Hill had come out of prison in 1978 he was in need of a job to show his parole officer that he was doing legitimate work. Of course, Hill had no intention of going straight and at that point was orchestrating drug deals on Long Island. Through Philip Basile, the owner of a nightclub, Vario got Hill a no-show job in a company in Island Park.

When it came time for Vario to stand trial in the fake-employment case, Hill testified that it was his old mob mentor who had ordered Basile to take him on as a sham employee, complete with phony pay stubs to trick federal parole officials. Basile, Hill testified, had been paying Vario large amounts of money for years. While defense attorney Joel Winograd told jurors that Hill was a person who would lie to anyone in authority when it suited him, Vario was nevertheless convicted.

Both federal convictions effectively put Vario, the man who gave the nod of approval to Burke to do the Lufthansa job, in prison for what would turn out to be the rest of his life. It was a consolation prize of sorts for the government, which was unable to bring the elderly mob boss to justice for the heist. Vario would die in federal custody at a prison in Fort Worth, Texas, on May 3, 1988. He was buried in a family plot in St. John Cemetery in Middle Village, Queens. Just like the secretive way he lived his life, in death Vario's final resting place is easy to overlook. His name is etched into the concrete base of the tombstone at the very bottom in small letters.

Jimmy Burke might have been able to see the light of day after his conviction in the Boston College basketball-fixing trial. But then Hill put freedom out of reach for him for good. It all came down to the murder of Richard Eaton in 1979, a killing that Burke thought he might get away with.

After Eaton had provided Hill and Burke with some poor-quality cocaine, he wound up dead in a trailer in Brooklyn. When Hill turned into a cooperator, he told investigators what he knew of the killing. Hill was not around when Eaton was murdered but he had been part of the drug deal and knew the extent of Burke's anger over being screwed by what Eaton had provided in terms of the cocaine and not getting a full refund payment. Not only did Hill recall Burke's remarks in February 1979 about having "wacked" Eaton, Burke also said, "This would be a lesson to Buzzy [another drug dealer] and the other guy and I will get the balance of my money." As it turned out, the killing of Eaton was a sufficient lesson because, according to Hill, Burke did get most of his money back.

Burke was indicted for Eaton's murder in 1984, and Hill was a key witness for the prosecution when the case went to trial in 1985 in Brooklyn state court. Hill's testimony was the only thing tying Burke directly to the Eaton killing. (At the time of the trial, prosecutors did not have the benefit of Valenti's cooperation, and if they had, they would have heard him say, as he later told the FBI, that Vincent Asaro told him that Eaton was murdered by Burke at his home.) To buttress their case, prosecutors also tried to show Burke's previous business dealings with the dead man as well as autopsy findings on how Eaton died. Eaton and Burke clearly knew each other, witnesses stated. The issue of how Eaton died was important because the prosecution alleged that he had been strangled and beaten.

According to then-deputy medical examiner Michael Baden, Eaton was already dead from strangulation when he was placed in the cold trailer, something that conflicted with the earlier prosecution claim that he froze to death. Burke seemed to favor strangulation as a way of dispatching people. He had done it with trucker Paul Katz years earlier. Baden's finding, based on a review of the autopsy report, was at odds with that of defense expert Dr. Milton Wald, who believed Eaton died from exposure to the cold. In another wrinkle, cops didn't find any of Burke's fingerprints on a rope found around Eaton's neck or in his apartment.

Nevertheless, Burke was convicted by a jury on February 25, 1985. He appealed his conviction to both state and federal judges, raising the issue of the circumstantial evidence being flimsy and the fact that the autopsy didn't support the prosecution theory that Eaton was strangled and beaten. For good measure, Burke complained that he had an ineffective defense attorney. The judges didn't buy Burke's arguments and he was consigned to state prison to serve a twenty-five-years-to-life sentence for Eaton's murder

Burke died on April 13, 1996, from the effects of cancer while he was at an upstate New York prison hospital. By the time he died, Burke had already lost his son Frank, who was killed in May 1987 after being shot on a Brooklyn Street. He was survived by three other children, his daughter Cathy who was married to Bonanno crime family soldier Anthony "Bruno" Indelicato, another daughter Robin or Robina and a second son Jesse James Burke who went on to be a real-estate attorney on Long Island.

James "Jimmy" Burke was never prosecuted for the Lufthansa heist. The rumors were that he had stashed millions of dollars of the loot in a bank safe deposit box, a fortune allegedly squandered by his son-in-law Anthony and his crime family captain Vincent Basciano. That claim of the secret fortune and its loss was made by Basciano's former close associate Dominick Cicale in an e-book he published in 2015. It was an allegation never proven, although it was entirely possible that Burke did stash cash he had accumulated from a life of crime—be it from Lufthansa, drugs, cigarette smuggling, or hijacking—in such a repository. Burke is buried at Saint Charles Cemetery in East Farmingdale, Long Island. He and his son Frank share a plot in the western area of the cemetery which happens to be across the road from a small airport. The headstone is modest. Old flowers and faded notes show the grave still gets visitors.

CHAPTER THIRTEEN
THE SHAKEDOWN GUY

THE EASIEST WAY TO BECOME A CRIME VICTIM in the Borough of Queens in the 1990s was to own a car. Auto theft was simply out of control in many parts of New York City. In 1990, over 145,000 vehicles were reported stolen, and in some parts of Queens cops would monitor shopping-mall lots and nearby streets with binoculars to get a jump on the car thieves. By 1994, things had improved somewhat with police logging in a reduced number of stolen cars, nearly 95,000 or almost 260 vehicles a day on average.

Auto theft had been a gravy train for the mob. Before he was assassinated, the late Gambino boss Paul Castellano lorded over a stolen car ring that from about 1977 to 1982 stole hundreds of cars per day. The vehicles were taken off the streets of Brooklyn and shipped to Kuwait. Castellano didn't get his hands dirty, but instead reaped the cash from the operation, money that was brought to him in big wads at his palatial home known as the "White House" in the Todt Hill section of Staten Island.

Castellano was ultimately indicted on charges he ran the ring and was actually on trial in Manhattan federal court in late 1985 when he was gunned down on December 16 outside Sparks Steak House on 46th Street in Manhattan. Six of his associates, including Gambino captain Anthony "Nino" Gaggi, were convicted of being part of the car-theft conspiracy on March 1986. Thieves were paid $150 for each car, which had their vehicle identification numbers changed before they were taken to Port Elizabeth in New Jersey for shipment to the Middle East.

The profits in stolen cars were also attractive to the Bonanno crime family. One operation run in part by family associate Gaetano Peduto had stolen over 2,100 vehicles, retagged them, and resold them to an army of willing buyers. Investigators believed the cars had an estimated value of $20 million. Even Albanian gangsters got involved. According to testimony given by Peduto in federal court as a government witness during a racketeering trial, Bonanno crime family captain Vincent Basciano, got kickbacks of between $1,000 to $2,000 for each stolen car.

For Vincent Asaro, the benefits of stolen cars were in the steady stream of income he could get if he offered his protection to those who actually did the dirty work. By 1994, Asaro was one of the last denizens of Robert's Lounge out on the street. Jimmy Burke was in prison and Henry Hill was living out west, courtesy of the witness protection program. Most of the others were dead or missing. As a member of the Bonanno family, Asaro had to keep his stature and earn money, for himself and his new boss Joseph Massino.

If truth be told, Asaro wasn't the apple of Massino's eye. Part of the problem was Asaro's volatility and temper, which pushed him to almost uncontrollable fits of anger in which he abused the men working under him. He also threw away money as fast as he made it at the race tracks, either Aqueduct or Belmont, both of which happened to be close to Howard Beach. Like many in the mob, notably the elder John Gotti, Asaro seemed to have a gambling compulsion, which for years kept his finances in peril and forced him to live close to the bone.

After getting out of prison in 1992, having served six years for labor racketeering, Massino had taken over command of the Bonanno group after the death of long-time boss Philip Rastelli in 1991. Although Massino didn't seem to care much for Asaro's demeanor and busted him down from the rank of captain, he still saw usefulness in the aging soldier, particularly with what he was getting from certain stolen car operations in Queens and Long Island.

While car thieves often took vehicles to sell to willing buyers in the United States or abroad, some of them saw just as lucrative a racket in chopping up the vehicles and selling off their parts. The places where this breaking apart of vehicles was done is known on the street as a chop shop. Sometimes the thieves would take orders for a particular component of a car and have a model stolen to order that could provide the part. The rest of the vehicle would be dismantled, or chopped, with parts stockpiled as needed. A car in pieces was worth more than the price of the vehicle new.

Guy Gralto, one of Asaro's associates from Ozone Park, knew the virtues of a well-run chop shop. Asaro knew Gralto from knocking around the auto-body business. The thing was that Gralto's auto businesses weren't all legitimate; he had his own chop shops. One was on 101st Avenue near Rockaway Boulevard and another was on Wood Street in Oceanside on Long Island. Between his chopshop actions and his regular auto parts, Gralto made a good living.

"I was a good earner," Gralto recalled in court testimony.

Gralto had started in the chop-shop business in 1987 at a cousin's junkyard in Jamaica, Queens. After a few years of dismantling cars, Gralto struck out on his own around 1992 and opened up Conduit Auto Parts on Cohancy Street in Ozone Park. His partner was his live-in girlfriend Vera who ran the office and answered the telephone. Eventually, Gralto took in Martin Bosshart and Darin Sirrota to get cars.

But in this industry, which prospered in New York City from auto theft and chop shop action, the reality of the business was that you could expect a visit from the mob. So on a day in 1993 when Vincent Asaro stopped by and paid Gralto a visit, the businessman knew that he was talking to the Mafia. Asaro wanted to be paid for protection, Gralto remembered. At first Gralto blew off Asaro and refused to pay. Asaro yelled and screamed and even struck Gralto. But the chop-shop merchant still refused to pay.

On Asaro's second visit, Gralto recalled, his old Ozone Park acquaintance showed up and announced his visit by driving through the fence at Conduit Auto. Gralto still wouldn't pay. Finally, Asaro called Gralto down to his club The Triangle and gave him a few smacks. According to Gralto's later testimony in a federal court case, Asaro yelled that if he didn't pay, Gralto's mother wouldn't be able to identify his body when he was done beating him. Hearing that, Gralto thought it best to start paying the guy.

Asaro got $400 a week from the chop-shop action, Gralto would recall later. He had no recourse but to pay: "So no other thieves robbed me, and no other wise guys would shake me down." Gralto usually paid Asaro at The Triangle at 101st Avenue and Rockaway Boulevard. Seeing that he and Vera were splitting their weekly profit from the chop shop of $12,000, what Gralto paid Asaro seemed like a small amount to keep trouble off his back.

Although Gralto remembered having to pay Asaro a good $1,600 monthly in protection, the relationship wasn't all a one-way street. By being under Asaro's wing, Gralto was protected from being preyed upon by other Mob associates and crime families. Asaro also on occasion would refer thieves to Gralto who needed to dump stolen cars from which parts could be harvested.

But the payments Gralto was making to Asaro were like throwing money away. He wanted out of the arrangement and had Vera talk to her friend Ronald Trucchio, a Gambino crime family soldier. Trucchio was willing to talk with Asaro and maybe split the $400 weekly payment with him.

When he heard that Trucchio had been approached, Asaro, in the words of Gralto, "pretty much went nuts." Asaro reminded Gralto that Trucchio was a mere soldier and that he, Asaro, was a captain who didn't have to talk to him. Trucchio would have to speak with his own boss, who at that point in time on the street was Joseph "Jo Jo" Corozzo. Gralto explained the situation with Corozzo who diplomatically said he would speak to Asaro.

But for reasons that were never made clear, Asaro wouldn't agree to work with Trucchio, and in the end a deal was struck for a buyout of sorts: a lump sum payment of $5,000 to Asaro to end the relationship. Gralto took the deal, and in late 1993 closed down Conduit Auto, moving his chop-shop operation to Oceanside in Nassau County, closer to where he lived. He continued to take stolen cars and parts from Bosshart and his cronies.

Yet Gralto's freedom from the mob was short-lived, and in the end it might have been better for him to have stayed with Asaro, the devil he knew. Once Gralto was no longer under Asaro's protection, he became easy prey for other gangsters, namely Bosshart and his crowd who in February 1994 abducted Gralto at gunpoint and took him to a warehouse in Maspeth where he saw to his horror that his worker David Torres had been tied to a pole and was screaming as he was being cut with a small saw. Bosshart and his people believed Torres had been stealing car parts from them on Gralto's orders and wanted to punish him.

For good measure, they started hitting Torres with a cable. Someone struck Gralto on the back of his head with a gun. With Torres screaming for his life, Gralto yelled at the attackers to leave the poor guy alone, that he had a family. What are you going to do, said Gralto, kill him over car parts? Then Bosshart shot Gralto in the calf, and the chop-shop owner crumpled to the floor bleeding. Everybody then drove Gralto to his home on Long Island, locked him in the bathroom and then herded Gralto's four kids, the youngest being a one-year old and the oldest age eleven, into the kitchen.

There is little gangsters won't do when they smell money. In Gralto's house there was a safe that was anchored to a wall. There was about $50,000 in cash inside, as well as about $30,000 in jewelry owned by Gralto, Vera, and the children. One of the home invaders took a crow bar and in a feeding frenzy pried the safe from the wall and carried it out of the house. It was a fairly big safe, about two-and-a-half feet square. Gralto was left on his own to stanch the bleeding from the bullet wound.

When Vera found out about the robbery she went straight to Trucchio who apologized and said the two men who were with Bosshart shouldn't have abused Gralto and ripped him off. Bosshart wasn't under the wing of the Gambino family, so there wasn't much he could do about him. Trucchio eventually got back $30,000 in cash and the jewels and returned it. He was sorry about everything that had happened.

Clearly, Gralto wasn't going to be able to go it alone without any protection. He decided it was best to stay under Asaro's wing and, as he would later testify, resumed paying him protection money.

This time Gralto would deliver the payments of about $500 a week to Asaro at a pasta restaurant in Hewlett, Long Island, where he liked to spend time. But by December 1994, Gralto again wanted out and paid Asaro another $5,000 buyout fee, a rather modest sum considering how lucrative his chop shops were. Detectives who investigated Gralto estimated that his illegal businesses were raking in millions of dollars from stealing and cutting up about twenty cars a week.

By 1995, Queens prosecutors and the NYPD had been making concerted pushes in an effort to get a handle on the stolen car rings plaguing Queens, and after months of surveillance and gathering of wiretap evidence indicted Asaro, Gralto, and ten others on charges they ran a multi-million-dollar car-theft ring. The criminal combination stole cars all over the metropolitan area. It was the first time prosecutors had used the state's organized crime control act to go after such a ring. Asaro was named by Queens District Attorney Richard Brown as the man controlling the operation even though he was only taking protection money.

The Queens case was quite serious for Asaro. He faced a possible maximum sentence of twenty-five years in prison under the organized-crime law. New York City officials were fed up with the level of car thefts, and they were going to make examples of Asaro and his co-defendants such as Gralto. One by one, those arrested in the case saw the futility of fighting the indictment and pleaded guilty. Gralto was among them and although he got a three-to-nine-year prison sentence after pleading guilty, he agreed to testify against Asaro. In return, prosecutors agreed to recommend that his sentence be reduced to a maximum of only three years.

For a while, the justice system gave Asaro a break. In a surprise ruling, the trial judge dismissed the case against Asaro. But an appeals court reinstated the indictment. Gralto was the prosecution's star witness against Asaro, and he rehashed his history of payoffs and the operation of the syndicate. In an effort to paint Gralto as unreliable, defense attorney Steven Mahler had Gralto's ex-wife testify how miserable he was, calling him a cocaine addict and a habitual liar.

As compelling as Gralto's testimony and wiretap evidence was, the jury couldn't come down with a unanimous decision and wound up split ten votes to two for conviction in June 1998. Asaro had dodged a bullet. But with his notoriety and the need to show they were serious about auto thefts, prosecutors retried Asaro in November 1998 and that time got the result they had wanted. Asaro was convicted of enterprise corruption, the New York State version of the tough federal racketeering statute. Thirteen of a total of sixteen defendants in the case had been convicted of a felony charge and Queens District Attorney Richard Brown said that the victory had helped in some measure to stem the once out of control car theft problem in his borough, making Asaro an unwitting poster boy in the war on crime.

"In my view, the huge decrease in auto theft in Queens that we have seen between 1990 when over 50,000 vehicles were stolen here in Queens County and last year (1997) when there were 19,981 such thefts, is due, at least in part, to our success in this and similar cases," said Brown after Asaro was led away to a cell to await sentencing.

In New York State, the majority of sentences are indeterminate, meaning there is a range of years and months with a maximum set in the law. Unless there is a mandatory minimum term, a judge is free to set a range up to the maximum, which in Asaro's case was twenty-five years. When it came time to give Asaro his just desserts, Judge Robert McGann served up a prison sentence of four to twelve years, about the middle range for the top enterprise-corruption count. Asaro was shipped off to Clinton Correctional Facility, a maximum-security prison in the upstate New York village of Dannemora. From there, Asaro filed various legal writs in Brooklyn federal court to get his sentence overturned. But by late 2002, Asaro had exhausted all of his legal options and had to serve his sentence of four to twelve years. In prison, Asaro was effectively out of crime-family business, and his son Jerome took over for him as an acting captain.

CHAPTER FOURTEEN
"WE'RE IN TROUBLE"

THE MORNING OF JANUARY 9, 2003, Joseph Massino, the boss of the Bonanno crime family, answered a knock on the front door of his Georgian-style home in Howard Beach to find FBI agents Kimberly McCaffrey and Jeffrey Sallet with a warrant for his arrest. It was hardly a surprising development for the portly Massino, who over a period of several days had seen various agents in surveillance mode around the neighborhood and knew that some of his compatriots had been talking to investigators.

"I was expecting you yesterday," Massino told both young agents as they flashed their badges and prepared to take him into custody.

Massino's arrest came as other federal agents that morning were rounding up other Bonanno crime family members, including his brother-in-law Salvatore Vitale and Frank Lino, one of Massino's captains. Lino had been a survivor of sorts, having escaped the bloody murder scene in May 1981, when the Three Captains—Dominick Trinchera, Philip Giaccone, and Alphonse Indelicato—were slaughtered in an old Brooklyn social club in a preemptive strike by Massino against a potential takeover of the crime family.

The Massino arrest was the culmination of a lengthy historical investigation by the FBI in which McCaffrey and Sallet, both accountants by training, followed the money trail and steadily built a case against the crime boss. By the time they took Massino out of his house, the crime-family probe had already led to the arrests of Bonanno captains Frank Coppa, Richard Cantarella, and Anthony Graziano. In total some twenty-six crime-family members had been nabbed in the preceding months. Once a group that prided itself on surviving so many law-enforcement investigations, the Bonanno family was now under siege.

Things quickly went further downhill for Massino. On February 28, 2003, just two months after the indictment had landed, word leaked out that Vitale had decided to become a cooperating witness for the government. It was the worst possible news for Massino because Vitale, aside from being his wife's brother, had been one of the men closest to him in the affairs of the crime family. Vitale had evidence about Massino's role in a number of mob murders and all sorts of other illegal activities. Vitale would be the guide for the FBI through the machinations of the Bonanno family when it came time for Massino to stand trial. By May, with so many cooperators providing information about him, Massino was hit with additional charges, including that of the murder of crime-family member Anthony Mirra.

About the time Massino was absorbing all of the bad news and the prospect of having to spend the rest of his life behind bars, Vincent Asaro was walking out of upstate Shawangunk Correctional Facility, where he had been transferred, as a free man after serving about four-and-a-half years for his chop-shop conviction. His discharge from prison took place in May 2003, and he was returning to a Mafia scene in Howard Beach that was markedly different from the one he had left behind in 1998. The Bonanno family had worked for years without being attacked by the government to any significant degree, and its rackets, as well as the power of Massino, had made the family a force to be reckoned with after years on the outside of the official Mafia ruling Commission. But by 2003, the hierarchy of the Bonanno borgata was running scared, afraid of informants and scrambling to keep a power structure to control the members.

As Sallett and McCaffrey were bundling Massino into their official car for the drive to FBI headquarters in Manhattan, Vincent Asaro was getting closer to becoming a free man. Asaro would officially be released from state prison in May 2003 after serving over four and a half years, the time he was required under the minimum range of his December 1998 sentence for enterprise corruption. He had been a well-behaved prisoner, and that had also worked in his favor. Back on the street, Asaro was still a soldier in the Bonanno family, and it would be a long time before he regained his status as a captain.

Massino didn't hold Asaro in very high regard. But when the crime boss was arrested Asaro's world in the mob faced new uncertainty. With Massino off the street and in a federal detention center in Brooklyn, the Bonanno family would have to be run by a committee of other captains. As John Gotti found out before he died in June 2002, it is difficult for a boss to keep tabs on his men. It is also sometimes difficult for a boss to keep the illegal money flowing to his coffers, although in Massino's case, he had a stockpile of millions of dollars in cash in his house and there was additional income from his legitimate businesses.

Asaro was not a wealthy man, and after coming out of prison, he had to work hard to earn a living, either legitimately or otherwise. He was sixty-eight years old when he walked out of Shawangunk prison, and his big earning days were behind him. Asaro still had an interest in a legitimate fence company, and he was eligible for Social Security. But it seemed that money and Asaro always parted ways quickly. He either would spend his cash on drinks or at the race track: gambling was his curse, and Asaro knew it.

On Long Island, the Sea Crest Diner in Westbury has the dubious distinction of being known to some as the "Rape Diner," so called because it was the site in 1982 of a horrendous crime. Five attackers forced nearly 100 patrons to strip and in some cases have sex with each other. The attackers shot two people and raped a waitress. It went down as one of the most brutal and horrendous crimes in Long Island history. The five suspects were caught and convicted for over 800 counts of rape and other crimes. So, when anybody mentioned the Rape Diner as a meeting place, the location was the Sea Crest. Enough said. Even mobsters referred to it that way.

With Massino behind bars, his crime family was ruled on the street by a special committee of three gangsters: Anthony Urso, Joseph

"Joe Saunders" Cammarano, and Peter "Peter Rabbit" Calabrese. When Calabrese had some family issues he had to deal with and couldn't spend the time on the committee, informants said that Vincent "Vinny Gorgeous" Basciano acted in his stead. All committee members were answerable to Massino but had wide latitude to take care of crime-family street business. The committee knew that the government had the help of jailed Bonanno captains Frank Coppa, Frank Lino, Joseph D'Amico, and former underboss Salvatore Vitale. So if the three committee members had to meet, they did it face to face and in a surrounding where they didn't think it would be possible for the FBI to listen to them. A public place like the Sea Crest Diner filled the bill. So did the Greenview Town House Restaurant in nearby Orange County. The committee moved around when it had to for security.

Of course diners and public restaurants are open to anyone, and the FBI could easily spot a mobster entering an establishment and see who he was sitting with. But eavesdropping on a table conversation would be difficult, unless there was a spy in the group. Well, for several months in late 2003 the FBI had the good fortune to have the cooperation of James "Big Louie" Tartaglione, a Bonanno captain who had decided to come back to New York, ostensibly because Massino wanted him to help with a crime family in disarray. Tartaglione, under the guise of trying to sort out the Bonanno family problems, went to see ruling committee members at both the Sea Crest Diner and The Greenview while wearing a body recorder. Cammarano, Urso, and Basciano spoke freely about crime-family business, including the latest gossip. One of their recurring subjects was Vincent Asaro.

According to recordings Tartaglione made on September 13, 2003 and turned over to his FBI handlers, the conversation about Asaro portrayed him at that point in his life as a man who was broken and dispirited.

"Talking about Vinnie Asaro, how is he doing?" asked Tartaglione.

"Vinnie's sick," answered Cammarano.

"Is he very sick?" Tartaglione wanted to know.

"Got the cirrhosis of the liver," said Cammarano.

That condition didn't surprise Tartaglione who remembered Asaro as being a heavy drinker back in his younger days, although he had more or less gone on the wagon and had tried to clean up his act.

But for Urso, drinking wasn't the only problem for Asaro. He was so broke that being in the crime family wasn't doing much for his self-esteem or reputation among his so called peers. It seemed as though Asaro's lack of money had made him abusive as a captain, a "skipper" as the rank was called.

"It's like our friend said, when you make a skipper and you make a skipper that's broke, he abuses his men for this," said Urso, quite possibly referring to something Massino was known to have said about others. "That is the God's honest truth. And that's what he did, abused everybody."

"Well is he still at the track every day still?" asked Tartaglione

Sure, said Cammarano, who knew how much money Asaro had squandered on the horses. The track certainly killed Vinnie was how Tartaglione saw things.

The money Asaro was throwing around at the racetrack was cash he couldn't really afford. As soon as a dollar bill landed in his hands it seemed to fly away in the vain hope of following a winning horse. Urso said Asaro owed people money, and he wasn't paying his debts. Urso was going to call him in and tell him to start paying off people.

"Gotta start with Vito. He owes Vito sixteen thousand," remembered Cammarano, without further identifying the lender.

Asaro had borrowed frequently over the years from fellow gangsters, the FBI had heard. One informant had related to agents that Asaro had taken up to $30,000 over the years from Massino, who had a significant loansharking business. Some crime family members were into Massino for over $100,000, so Asaro's amounts were relatively small. Asaro owed a number of people, and there was little sign that he was paying it back, according to Cammarano.

"Is he earning?" said Tartaglione.

"Is he earning? Who the fuck knows, Lou, I don't know," said Urso.

Certainly in the 1990s when he had the chop-shop income Asaro had some money coming in. Gambling also seemed a source of income. Vitale had recalled for the FBI that also during the 1990s after the death of a bookmaker known only by the name "Stretch" that the operation was turned over to Asaro who allegedly ran it with his son Jerome. Although the Asaros may have run the business on a daily basis, Vitale told the agents that he actually owned the operation.

Well, Asaro just got home from prison about two months ago so, no, he wasn't doing anything yet to earn money, explained Cammarano. To get Asaro back on track, they needed to put him under somebody's command so Cammarano was going to have to include him as part of his crew.

A month later, the same three old timers met at a diner, and again Asaro's woes came up in the conversations. He was definitely on everybody's radar but not in a good way. Asaro may have been going back to the track, but if he couldn't kick in $25 a week to the Bonanno-family war chest, a fund to help members who needed help paying for lawyers, which were quite in demand, he should stay away from the horses, said Urso.

"Let me tell you something," said Tartaglione in agreement with Urso. "If anybody like him can't give twenty-five dollars a week, he shouldn't be in this life. Not unless he's got cancer, he's dying, not unless he's definitely sick and there's no way for him to earn something like that."

But the fact of the matter was that Vincent Asaro was in "the life." It was just not a life that was doing him any good. Aside from being broke, Asaro's stature had been reduced. He had once been a captain. But when he went to state prison, he turned over his meager crew of soldiers to his son Jerome, who was made an acting captain. Jerome Asaro was the latest of the Asaro men to become blooded to the Mafia and was one of a number of them who followed in their fathers' footsteps to join the Bonanno family. There were at least nine father-and-son combinations in the borgata at that time. Massino is believed to have wanted to have such familial pairings because it gave him more power over the fathers. Informants said Massino had been the one to approve the induction of the sons, including Jerome, into the crime family and in some cases presided over the ceremonies.

After Vincent Asaro was released from prison, he had to eat crow and as a soldier was placed in the crew of his son Jerome, who by that time had been promoted to official Captain position by Massino. So, after years of having his son do his bidding, Vincent Asaro found himself under his son. The relationship between them was fraught with tension, with Vincent resenting his son for his ambition and tightness with money.

For the most part, Tartaglione was a convincing double-agent. He made recordings of Cammarano, Urso, and Basciano in which he put them at ease and drew out useful tidbits of information that helped the FBI in its understanding of the Bonanno family and the instability it was suffering since the arrest of Massino and some others. At one meeting at the Sea Crest Diner, the conversation among the four men led to their commiserating about the way informants had riddled the ranks of the family, with Tartaglione saying over coffee, "We're in trouble, we're in trouble."

However, Basciano had a nagging suspicion about Tartaglione and wondered why he had suddenly returned from Florida to hang around with his old Bonanno friends, action which could easily get him nabbed on a parole violation.

"It was strange. All of a sudden, out of the clear blue, Big Lou wanted to come around and start running the Bonanno crime family," Dominic Cicale, a then-up-and-coming member of the crime family would recall later.

So, for a meeting Tartaglione had with the three ruling members of the Bonanno family on January 18, 2004, at the Sea Crest Diner, Basciano had Cicale conduct a counter-surveillance on the diner. Cicale was to watch for any law-enforcement cars outside the diner, and if he spotted any he was to signal Basciano with the pager code "5050." After noticing a number of clean cars, devoid of any winter road splatter and salt, Cicale went to a pay phone and entered the code.

Tipping off that the meeting was under surveillance and that

Tartaglione was an informant, Basciano moved the conversation at the table away from anything incriminating. Sensing a sudden coolness of the three other men, Tartaglione left the diner and later reported to his FBI handlers. Two days later, Urso, Cammarano, and some other Bonanno crime-family members were arrested on racketeering charges. The leadership of the family had all but been decimated. Only Basciano wasn't charged and in effect he became Massino's acting street boss. His time for a jail cell would come later.

After the ruling committee members were arrested on January 20, the crime family Vincent Asaro and Jerry Asaro knew was in disarray. Dozens of members and associates had been arrested. No one could trust anyone and Basciano even held meetings with captains in which he asked them all to strip to their underwear in case any of them were wearing a secret tape recorder or transmitter.

The FBI had already harvested a basket full of cooperating witnesses who were giving evidence against Massino, Urso, Cammarano, as well as Canadian gangster Vito Rizzutto. The agency strategy of building an historical case against the family that included numerous murders and other crimes was paying off. Agents also were gleaning information from informants about the Asaros, father and son. Jerome Asaro was established as an acting captain, soon to be full captain, the agents learned. There was also an intriguing tidbit about Vincent.

Joseph D'Amico, one of the turncoats who had gone over to help the FBI, had an interesting pedigree with the mob. He was the cousin of Bonanno captain Richard Cantarella, who also became a cooperating witness. Know by the nickname of "Mouk," D'Amico got his hands bloody for the crime family in February 1982 when he shot Bonanno captain Anthony Mirra at point-blank range as both men were exiting an underground parking lot in Manhattan. Mirra had been suspected of being an informant at a time when the crime family was paranoid over FBI activity. It had surfaced months earlier that a brash wiseguy named Donnie Brasco had actually been an undercover FBI agent with the real name of Joseph Pistone. Working for many months undercover, Pistone had penetrated the Bonanno family, particularly the group run by Sonny Black Napolitano. Mirra had even used Pistone as a driver, which showed how convincing the FBI mole had been in his undercover role.

In a debriefing with agents on April 14, 2003, Joseph D'Amico talked to them about a number of things such as gun trafficking, the assassination in 1979 of Carmine Galante, and gossip about who was who in the Bonanno family. He had also heard something none of the other big cooperating witnesses had apparently reported to the agents: Vincent Asaro was involved in the "Lufthansa heist" with Jimmy Burke, who was around Paul Vario.

CHAPTER FIFTEEN
NEVER SAY NEVER

WHEN HE WAS ARRESTED ON JANUARY 23, 2014, there was no way that Vincent Asaro was going to be living anywhere else for the foreseeable future other than the Metropolitan Detention Center in Red Hook. Given the ugly things said about him in the prosecution's fifty-three-page detention memorandum, Asaro was not going to get bail. In fact, defense attorney Gerald McMahon didn't even try to get him out: any effort would have been an exercise in futility. Vincent was going to be a guest of the Bureau of Prisons until at least his trial—whenever that might be.

As it turned out, McMahon was the one who got out first, in a manner of speaking. He didn't stay with the case for very long. Asaro didn't have any money to retain a private attorney and McMahon, although a tenacious lawyer who had bested Brooklyn federal prosecutors in a number of mob cases, couldn't stay with the case. So, on February 12, 2014, Judge Allyne Ross appointed Elizabeth Macedonio of Queens to take on Asaro's defense. A petite blonde with long straight hair, which fellow attorneys said never seemed anything but well-coiffed, Macedonio had cut her eyeteeth on some mob cases. A graduate of New York Law School, solo-practitioner Macedonio quickly earned a good reputation among her peers as she wrangled some very good plea bargains for her clients.

The indictment in the Asaro case was really a legal hybrid. It contained the overall racketeering conspiracy charge and along with it a series of extortion and gambling counts involving a total of five defendants. But even a quick reading of the indictment showed that the main charges were those against Asaro: The Lufthansa robbery and the murder of Paul Katz for which the other defendants weren't named, save for Asaro's son Jerome who was fingered as an accessory after the fact in the murder for moving Katz's corpse.

To the defense attorneys for Thomas DiFiore, Jack Bonventre, and John Ragano, the early strategy was to get the case against those defendants separated or severed from Vincent and his son. The Asaros were charged with the most serious crimes, including in addition to the Lufthansa heist counts of robbery, arson, and murder solicitation. The Asaro counts spanned nearly forty years. DiFiore, although said by prosecutors to be the new street boss of the Bonanno crime family, faced only an extortion charge involving one debt and attempts to collect it over a four-month period in 2013. Ragano, a big man nicknamed "Bazoo," who looked like a mob tough and was considered by law enforcement to be a Bonanno soldier, was also only named in the one count with DiFiore. Bonventre, a reputed Bonanno captain, faced an extortion charge and claims that he ran an illegal gambling business from 2007 to 2008.

In March, Ragano's attorney Charles Hochbaum moved to have his client's case severed from that of Asaro. The other defense attorneys didn't want to join in that maneuver until they had learned more about the government's case. Attempts to get a severance are difficult tactics for a defense attorney to try generally. Hochbaum argued to Judge Ross that if Ragano had to go to trial with Asaro there would be "spillover prejudice" because he would have to do more extensive trial preparation than if he was tried separately. There were counts that Ragano was not charged in so it would be unfair to have him tried with Asaro, the defense argued.

Ross made quick work of Ragano's argument and in a short, four-page ruling on April 7, 2014, denied his motion. The indictment wasn't so complex that the jury wouldn't be able to weigh the evidence against each individual defendant on each charge, said Ross. The judge also said there was significant overlap in evidence on the charges facing Asaro and the few in which Ragano is mentioned. If she gave the jury proper instructions about considering evidence separately against each defendant, Ross didn't think there was any risk of spillover prejudice. So for the time being, all of the defendants including Asaro would face the music of a trial together.

The U.S. Supreme Court has said that "there is a preference in the federal system for joint trials of defendants who are indicted together." But that preference wasn't absolute, and if there is a risk that a defendant would be prejudiced by a joint trial, the court could grant a severance It was a tough burden, but it has happened that one or more defendants were tried at a different time from someone else.

Ross's decision showed that DiFiore, Ragano, and Bonventre would not have an easy time if they tried again to get separate trials. Meanwhile, Assistant U.S. Attorney Nicole Argentieri, as was routine in Mafia cases, made some plea bargain offers to DiFiore, Ragano, and Bonventre. But as one defense attorney remembered it, the government offers on prison sentences if those defendants plead guilty were "nonsensical." None of the defendants took the government offers.

Argentieri and her co-counsels also began turning over evidence to the defense teams, which the government intended to use at trial. This was a routine procedure required under federal law, justified by the rationale that there shouldn't be any trial by ambush in which a defendant was delayed in seeing and assessing the prosecution's evidence. After about five months of getting evidence dumps, the defense attorneys believed they had a shot at getting Asaro's trial separated from those of DiFiore, Ragano, and Bonventre. The chance of success still didn't seem great but it was worth taking.

To movie fans, particularly those of actor Bill Murray, the name Steve Zissou might just ring a bell. In 2004, Murray starred in the comedy *The Life Aquatic with Steve Zissou*, about an oceanographer who wants to avenge the death of a friend by a terrible shark. The film was a parody of sorts of the life of famed French oceanographer Jacques-Yves Cousteau, although it was a fictional account. But as it turned out, the main character name of "Steve Zissou" happened to be that in real life of a Bayside Queens criminal defense attorney named, well, Steven Zissou.

Because of the match between the name of Murray's character and Zissou, Buena Vista Pictures came to a confidential agreement with the attorney in which the company could use his name. At the end of the film, there is a comment on the screen that reads, "The filmmakers acknowledge that the real Steve Zissou is a prominent attorney in New York City specializing in complex federal litigation." That was not a bad plug for Zissou and most likely his deal with Buena Vista Pictures also proved financially rewarding.

Still, Zissou, whose name is of Greek origin, had to continue to earn a living no matter what he got from the film. As a regular in Brooklyn and Manhattan federal courts, Zissou had a busy caseload of mostly criminal clients. He had shared a suite of offices for years with Macedonio, and both trooped from Bayside to the courts to handle a steady diet of cases. Zissou had represented some high-profile cases, notably that of a Guyanese immigrant accused of having people killed in an insurance scam. (The defendant, Ronald Malley, was convicted but spared the death penalty.) And he represented terror defendant Ahmed Khalfan Ghailani, who was convicted of conspiracy in the U.S. embassy bombing in Kenya but acquitted of all other charges.

Among the federal criminal bar attorneys, Zissou was well regarded, and he had experience in complex criminal cases, experience which helped him to see down the road and anticipate possible moves a court might make and how it all might impact his clients. Criminal cases are as much about gamesmanship, and a favorable ruling by a judge could have far-reaching repercussions for both sides. The other defense attorneys involved, Gordon Mehlman and Diane Ferrone, who represented Jack Bonventre, and Charles Hochbaum who represented John Ragano, were also experienced in complex cases. All of the lawyers crafted their motion papers for the severance, with Zissou doing the bulk of the work and taking the lead in court.

The papers for the new severance motion were filed on July 28, 2014, with Argentieri and her team filing their opposition a short time later. In a nutshell, DiFiore and Bonventre wanted Ross to sever their trial for the extortion counts from that of the Asaros, who as mentioned previously faced a more serious group of charges ranging from the Lufthansa robbery to arson and murder solicitation. Bonventre also wanted a severance for the gambling charges he faced.

Severance motions are always a long shot. The tactic had already failed once in the Asaro case. Even prosecutor Argentieri predicted it was a lost cause, saying, "Oh, Steve you know she will not grant your severance motion," the defense attorney remembered. Zissou knew the odds were against him but still held out hope. He then left for a vacation in Europe with his family.

It was while he was at the Sofitel Hotel in Rome, having a cup of cappuccino at about 11:00 A.M. that Zissou noticed his iPhone ping, indicating he had a text message from his office. The message stunned him. In a short text, Zissou learned that the defense motion for severance had been granted by Ross, despite the fact that the odds were against a judge going along with the defense in such cases. In a twelve-page decision released on August 20, Ross said she agreed that some kind of severance was needed, particularly because the case had allegations of violence—the Lufthansa robbery and the Katz murder—which were inflammatory and likely to cause a greater "risk of substantial prejudice" to the defendants like DiFiore and Bonventre. While agreeing that a charge of extortion was a crime of violence, Ross said that particular allegation in the case was "starkly different in quality and nature from the violent and heinous acts spanning a forty-year period that Vincent and Jerome are charged with." The risk of prejudice was so great that the case of DiFiore and Bonventre had to be severed, said Ross. Then, she allowed Ragano, the defendant who had made the earlier unsuccessful move for a severance, also to be tried separately from the Asaros.

The defense had a nice, unexpected victory in the severance. But it was not the only thing Ross did that would have implications for the government's case. She also ruled that the trial of DiFiore, Ragano, and Bonventre on the extortion counts should take place *before* the trial of the Asaros on the main racketeering count, which included the Lufthansa heist and everything else they were accused of. While at first glance that might not seem like a big deal, such a trial occurring before the main Lufthansa event would give the world—and the Asaros—a preview of Gaspare Valenti's testimony and also show how well he stood up on the witness stand. The government would then lose the element of surprise and by testifying first in a sort-of preview trial, Valenti would be locking himself in to his testimony. Ross did give Argentieri and her prosecution team that option of trying the Asaros on the *extortion* charges along with the other defendants. But that would have to be the government's decision. Otherwise, Argentieri and company could wait and try the Asaros later.

Faced with the prospect of two trials, prosecutors decided to push for more realistic plea bargains with offers the defendants would find more appealing. Given that DiFiore, Ragano and Bonventre were said by investigators to be members of the Bonanno family, the government wanted a so-called "global plea" to involve some prison time for each. Bonventre had been lucky enough to make a $2 million bail, but DiFiore, who suffered from health issues, and Ragano, had both been in custody since January 2014. DiFiore in particular had tried a number of times to get bail, arguing that his health wouldn't improve while in jail, but hadn't been able to convince Ross to spring him. What seemed to work against DiFiore was the fact that NYPD and federal surveillance had shown that he was a member of the administrative committee leading the Bonanno family. No longer was the borgata under the command of a single man like Massino. After being decimated by so many federal prosecutions, the crime family was being steered by DiFiore and Vincent Asaro, For Asaro, such a leadership role was something that was quite a change in stature for a man who had once been busted down to the lowly rank of soldier.

During plea negotiations, it became apparent that DiFiore wanted any deal to include Jerome Asaro, if the younger Asaro wanted to be included. As Zissou recalled, DiFiore's sense of camaraderie made him look for a way of getting Jerome out from under having to endure a trial and going down with his father, who was facing big troubles and on paper looked like he would be convicted. Vincent

Asaro was also involved in these meetings for a global plea and complained that he wanted to be covered as well. But given the gravity of the charges against him, Vincent Asaro wasn't going to be getting any meaningful plea. By late September, the plea bargaining intensified and Zissou wrote Ross to say everybody had made "considerable progress" and believed that the remaining issues didn't present big obstacles to a deal.

So, it wasn't terribly surprising that over a two-day period between October 7 and October 8, 2014, DiFiore, Ragano, and Bonventre appeared before Ross and separately entered pleas of guilty to a single count of conspiracy to collect an unlawful debt. The victim who owed the money was a car-wash employee and debt was at a criminal usury loan rate, which in New York State meant that the interest rate was more than an annual rate of 25 percent. The victim had borrowed from a Bonanno family associate and owed $30,000, an amount that was eventually paid. Bonventre entered his plea first on October 7, while the other two followed a day later.

The plea situation for Jerome was different than the other three. He faced more serious racketeering charges, mostly notably a case of arson involving a black nightclub and his having a role in the surreptitious moving of Paul Katz's remains. The prosecution wanted his plea to carry more weight at sentencing. So Argentieri insisted on Jerome pleading to the Katz and arson counts.

Jerome was one of the crime family's younger powers, something underscored by the way he had supplanted his father, becoming a captain and then having his father report to him. The relationship between father and son had gone sour over the years, with Vincent lashing out at Jerome and his ambition. In one conversation taped by Valenti, Vincent saw his son as greedy and power hungry, regretting that he had made him a captain.

"Fuck Jerry," said Vincent about his son. "Fuck him in his ass. Fucking Jerry is for Jerry. Jerry's for Jerry. I lost my son. I lost my son when I made him a skipper. I lost my son when I put him there."

The way Vincent saw it, Jerome was avaricious. He railed about him, calling him a "greedy cocksucker" who was ungrateful for the fact that he had secured his son what amounted to a no-show job for $600 a week.

But there seemed to be other things at work that fractured the relationship between Jerome and his father. His parents divorced in 2005, and it appeared that Jerome took the side of his mother in the marital fight. Jerome also had a more significant work history than Vincent, from that of a laborer at a shipping company to construction and then as a dispatcher at a concrete firm. These were all things that made Jerome appear more financially stable.

Although he was a working family man—he had raised three daughters before divorcing his first wife Susan—Jerome got involved willfully in the mob. When it suited him, Vincent had used Jerome as a willing acolyte for crime family business. When it came time, Jerome pleaded guilty before Ross to the nightclub arson, admitting he torched at his father's direction the night club Afters, which had once been a mob watering hole, at 8601 Rockaway Boulevard, Ozone Park but became disliked by Italian gangsters after its new owners wanted to cater to African-Americans. By his plea, Jerome admitted he and another man got inside the club and helped start a fire that caused considerable damage.

In terms of the Katz murder, Jerome didn't admit to killing the hijacker. But he did say that "in fact knowing that a murder had been committed, I assisted persons in moving the body of that person after the fact." Jerome also admitted that he dug up the body to prevent "the apprehension of the individual who committed that murder."

Some interesting things seem evident about the allocution Jerome made in court about the Katz body. First it was clear that he knew who might have committed the murder. Second, he didn't name his father Vincent as the killer, as the government had alleged he had. Third, he did not agree to testify against his father. Fourth, Jerome didn't admit to being a member of the Bonanno crime family but rather an associate, which is a lesser status. Yet taken together, the arson and the murder accessory charges listed in the new criminal information nailed Jerome on a racketeering conspiracy charge, the same one his father had been charged with in Lufthansa and other crimes. This had the effect of pushing the suggested prison sentence for Jerome to the range of seventy-seven to ninety-six months, in part because he already had a previous federal guilty plea to racketeering some years earlier.

Over a period of two days in October 2014, DiFiore, Bonventre, Ragano, and Jerome Asaro pled guilty before Ross to the negotiated plea deals. Then in 2015, Ross doled out the various sentences and gave DiFiore twenty-one months, which in his case was a bargain because he got credit for time served and would be out in a year. Bonventre got twenty-one months and Ragano fifty-one months, much better than if had they gone to trial and lost on the racketeering case.

In Jerome Asaro's case, defense attorney Lawrence Fisher submitted papers that described his client's work ethic and his regret about his life of crime. Fisher also attached letters from family members, including his current and former wives, his children and other relatives asking for a lenient sentence. Particularly poignant was a note written by his mother Theresa who was suffering from blindness and had to dictate her words to a daughter. Theresa Asaro said that in her failing health she relied upon Jerome and hoped that Ross would take her needs into consideration.

But when Jerome Asaro was sentenced on March 26, 2015, there was another family in court whose members Ross had to consider: those of murder victim Paul Katz. Before he disappeared on December 6, 1969, Katz had fathered five children with his wife Delores. His life had been one in which he was mixed up with Burke and his crew in all kinds of hijackings and other thefts, and when Katz left the house for the final time, both he and his wife knew he might never return.

When she was given a chance to speak in court, Katz's daughter Ilsa remembered how she and her brothers and sister had been watching an episode of *Frosty the Snowman* on television when her father walked out the door. Her mother, Ilsa said, had begged Katz not to leave.

"He never came back," Ilsa said to Ross.

Actually the remains excavated by the FBI team from the basement of the house in Ozone Park did make it back to Katz's family after the bones, hair, and other bits of tissue were analyzed for DNA comparison. The remains were turned over to Katz's son Lawrence by the FBI.

"He came home with me carrying him in an evidence bag," Lawrence told Ross.

Adding a macabre element to the entire sentencing proceedings was the fact that as Ilsa tearfully addressed Ross she said she was carrying some of her father's cremated remains in a cloth bag inside her handbag. She did not actually take the remains out as she spoke. The torment of not knowing for years about what had been her father's fate had led Ilsa to have to come up with a fiction about his demise.

"When we were asked, 'Where's your father?' we'd say he died in a plane crash," Ilsa said.

Asaro offered no apology to the Katz family members, but did so to his own family. When it came time for Argentieri to speak, she reminded Ross that Jerome had lived a life that had been steeped in Mafia involvement.

In sentencing Jerome, Ross didn't give him a break. She hit him with ninety months or seven-and-a-half years, not much under the sentencing guideline maximum recommendation of ninety-three months. Judges don't have to stick to the guidelines, but in this case Ross saw no reason to go to the low end of the range. Seeing that Jerome didn't have the ability to pay a fine, Ross didn't impose one but did hit him with the mandatory special assessment of $50, half of the usual $100 levy.

With four of the five defendants convicted, the government could now turn its attention to Vincent Asaro, the last man standing and the main attraction who prosecutors said was intertwined with the Lufthansa heist. Asaro wasn't going to take a plea deal, certainly not one that gave him a twenty-year prison sentence and that meant he would die behind bars. At the age of eighty, Asaro was going to trial.

CHAPTER SIXTEEN
DEAD MEN TOLD
NO TALES

NOBODY KNOWS HOW MANY HOMICIDES Jimmy Burke had committed in his decades-long criminal life. Some in the FBI thought it could be as many as thirty. The bloody trail after Lufthansa accounted for the deaths of at least five direct participants in the heist, not counting the death of Anthony Rodriguez who died after one of his poisonous pet snakes bit him. As Henry Hill would tell investigators, Burke saw informants all around him and sometimes—as in the case of Paul Katz—he was right and had no qualms about killing.

Anyone who watched the film *GoodFellas* saw slayings by Burke's crew at Robert's Lounge done by garroting, stabbing, or gunshots. Bodies went missing, were tossed into hastily dug graves or else left in the street. Murder gave the edge to Scorsese's cinematic version and the public and news media were waiting to see what Vincent Asaro's trial would bring out about all the blood and gore. Katz's murder would certainly be part of the case because it was listed in the indictment. But what about all of the other killings? Could they be linked somehow to Asaro?

Prosecutors did not disappoint. In March 2015, with a trial still some seven months away, Argentieri and her staff crafted a seventy-two-page special court document known as a motion *in limine,* a term that comes from the Latin and means at the "threshold" and refers to a request before trial to either bring in or keep out certain evidence. They would follow it up with additional filings. In Asaro's case, the prosecution wanted to *bring in* certain evidence to show how he had been continually involved over forty-five years with the Bonanno family and bring in evidence of other acts—all bad—not charged in the indictment but which showed his criminal intent and motives. Among those were Asaro's history of heavy drug use, gambling, stealing, assaults, threats of violence, and shakedowns. But added to the government's list were a number of murders linked to the period after Lufthansa that had widely been tied to Burke: Martin Krugman, Joseph Manri, Robert McMahon, and the disappearance of Thomas DeSimone, as well as the killing of Richard Eaton.

The government wasn't trying to pin all of those murders on Asaro. Not by a long shot. Instead, prosecutors hoped that remarks Asaro made about the killings to certain potential witnesses would show how trusting he had been of them. It was a way of bringing into the courtroom through the back door the Lufthansa killings, which had captivated New York for so long. It may not have been the prosecution's intent to stoke such interest in the case, but reporters began to salivate over the prospect of seeing life imitate art in the courtroom. "RealFellas Revealed: Secrets of Lufthansa heist double-cross & slays," blared the *Daily News* in one headline after prosecutors filed their papers.

Of course, Asaro wanted to have that evidence kept out. His attorneys said that evidence of the *GoodFellas* murders was not only irrelevant to the case but raised the likelihood that the jury would be confused or prejudiced against Asaro. It would be hard, the attorneys argued, to keep the lurid details of the violent deaths of those involved in Lufthansa from tainting Asaro and bolstering the argument that he was a killer of Katz as the government alleged.

But if the world was waiting to see a reprise of tales of infamous murder in the Lufthansa trial, Ross throw cold water on that notion. Going through each of the murders and disappearances prosecutors wanted to introduce into the Asaro trial, Ross found some compelling reasons to keep most of it away from the jury and the public. The fact that wig merchant Marty Krugman had been a pest to Burke by asking about the robbery and other things was okay to come before the jury because it showed the existence of the Lufthansa robbery conspiracy charged against Asaro, reasoned Ross. But evidence that Burke had said to Valenti that Krugman was killed for complaining about the way the loot was split was another matter. The fact that Krugman had been killed wasn't really part of the robbery conspiracy, she said.

"At some point the collapse of relationships and murder of co-conspirators after the heist ceases to be an epilogue to the heist, and begins to tell the story of a whole new set of crimes," reasoned Ross in her ruling on the evidence. "Marty's murder does not mend a 'break in the natural sequence of the narrative of evidence' about the Lufthansa heist. Nor is it required to show trust between Burke and [Valenti]."

There was just too great a risk of confusing the jury and prejudicing it against Asaro to refer to a murder "possibly ordered" by his associates so Ross decided that part of the evidence about Krugman's death had to be kept out of the trial.

Thomas DeSimone's disappearance caused similar problems for Ross as she found in the Krugman case. Ross, like most people, assumed that DeSimone had been murdered after the heist. But again she found that his presumed homicide had no bearing on the planning and execution of the Lufthansa robbery. Valenti could testify about his closeness to DeSimone but didn't have to tell a story about another murder, which if the jury learned of it could confuse the panel and prejudice it against Asaro by raising the implication that his "associates tended to meet violent deaths."

The double homicides of Joe Manri and Robert McMahon weren't killings the prosecution had accused Asaro of having a role in. In fact, according to court papers, gangster Anthony Stabile was the one who killed the pair on Burke's orders, information that contradicted Henry Hill's earlier claims that Paolo Licastri had admitted he was the triggerman. Argentieri had argued in her court papers that information about the double murders would help relate why Valenti was afraid to meet with Stabile and confided such apprehension to Asaro. The government's argument was that Valenti's confiding to Asaro was evidence of the relationship that existed between the two men.

But for Ross, evidence of the Manri-McMahon killings was essentially overkill if the prosecution was trying to show the level of trust between Valenti and his cousin Asaro. "I find that [Valenti's] request for defendant's advice is of low probative value given the other evidence available in this case," said Ross. There was just no justification for using evidence of two murders, which again would create an "aura of extreme violence" around Asaro, she ruled.

The government had also wanted to use evidence about the murder of Louis Cafora to prove the Bonanno family link to the heist and as a roundabout way of proving the general proposition that gangsters consult their superiors before doing killings. In the case of Cafora, who disappeared with his wife, the government specifically wanted to show that Asaro, Valenti, and Michael Zaffarano had talked at one point about the fact that Asaro did want to help out in the killing. But to Ross, such evidence didn't show any connection between the Bonanno family and the actual Lufthansa heist itself and information about the Cafora killing was not to come before the jury.

So by her ruling, Ross knocked out evidence about the Krugman, DeSimone, Manri, McMahon, and Cafora homicides. For the most part, the gory aftermath of the Lufthansa robbery was not going to see the light of day when Vincent Asaro went on trial. But one Lufthansa-era killing could make its way into the case, that of Richard Eaton, who had died because of the way he had stiffed Jimmy Burke over money from a drug deal. In his debriefings, Valenti had told the FBI that after Eaton had been killed he was enlisted by Jerome Asaro to dig a hole to bury the corpse but that the cold ground in February prevented that from happening. The body was then taken to a trailer on some Brooklyn property Valenti's family owned for storage until a backhoe could be found to dig the grave. However, Eaton's body was discovered by police in the trailer and afterward, according to Valenti, Vincent Asaro told him where and why Eaton had been killed by Burke.

For the prosecution, evidence of the Eaton murder not only helped to prove the Lufthansa heist charge but also the allegation about the murder of Paul Katz some ten years earlier. Evidence of the Eaton slaying helped show the close relationship between heist organizer

Burke, Asaro, his son Jerome, and Valenti, prosecutors maintained. All those men had developed a trusting relationship, which allowed them "to successfully execute and cover up the most risky and violent offenses, including the Katz murder and the Lufthansa Heist," the government argued.

Ross also said some other Lufthansa-related evidence could come into the case. The late Gambino crime captain Anthony "Fat Andy" Ruggiano had a girth that matched his nickname. Ruggiano's widening waistline came from the fact that he liked food, so much so that he opened a popular café in Ozone Park, which became something of a crime-family hangout. Ruggiano had a jewelry business where he sometimes fenced stolen jewels and according to the FBI had been approached by Burke and Asaro to put some of the jewelry stolen in the heist into play. The FBI knew this because Ruggiano's son, also named Anthony, had been told the details by his father. While Fat Andy, who died in 1999 of a heart attack, may have been an old-school stand-up gangster who never squealed, his son, a Gambino associate, was made of different stuff and eventually became an FBI cooperating witness to save his skin after participating in a number of crimes, including the murder of his own brother-in-law, Frank Boccia.

Prosecutors wanted to use Junior Ruggiano's testimony against Asaro for the reason that it showed more about the Lufthansa conspiracy and the attempts by Asaro and Burke to fence the stolen property without having to share more than they had to with their Bonanno and Lucchese crime-family bosses—notably Philip Rastelli and Paul Vario. Junior Ruggiano's testimony was needed because his father was dead and couldn't be called as a witness. Normally the younger Ruggiano's recollections would be hearsay. But Ross, noting that Fat Andy was dead, ruled that Junior Ruggiano's recollections about his father's statements to him could be used as evidence. By talking to his son and admitting that he had obtained some of the stolen Lufthansa jewelry for his store, Fat Andy was admitting that he not only was a jewelry fence but shared in some of the Lufthansa spoils. For Ross, those were statements against Fat Andy's "penal interest" meaning they implicated him in wrongdoing and could be used by the government as evidence even though they might be hearsay.

So, in the final analysis and to the media's disappointment much of the sensational blood and gore surrounding the Lufthansa heist would be kept out of the case. That was a clear win for Asaro's defense team. But Ross did permit some old Lufthansa evidence to come in. There was another interesting wrinkle that could prove helpful to Asaro. Ross also permitted his lawyers to use some NYPD reports and documents about the disappearance of Paul Katz. Consisting of the original missing person's report and additional materials, the police documents added a new name to the disappearance of Katz: Joseph Allegro. The police documents showed that on the afternoon he left the house for the last time, Katz had told his wife Delores he was going to meet Allegro, one of the men arrested with Katz in an earlier hijacking case. Katz never returned that day. For a number of legal reasons, Ross said Asaro's lawyers could use the police documents as evidence and by implication put before the jury the name of Allegro as another person who might have been involved in Katz's disappearance and death.

As the trial date of October 19, 2015, approached, Asaro had been in federal custody for twenty-one months, and the time of incarceration was wearing on him. He had suffered from heart trouble, having received a bypass operation and if his old gangster friends were right had liver troubles. Asaro had not lived a healthy life, even as a young man when he struggled with drug addiction and alcohol. It had worn him down. His face was angular and thin, making him look every bit of his octogenarian self. Also fatiguing for Asaro were the early 5:30 A.M. wakeups at the detention center whenever he had to be bussed to court. "This 'Sleepfella' wants to catch a few more winks before going to court," joked one *Daily News* story.

Through his attorneys, Asaro sent a letter to Ross claiming he should be released on bail because of his health issues and the strain of having to go back and forth to court. Asaro proposed that he be let out on bail to live under conditions of home confinement—meaning with an ankle bracelet monitoring device—at his girlfriend's home, what better way to get your vigor and vim back. Besides, at his advanced age and with the Lufthansa and Katz murder allegations over four decades old, Asaro said he wasn't a danger to anybody.

No way, said prosecutors about Asaro's request for bail. In a letter to Ross, Assistant U.S. Attorney Alicyn Cooley said that Asaro was still a violent man well into his seventies and that Valenti's taped conversations proved it.

"Even with home confinement and electronic monitoring, the defendant would have unfettered use of telephones and smart devices while at his girlfriend's residence and could easily conduct the Bonanno family's business with those resources and his newly obtained freedom," wrote Cooley.

Asaro could still try to intimidate witnesses either directly or indirectly, Cooley continued. She added that since Asaro was now aware of the strength of the government's case, his incentive to flee was stronger than ever and he could rely on the resources of the Bonanno family to do so. In reality, the Bonanno family didn't seem to hold Asaro in high regard, particularly after his coarse comments about his son and DiFiore had surfaced, so it is doubtful anyone in the borgata would have risked helping him to flee. The crime family also didn't have the kind of financial resources anymore after years of prosecutions to help Asaro even if it wanted to. Nevertheless, Ross played it safe and kept Asaro in custody, but indicated to both sides that they might have to try and sort out a later jailhouse wakeup call for him on the days he had to come to court if things got too tiring for him.

The solution that emerged to save Asaro some sleep time and make the day less stressful involved the U.S. Marshals Service. Instead of bundling Asaro on the regular Bureau of Prisons bus for the ride from Red Hook to the courthouse, the marshals awoke Asaro separately and then drove him in their vehicle to downtown Brooklyn. It might not sound like a big deal, but the arrangement saved Asaro from the fatiguing early wakeups at the jail. He also was able to strike up friendly banter with the marshals escorting him. When the trial day was finished, Asaro would then be put back on the regular bus for the ride back to the Metropolitan Detention Center.

Jury selection in the Asaro trial took about two days and by October 15, 2015, a panel of six men and six women, along with four alternates had been selected from the hundreds of potential jurors who endured the selection process. Despite concerns about the impact the movies *GoodFellas, The Godfather,* and other mob films might have on juror impartiality, Ross and the attorneys quickly found a panel that seemed acceptable. Jury selection is always an important part of a big trial and both defense and prosecution want jurors who don't appear biased and can keep an open mind—and will follow the law as laid out by Ross.

On the defense side, Macedonio and Ferrone used their gut sense about the jurors and looked for candidates who showed some sense of independence, a certain swagger as she called it. The defense also didn't want a panel composed of white-haired elderly women who might be turned off by the allegations of violence. The result was a fairly diverse panel of what Macedonio later said were mostly working-class people. Sometimes the selection process can drone on for days. But for Asaro, things went quickly and smoothly.

CHAPTER SEVENTEEN
"SCORE OF SCORES"

ANYONE WALKING INTO COURTROOM 8C in Brooklyn Federal Court—known officially as the U.S. District Court for The Eastern District of New York—at 9:30 the morning of October 19, 2015, would be struck by the fact that Vincent Asaro's destiny was going to be determined by the hard work of a number of women. The prosecutors were all women. Asaro's defense attorneys were all women. Lastly, there was Judge Allyne Ross.

A native New Yorker, Ross had been on the court since 1994 when she was nominated for a judgeship by President Bill Clinton. Educated at Wellesley College and Harvard Law School, Ross eventually landed a job at the same Brooklyn U.S. Attorney's Office that was prosecuting Asaro. After about ten years as an assistant U.S. attorney, Ross became a magistrate judge for eight years before Clinton nominated her for the bench. She had a reputation for being an even-tempered jurist and despite her past career as a prosecutor didn't seem to have a pro-government bias. She was on senior status, meaning she could pick what kind of cases she would accept and had as much as three months off. But Ross, like most of the senior judges in Brooklyn federal court, kept a large workload. Ross liked to work full days when she was on trial and often held court five days a week. That is how things would go for Asaro's case.

Arrayed at tables directly in front of Ross's bench were the prosecution team of Nicole Argentieri, Alicyn L. Cooley, and Lindsay

K. Gerdes, as well as paralegal Teri Carby and FBI agents Robert Ypelaar and Adam Mininni. Argentieri, at the age of thirty-eight, was the senior attorney on the case and had been a prosecutor in the office since 2007, having worked previously as an associate at a prestigious Manhattan law firm. She had earned a law degree from the University of Pennsylvania Law School. As a prosecutor, Argentieri earned a reputation among defense lawyers as being aggressive, perhaps a bit strident and had garnered experience in the prosecution of a number of Mafia cases, notably that of Bonanno captain Vincent Basciano who was convicted of racketeering in 2011 but escaped the death penalty despite her vigorous argument to the jury for his execution. After eight years of experience, Argentieri rose to the position of acting chief of the Organized Crime and Gangs section of the office and secured convictions in most of the cases she handled, according to government data analyzed by Transactional Records Access Clearinghouse, a non-profit group that crunches the numbers of a wide variety of Department of Justice data. One case that got away from Argentieri was that of Anthony Romanello, the reputed gangster who was acquitted of extortion charges despite the testimony of Massino.

The other two attorneys at the prosecution table were less experienced than Argentieri but deemed up to the task of handling the case with her. Gerdes, thirty-four, was a product of the University of Cincinnati College of Law and had done a stint at the Brooklyn District Attorney's Office where she worked on homicide prosecutions before joining the U.S. Attorney's Office in Brooklyn. Cooley, thirty-two, was Ivy League through and through. She graduated from Yale University and was also a graduate of its law school. Cooley was the youngest of the prosecution team but had earned legal experience at the high-powered Manhattan law firm of Davis, Polk & Wardell.

Ever since she graduated from New York Law School, Macedonio had wanted to be a trial lawyer. She didn't take the traditional route of working at a big law firm, which could have kept her out of the courtroom, but instead opened up her solo practice in Queens where she took office space in the Bayside firm of Steven Zissou. If it was criminal work she wanted, Macedonio got it in large quantity.

She represented mobsters Jack D'Amico, once the close friend of the late John Gotti, as well as Joseph Cammarota Jr., a Bonanno family captain. Most of Macedonio's cases resulted in plea bargains, and she earned a reputation for working out good deals for her clients. She had yet to win a complete federal acquittal.

But as experienced as she was, Macedonio was just one attorney facing an entire prosecution team. Aside from paralegal Sam Tureff and investigator Ron Dwyer, Macedonio seemed out-matched in terms of the personnel the government had. At one point, Macedonio asked Ross to appoint her a co-counsel who would be paid by the court, the way Macedonio was being compensated. But Ross, apparently for budget reasons, balked at that suggestion. Finally, Macedonio turned to colleague Diane Ferrone to see if she would accept appointment at a lower "mentor" rate, which Ross approved.

Tall and dark haired, Ferrone, thirty-nine, already had experience in the Lufthansa case, having worked on the defense of Jack Bonventre, one of Asaro's co-defendants who got out of the case with a plea bargain in late 2014 and a sentence of twenty-one months and a $40,000 fine. Ferrone was a native of Long Island, growing up in North Bellmore and then going to high school in Syosset. Like Argentieri, Ferrone was a graduate of the University of Pennsylvania Law School, where they had been friends. After law school, Ferrone took a job with the well-known and highly respected white-collar defense firm started by the late Robert Morvillo, among whose clients was Martha Stewart.

Ferrone later worked at the criminal defense boutique firm of Sercarz & Riopelle, where she worked along with named partner Roland Riopelle defending Annette Bongiorno, one of financial criminal Bernard Madoff's employees who was ultimately convicted for her role in the fraud. After a couple of years at Sercarz & Riopelle, Ferrone eventually started her own solo practice. She seemed happiest as a lawyer working for herself. Ferrone was a good co-counsel choice for Macedonio since she had a mix of trial and extensive brief-writing experience. She also bonded with her clients, said a former colleague, something that could prove useful with a difficult client like Asaro.

Surrounded as he was by mostly women, Asaro was the oldest person in the well of the courtroom, a fact that was obvious to even the most casual observer. To soften his image at the defense table, Asaro wore sweaters which made him look even more grandfatherly. If anyone was expecting to see a thuggish-looking man facing the jury, they were mistaken.

The first order of business on the opening day of the trial was a skirmish among the attorneys over money—not theirs but rather what the U.S. government had paid the cooperating witnesses. The witnesses had been paid varying amounts, and Macedonio and Ferrone computed that the total was around $2 million, including $250,000 for the first witness Salvatore Vitale, an amount paid shortly before trial.

Argentieri didn't think the payment had to be brought up in the testimony. Macedonio thought otherwise. Ross said she was troubled by it but wanted to read some other documents first before making a decision.

It fell upon Assistant U.S. Attorney Lindsay Gerdes to give the government's opening statement and as she faced the jury she wanted to make sure from her very first words that each of them knew that Asaro was no soft and cuddly granddad but a dyed-in-the-wool gangster who lived by the rules of the mob.

"Omertà, the code of silence. Death before dishonor. Never talk to the police. These are the mottos of the Mafia," Gerdes said. "And punishment for disobeying that code is death."

Right from the start, Gerdes brought up the most vile of the allegations against Asaro: the murder and anonymous burial of poor Paul Katz, the misguided hijacker and mob associate whose bones were sifted from the soil during the FBI dig at the house on 102nd Road

Opening statements are not evidence, but prosecutors try to make them compelling and shocking, dripping the proceedings in blood so that a jury will wonder from the very start just what kind of defendant sits before them. Katz went out of the house one day in 1969 and never returned to his family, said Gerdes, adding that there was a simple reason for that: he was cooperating with police after being arrested.

"After 44 years, all that remained of him, all that could be returned to his children were pieces of the man he once was; bones, hair, and teeth," Gerdes continued. It was a horrible ending for any human being and the prosecutor then turned toward Asaro.

"One of the men who killed Paul Katz, who murdered Paul Katz, who strangled him to death with a dog chain, who hid his body away from his family, the man with death before dishonor tattooed on his forearm sits in this courtroom today. That man is Vincent Asaro, the defendant," she said.

Opening statements are useful because they can whet the appetite of jurors and ready them for what may come. A good opening can point out weaknesses in a case as well as strengths. But one thing is clear. If an opening statement promises too much it can come back and haunt the lawyer when it comes time to sum up everything at the end of a trial and what was promised in the opening never materialized in the proof.

Gerdes's job for the nearly forty-five minutes she spoke to the jury was to make sure that it was clear what she and the prosecution team believed they could prove. In broad strokes, she said Asaro was a Mafiosi who came from a long line of mobsters and was wedded to the life of La Cosa Nostra.

"The defendant is a gangster through and through. He lived and breathed the mafia. He was proud to be a made member, but one thing that always defined him was that he always did things his way," Gerdes explained.

Of course, the most serious crime in the case was the Lufthansa heist and operation pulled off by Asaro and Jimmy Burke, "truly the score of all scores," said Gerdes about the bold and nearly flawless robbery at Building 261 at JFK the morning of December 11, 1978.

Gerdes painted a very cinematic description, based on what Valenti had told the FBI, about what had happened when the Asaro-Burke crew sprang into action. Burke and Asaro lay in wait a short distance away in a crash car just in case the cops arrived.

Her description was vivid and fast-paced. "The rest of the team piled into the stolen van and headed for the cargo terminal. They cut the chain-link on the fence and got inside, and there they huddled the employees together, and held them at gunpoint. They quickly made their way to the high-value vault. Jackpot. Boxes and boxes and boxes of money and jewelry, more money than everyone could have ever, ever dreamed."

Lufthansa made Asaro a rich man, said Gerdes, to the tune of a nice $500,000 share, money she said he used to fund his loansharking business well into the 1980s, increasing his street cred in the mob. Along the way, Asaro passed up some of the proceeds to his bosses in the Bonanno family, $100,000 to one and jewelry to another, Gerdes told the jury.

"Life was good. It would be for the defendant," she added.

Gerdes wasn't going to go into everything Asaro was charged with, but she told the jury that there had been much to his life of crime.

"The defendant stands charged with his involvement in over 40 years of criminal activity, 40 years of conspiring to commit crimes for and at the direction of the Bonanno crime family," Gerdes stressed.

The prosecutor noted that the case was also about extortion, shakedowns in the Times Square porn industry, and of course the murder of Katz. All of this would be proved through Valenti's testimony and the myriad tapes he made that depicted Asaro reminiscing about his gangster life and then revealing the callous, brutish way he tried to intimidate people for money, said Gerdes.

"You will hear him say 37 years a wiseguy, referring to the 37 years he spent as a made member of the Bonanno crime family. Then he says and another 50 years before that, referring to the 50 years his father spent in the family," Gerdes continued.

"You will hear the callousness and the ruthlessness of this man, how in talking about one victim he tells another soldier below him in the crime family to stab him, give him a beating, give him a beating," added Gerdes.

The prosecutor ended her opening as prosecutors always do, with the fervent hope that the jury would find the evidence against Asaro compelling and convict him of the 16 crimes for which he had been indicted.

In the face of Gerdes's drama, Diane Ferrone carried the weight for the defense when it came time for her to speak. She told the jurors that Vincent Asaro enjoyed the presumption of innocence, no matter what the prosecution had just said. That was a stock argument by defense attorneys but it was true: The American legal system presumed all defendants accused of a crime by prosecutors and police were innocent until proven convincingly that they weren't.

There would be at least four mob turncoats who were expected to testify and Ferrone went after the one who could do the most damage: Gaspare Valenti, the broken, deadbeat of a man who turned to the FBI in financial desperation.

Valenti spied on Asaro for the government for well over six years, and it was strange, said Ferrone, that it took the FBI so long to arrest the old man. More to the point, why did Valenti decide to do what he did to his cousin, become a sort of Mafia fifth-columnist who led Asaro down the garden path.

"Gaspare Valenti has a long history of borrowing money from people and never paying it back," said Ferrone. After running out of cities where he could make money, Valenti "embarked upon a new plan for making a buck. His new source of cash: the U.S. government."

The only evidence in some instances against Asaro was the testimony of Valenti, and that, Ferrone said, had to be analyzed very carefully.

"After you hear from Gaspare Valenti, you'll quickly determine he's no star; he's more of a black hole," Ferrone added. "Listen carefully to what Gaspare Valenti has to say, and if you wouldn't believe him in your ordinary life, then you shouldn't believe him just because his latest con victim happens to be the United States government."

*   *   *

When all of the money and assistance that the government gave to cooperators like Valenti, former Bonanno underboss Sal Vitale, former boss Joseph Massino, and others was added up, it would total $2 million, said Ferrone.

"The criminal cooperators the government will put on that stand, Joseph Massino, Sal Vitale, Anthony Ruggiero, Peter Zuccaro, they've lied to government officials and manipulated the criminal justice system their entire lives," Ferrone argued. "The evidence will show they are accomplished criminals who began committing crimes as teenagers and never stopped."

"Just because someone is called as a government witness doesn't mean they're telling the truth," Ferrone reminded the jury. "Once a liar, always a liar. A leopard never changes its spots."

With Lufthansa the first thing on everyone's mind, the prosecution called as its first key witness Vitale, the ex-Bonanno mobster who became a turncoat in 2003. To some, calling Vitale seemed a move strangely out of place in the sequence of the crime. He wouldn't know anything about the actual heist in December 1978 but could only testify about what he said was the way some of the jewelry loot had been handled. Vitale had testified in numerous trials, so he seemed terribly self-assured, even smirking at times.

"You name it, I testified in it," Vitale said about his history as a turncoat mob witness.

Yet while Vitale has testified in a great many cases and helped the government to secure major convictions, including those of Massino and Bonanno captain Vincent Basciano, life for Vitale was a struggle. After being released from federal custody in 2010, Vitale was placed in the witness relocation program and given a new identity. But his marriage had collapsed, and he saw his four sons only sporadically. As a man with the new identity, Vitale soon learned that his life was a struggle, mainly because he couldn't get work.

"It's impossible for you to get a job. I mean, you could go work for the local hardware store if the guy's not going to ask no questions. But if you work for any kind of UPS, REA, or Target, Walgreens, I've been turned down by every company. You just can't get to a human being," said Vitale when he was questioned about his current situation by Argentieri. "Once you put in your information into a computer, the computer is set to knock out certain things. You got to bring a Social Security card. Who is going to hire a guy at 65 years old with a brand-new Social Security card?"

To make matters worse, Vitale said that the U.S. Marshals Service cut off his subsistence—"threw me out into the street" as Vitale put it—with no money and no way of making a living. Any time he searched for work, potential employers, seeing he had a recently issued Social Security card, figured he was a wiseguy from Brooklyn, Vitale said. Finally, the FBI gave him a $250,000 payment as a reward for helping the federal government not only convict big mobsters but helping to secure the forfeiture of as much as $20 million in ill-gotten gains.

Dressed in a suit and tie and looking relatively at ease, Vitale seemed comfortable on the witness stand even though he believed that he was in constant danger from the mob. He had the moniker "Good Looking Sal" from his days as a vain wise guy, although he insisted he didn't deserve such a nickname. He was remembered by some relatives for having an affection for the designer label Hugo Boss. Vitale had risen to the rank of Bonanno underboss at one point and had been a caretaker acting boss of the crime family during the period Massino was both on the lam and briefly in prison for labor racketeering.

Yet Vitale had a great deal of baggage as a witness, namely the fact that he had admitted to the government playing a role in at least eleven murders, many with Massino. He wasn't a killer as such who bloodied his hands from the evil deeds. Instead, sometimes Vitale's role was that of cleaning up the bloody mess, as he did when Massino had his cigarette-smuggling business partner Joseph "Doo-Doo" Pastore killed in an apartment in Queens in mid-1976. Other times, Vitale played the man who lulled a victim into a false sense of security, which is what happened in early 1984 to Cesare Bonventre. A stylish Sicilian transplant who was in the Bonanno family, Bonventre had been one of two men who were supposed to guard Carmine Galante when he was assassinated in the summer of 1979. In the byzantine world of Mafia life, Bonventre had been doing well in the crime family and was even promoted to captain when suddenly his star began to fade, and Massino, at the time a powerful captain himself, said Bonventre had to be killed.

The FBI believed that Bonventre was marked for death either because he distributed some poor quality heroin or was viewed as a threat to the power of then-Bonanno boss Philip Rastelli and Massino. In any case, Vitale was the one who got Bonventre to drive with him and mobster Louis Attanasio on the pretext that they were going to a meeting with Rastelli. As the car Vitale was driving entered a garage on Fifty-seventh Street in Maspeth, he said the code words "It looks good to me" and Attanasio, according to later court testimony, fired two bullets into Bonventre's head. While Bonventre struggled, he was ultimately finished off and disposed of in fifty-five-gallon drums of glue in New Jersey.

Vitale got into the Mafia through Massino, his brother-in-law and at one time his closest friend. It was Massino, once a muscular young man, who taught Vitale to swim at the public pools in Queens. Of the two men, it was Massino who had come to the attention of Bonanno boss Rastelli in the 1970s, and after a career as a hijacker and cigarette smuggler was initiated into the mob in late 1976 or 1977. By 1978, Massino was a captain and was visiting Rastelli in prison, passing him messages and considered a young mobster with an inside track to the boss.

Vitale tagged along on Massino's coattails but wasn't given quick mob membership like his brother-in-law. When Vitale had a run-in with Asaro, who was already a made man at the time, the latter pointedly reminded Vitale that he wasn't a Goodfella so he should watch his mouth. By 1984, after years of being Massino's acolyte, Vitale was given membership in the Bonanno family.

The prosecution wanted to use Vitale to show the structure of the Mafia and the Commission, stuff that he was qualified to talk about because of his past associations. Since this was a Mafia racketeering case, the prosecution had to prove the existence of the Bonanno family and that it was a racketeering enterprise, of which Asaro played a role. Vitale recalled a number of interactions with Asaro, some of which weren't good because Vincent had a temper and was volatile. Interactions with him weren't always pleasant, recalled Vitale.

Under questioning by Argentieri, Vitale related an incident in 1981 that had involved an unpleasant encounter with Asaro in a dispute. It seemed that a Bonanno associate named Jose Marsala had been making usurious loans in Howard Beach without clearing it with Asaro or anyone else. Asaro was furious and started giving Marsala trouble. Faced with a problem, Marsala turned to Vitale for help. At that point, Massino was a fugitive and living in the Pocono Mountains area of Pennsylvania where Vitale would visit him to give him updates on crime-family business. During one of those secret visits to Pennsylvania, Vitale told Massino about the problem over Marsala's loans. Massino's response was that he would be returning to New York soon and that Asaro should leave Marsala alone until then.

After returning to New York, Vitale said he met with Asaro at his club on Pitkin Avenue and gave him Massino's message. It did not sit well with Asaro. He got angry and said Marsala was pushing money out onto the street when he shouldn't be, recalled Vitale. But there was nothing Asaro could do.

A few days later, Vitale testified, he went to meet with Bonanno family boss Philip Rastelli in McCarran Park in the Greenpoint section of Brooklyn and discussed the Marsala problem. Rastelli had already talked to Asaro about the dispute and then told Vitale that both he and Asaro should get along. Besides, said Rastelli, the crime family was going to admit Vitale to Mafia membership and he would be a comrade of sorts with Asaro, who was already a made man.

"That Vinny is a made member, but you are going to be a made member some day and you should try to get along with Vinny," Rastelli said, according to Vitale.

Vitale then met Asaro for a second time at a diner on Cross Bay Boulevard to pass along the message that Rastelli also wanted Marsala to be left alone for the time being. Like what happened in the earlier encounter, Asaro went ballistic, swearing at Vitale and dressing him down, saying, "I'm the Goodfella here, not you!"

Vitale then played the one trump card he had, telling Asaro that the message was that time coming from Rastelli himself. That stopped a flustered Asaro short, who had to backpedal and sheepishly responded that Vitale should have said that from the beginning, according to the testimony.

"I said, 'Vinny, you didn't give me a chance. Phil said leave the guy alone until Joe comes home,'" Vitale recalled, adding "Then I just couldn't wait to get out of there. I got out of there."

There would be many episodes, including some taped conversations, which would show the angry nature of Asaro, and Vitale certainly had borne the brunt of some of his anger. But the real usefulness of Vitale would be to show how he linked Asaro somehow to the Lufthansa heist. It would be hard to dispute Asaro's ties to the mob or the existence of the Bonanno crime family. But the real test for the prosecution would be if he could be linked through Vitale to the robbery.

To do that, the prosecution questioned Vitale about a car trip he had taken with Massino shortly after Lufthansa. Vitale at that point wasn't a made man and served as his brother-in-law's driver. Vitale testified that he drove Massino to meet Asaro at a mechanic shop on Cross Bay Boulevard, a place run by Joe Marsala. Vitale said he waited in the car and watched in the rear-view mirror as Massino met Asaro outside the garage. Both men then went for a walk as he watched them in the mirror, recalled Vitale.

"What did you see?" Argentieri asked Vitale.

"I seen Vinny hand Joe a case," answered Vitale.

"Then what happened?" Argentieri said.

"They kissed goodbye," recalled Vitale.

After Massino returned to the car, Vitale drove away. As he drove, Massino opened the case and showed it was filled with gold chains and necklaces, saying "This is from the Lufthansa score," according to Vitale.

That night Vitale went to Massino's home in Howard Beach. Massino opened the case and spread the jewelry out on his dining-room table, according to Vitale. As a gift, Massino gave Vitale a gold chain.

"He was always a big spender," Vitale said sarcastically about Massino. "He gave me a chain as a gift."

That last remark showed the depth of the hatred that Vitale had for his former crime boss. Both were related by marriage and had been extremely close growing up. But when they were arrested and indicted in early 2003, Vitale decided to become a government co-operating witness, driven in part by the fact that Massino had recently put him on the shelf, stripping Vitale of his control over other members of the Bonanno family and depriving him of money from rackets. Massino had soured on Vitale because of the poor way he related to other crime-family members and because of the suspicion by some over the years that Vitale might be an informant—suspicion that at the time was a bit premature. Some in the crime family wanted Vitale dead, and at one point his wife Diana pleaded with Massino not to have him killed. Massino, whose wife Josephine was Vitale's sister, agreed to let him live.

The rest of Vitale's direct testimony dealt with a series of events in the history of the Bonanno crime family that he played a role in or knew about. He admitted to his share of extortions, loansharking, gambling, and homicides. In the latter, Vitale said the closest he got to pulling the trigger was in May 1981 during the killing of the Three Captains: Dominick "Big Trin" Trinchera, Philip Giaccone, and Bruno Indelicato. The three men were killed as a preemptive strike in a Massino-led operation because they were believed to have been plotting to take over the crime family from Rastelli. Vitale said he had a tommy gun during the incident at a club on 13th Avenue in Brooklyn but never had to use it since the three men were slaughtered quickly enough.

Vitale's cross-examination was handled by Macedonio, and her tactic seemed two-fold: to show the jury that Vitale had received "coverage" for a long list of crimes in his plea deal with the government and to spell out the various murders he participated in. Macedonio wanted to give names to the victims and to show the matter-of-fact way Vitale and the others in the Bonanno crime family took many lives. One New York judge once called Macedonio's method of questioning "snarky," and at a number of points she seemed to get on Vitale's nerves, as the following exchange showed about the way a nephew of mobster Pete Rosa had been marked for murder because he was suspected of being an informant.

"You couldn't care less if they killed this man," said Macedonio.

"If he was a rat, yes, I could care less," replied Vitale.

"You didn't make an inquiry, you just said do what you have to do?" Macedonio asked.

"If a captain comes in with an official beef that was put there by Mr. Massino, and he could prove it to the individual's relative . . . what, do I want it notarized? I mean what do I do? You are talking about street people here," a testy Vitale answered.

The long and the short of Macedonio's questioning was to show that in addition to the eleven mob murders Vitale had pleaded guilty to, there were at least two others that he didn't have to admit responsibility for under his plea deal. Going over the details of some of the murders, Macedonio was making it clear to the jury that government witnesses like Vitale had a great deal of blood on their hands, a lot more than had been alleged against Asaro.

Massino had always been a scheming, Machiavellian character in the Mafia, and during his cross-examination Vitale revealed how his brother-in-law used the murders of the Three Captains to secretly consolidate his power. After the murders there was a push by some in the Bonanno family to have Massino assume the throne as boss. But according to Vitale, Massino didn't want that but preferred to have the aging and tired Rastelli stay on as a figurehead boss. By keeping Rastelli as boss, Massino was keeping the FBI attention focused on someone other than himself.

"He didn't want the family, because he was getting the respect, he was getting the money, he was getting the notoriety without being in the seat," explained Vitale about Massino's plan for Rastelli.

At some points, Macedonio seemed to overdo it with her questioning, repeating lines of inquiry, particularly about the amount of money Vitale had received from the government as a stipend and what his family could keep. Finally, Vitale reminded the court that Macedonio had already questioned him about certain things and Ross agreed, telling the defense attorney to move on to something else. Ross even had to tell Macedonio during a sidebar that while she thought she cross-examined very well that she tended to be "argumentative" with the witness.

But in the time Macedonio spent with Vitale on cross-examination she had gone through years of his criminal life and spread out before the jury all of the murders he had been involved in. The jury also saw, unlike from the government's direct examination, that Vitale had received a great deal of compensation from the government, close to $900,000 for his cooperation, as well as his freedom. For someone who was a major Mafia player, Vitale had made out fairly well.

Toward the end of her cross-examination, Macedonio questioned Vitale about the treacherous nature of the Mafia. Friendship, explained Vitale, was a relative situation in the Mafia.

"You don't real have friends in organized crime," Vitale said at one point, "because some day you might be ordered to kill that individual. I was close to a couple of individuals, yes, but I didn't want to go beyond that."

"That is because it is a treacherous organization, correct?" Macedonio asked.

"Without a doubt," replied Vitale.

CHAPTER EIGHTEEN
"COME DRESSED"

AFTER A LIFE OF CRIME, SAL VITALE came to understand that in the Mafia the most dangerous thing could be a friendship, even a life-long one. During the time he testified, Vitale would be heard to say a phrase that was in some ways the watchwords for survival and caution in the gangster life: "Only your friend can hurt you." The next witness called by the government at the Asaro trial was a person who in his own way and by his own conduct illustrated the truth in Vitale's words.

It was the very next day after Vitale had testified that Gaspare Valenti took the witness stand. The time was just around 10:00 A.M. on October 20, and this was to be the premiere witness for the government, the man closest to Vincent Asaro who had turned against him and tape recorded him for three years. The thousands upon thousands of words captured on tape were the proof, prosecutors said, that Asaro was a thief, arsonist, extortionist, and killer—a mobster to the core.

When he entered Judge Ross's courtroom, Valenti looked like any aging, balding grandfather. He was nicely dressed in a jacket and tie and, like Asaro, didn't have the slightest air of malevolence. Of course, the very first question to him from Nicole Argentieri was whether he was involved with organized crime. Yes, was the reply. From the late 1960s until 2008, Valenti said he was an associate with the Bonanno crime family and was under the command of his cousin Vincent Asaro. Together, they committed a long list of crimes, he explained.

"What was the most serious crime you committed?" Argentieri asked.

"Lufthansa," answered Valenti.

"What did you do at Lufthansa?"

"We robbed the Lufthansa air freight company."

"Approximately when?"

"Nineteen seventy-eight."

"Who directed you to do that?"

"Vincent Asaro."

Argentieri had certainly jumped to the chase with that line of questioning, raising expectation that the heist would be the first thing to be illuminated. But just as soon as Lufthansa was brought up, the interrogation moved to the more historical as the prosecutor had to set the table through Valenti's testimony and show how both he and Asaro bonded over the years and carried out a host of crimes charged in the indictment. This was the foundation needed to prove the case, to show why Valenti was a reliable source of information and to reveal in graphic details the crimes Asaro was accused of committing.

Like many of the young men who grew up in the South Ozone Park area in the 1960s, Gaspare Valenti, who completed twelve years of high school but never got a diploma, was looking for a purpose to his life. Growing up in the area known as The Hole and across the street from Asaro, Valenti started committing crimes as a teenager. Nothing too serious. A burglary of a small store perhaps. But, eventually he graduated to things more serious.

One day, Asaro's father Jerome approached him and said, "We have a score," meaning a robbery and asked if he wanted to be part of it, recalled Valenti. The way Jerome Asaro pitched the idea was as if it was a rite of passage for an aspiring gangster.

"He explained it to me that everyone has lust sitting in their hearts. Some people have more lust. It's up to you if you want to commit this crime with two other people," Valenti remembered the elder Asaro telling him. Valenti agreed to join in, and he and two others robbed seventeen people in the office of the Long Island Press, a newspaper, of $63. What stood out in Valenti's mind was his naïveté about the ways of the street criminals. Just before the robbery, he was told to "come dressed" and Valenti said he did his best to do that.

"I wore a seersucker jacket, white and gray stripes, burgundy pants, a burgundy shirt and burgundy patent leather boots," said Valenti.

He was the best dressed robber on the scene, but when his fellow criminals saw him show clothed that way, they laughed. "Come dressed" means to come with a pistol, Valenti was told, and when he described the incident in the courtroom, there were chuckles. Valenti and his two cohorts split the cash with Jerome Asaro. Later, the elder Asaro asked Valenti if he wanted to continue in the life as a criminal, and Valenti said yes and learned he would be working under his uncle.

At that point, Valenti was a mob associate, someone who had to report to a Mafia member he was "on record" with to reveal what he was doing and to split some of the proceeds from any crimes. Valenti remembered that he had to clean up his act and shave his moustache and to make sure he acted respectfully. He spent more and more of his time with his cousin Vincent, drinking at the Colonial House, a bar in the nearby City Line section of old East New York. When the time came, Asaro told Valenti that they had to do a favor for an important Bonanno crime-family member named Michael Zaffarano. It was their first assignment together and it involved the sale of pornographic films.

In the annals of the Mafia, Zaffarano, who happened to be Asaro's uncle, was something of an icon. In a business career that spanned decades, Zaffarano became a well-known porn merchant who made a few shrewd real estate deals in the Times Square area. In the buildings Zaffarano purchased on Broadway, he established the famous Pussycat Theater and leased out some of his property for topless dancing venues and other sex businesses. When the area became targeted for a major urban-renewal project, Zaffarano's land would be worth over $15 million. So significant was Zaffarano's clout in the sex industry that he traveled back and forth to California to settle business disputes and sign deals with porn actresses.

Asaro brought Valenti a box of video tapes of porn films to sell with the admonition, "Don't screw up with these; these are Uncle Mickey's. You will get killed." Valenti said he sold the films, passed along the money to Asaro and got nothing in return.

Valenti said he did better financially with some other arrangements with Asaro. When Asaro and Jimmy Burke pulled hijacks together, Valenti said he sold some of the stolen goods for his cousin, including shirts. Burke was a good man to know because if you got on his right side you could make money with him. You wanted to be on Burke's right side because "he would kill you just as soon as earn with you," remembered Valenti.

But over time, Valenti got comfortable enough with Burke that he hung out several days a week at the Irish gangster's Robert's Lounge. There, Valenti would hobnob with other club denizens like Henry Hill, Thomas DeSimone, French McMahon, and Angelo Sepe. Robert's Lounge was like the alien cantina in the first *Star Wars* film, a place where the brigands, schemers and killers of the mob universe gravitated to make deals, plot the next score or just get drunk.

When committing so many crimes, the crew at Robert's Lounge would occasionally get caught and when they did they had to spend some time in jail, at least until they were able to pay a cop and get out, said Valenti. One incident in 1969 stood out in particular. Burke and a number of his crew including Asaro were arrested at a warehouse in South Ozone Park, which Paul Katz used to store hijacked goods, said Valenti. Everyone—except Asaro—was freed after Burke said "they paid their way out," which Valenti said meant they bribed a cop. It took a day for Asaro to get released and he was angry, recalled Valenti.

For years, Katz had been working with Burke's crew on hijacks across the city and floated between Robert's Lounge and Henry Hill's bar The Suite. But in October 1969, Katz's luck started to turn when he and four others were arrested in the Bronx after they hijacked an armored truck carrying $100,000 in gold and platinum. Katz, then twenty-eight-years-old, made bail and then appeared to start to secretly cooperate with police, according to law-enforcement records. The same records showed that detectives in Queens had a wiretap on Katz's home telephone. Around November 1969, Katz told his police contact about a drop site for hijacked goods, which police then promptly hit and apparently arrested Burke, Asaro, DeSimone, and the others, the records showed. But as it turned out, Burke was cut loose and not reported as being a defendant, allegedly because $5,000 was paid to a cop.

Katz continued to meet with his police contact, sometimes on the rooftop of a parking lot by his apartment on the Horace Harding Expressway, other times at a bar. If Katz believed his clandestine passing of information to the police would remain a secret, he was wrong. According to information later given by Hill to NYPD officials, Burke had a contact inside the office of then-Queens District Attorney Thomas Mackell. (While he had his own problems years later, Mackell wasn't implicated in the corruption Hill alleged in his debriefings.) The contact would pass along information whenever an informant gave information to detectives. Burke soon learned of Katz's cooperation, and his fate was sealed.

It was a Saturday, December 6, 1969, that Delores Katz noticed her husband Paul acting nervously. The telephone at the couple's apartment had been ringing incessantly with one of the callers being Katz's detective contact in the NYPD and a man named Joe Allegro, a suspected hijacker who had been arrested in the Bronx earlier with Katz, according to law-enforcement records. At some point, Allegro had stopped by a drugstore near the Katz apartment and told Katz that Burke wanted to see him, the records stated. While Katz initially entered Allegro's car he had a change of heart and left, returning home and telling his wife that he believed Burke knew he had told the cops about the hijack drop point.

About 6:00 P.M. that night, Katz took another telephone call from Allegro, told his wife that he was going to a drugstore and that if he didn't return in about fifteen minutes to call the NYPD. While Delores Katz didn't want him to leave, her husband went out. She never saw him again. Mrs. Katz then filed a missing person's report with the police.

From the very beginning, as soon as Katz disappeared, allegations arose that crooked cops helped instigate Burke in carrying out the hijacker-informant's demise. Intelligence reports said "that Burke's entrée to police was set up by Vincent 'Jimmy' Santa, an ex-NYPD officer who left the force under a cloud. Police records show that Santa, also known on the street as "Santos," left the NYPD in April 1961 without giving notice to the department and forfeited all rights to any pay that was due. Santa was closer to Burke's age and to some seemed more simpatico with the Irishman than the younger Hill, who some saw as an errand boy, although a very trusted one. In any case, the intelligence reports said it was Santa who introduced Burke to cops at the Queens District Attorney's Office. This was the period of the 1960s when the police department in New York City was rife with corruption problems, when detectives were openly cozy with drug dealers, mobsters, and all manner of wise guys. Anyone who doubts that state of affairs only has to read the Knapp Commission report and the stories about cop Frank Serpico whose whistleblowing ripped the lid off the systematic corruption in the department at the time.

According to statements Hill later gave to investigators, the night after Burke had learned Katz was an informant, he came through the rear door of Hill's club The Suite on Queens Boulevard with an NYPD detective and Santa. After the chef was chased from the kitchen, Hill said he was given (he didn't specify by whom) Katz's wallet and a handgun to dispose of, according to law-enforcement records. Hill said among the papers in the wallet he noticed Katz's driver's license. The cop, Burke alleged, had told him about Katz's informant status and later was seen hanging around The Suite, getting patted on the back by patrons as they were having drinks. (About fourteen years after Katz's death, the detective in question told an investigator that Hill was a junkie and a liar. He was never charged criminally and died in 2007.)

It was under further questioning by Argentieri that Valenti recalled a telephone call he got from Asaro with a request to get him a place so he could have a meeting with Burke. The request seemed pretty straightforward, and to accommodate his cousin, Valenti selected a newly constructed and unoccupied home on 102nd Road. Valenti's father had constructed a row of houses on the street, and when he died management of the properties became his son's responsibility, so he had unfettered access to the buildings.

The next day was a Sunday and since no one was working, the homes were empty. Valenti remembered that Burke and Asaro pulled up in a car which they backed into the sloping driveway of the model home. Then, according to Valenti, Asaro told him the purpose of the visit.

"'We have to bury somebody,'" said Asaro, according to Valenti's testimony.

Valenti was taken aback and thought his cousin might be kidding. But then he went down to the basement where Burke told him to open the door and then stay outside to make sure nobody entered the premises. Valenti did what he was told and for about three hours stood guard outside the house. Valenti said that during the time he stood watch he heard the sound of a sledgehammer hitting concrete. Eventually, Burke left and Asaro drove his cousin to a fence company Asaro owned to get some concrete, according to Valenti.

"What did he say to you at that time?" asked Argentieri, referring to Asaro as they drove to the fence company.

"He says he did most of the digging because Jimmy had hurt his hand when he killed Paul," answered Valenti.

"What did he say to you about how Paul Katz was killed?"

"They strangled him with a dog chain," Valenti answered, although he didn't specify who he meant by "they."

Asaro inadvertently revealed the name of Katz during the drive and apologized to his cousin, telling him he shouldn't have ever mentioned the name, testified Valenti.

"'I'm sorry I said that name to you. Never, ever mention that name again or this incident,'" Asaro said, according to Valenti.

After returning to the basement grave, Valenti said he spread lime over the corpse to hasten its decomposition. Then he cemented over the hole, which he described as being oblong. The body had to be dropped in because of the shape of the grave, remembered Valenti. He also learned that a water pipe had been damaged during the digging, something that years later would bedevil the FBI evidence team when it re-excavated the grave.

A few days later, Valenti remembered visiting his uncle Jerome with Vincent at a diner on Cross Bay Boulevard. Jerome was apologetic, but told Valenti the issue was closed for discussion.

"'I am so sorry that this happened,'" Jerome said, according to Valenti. "'This should have never happened with you, but it did happen. We are going to discuss this one time and it should never be spoken about again with no one.'"

Jerome then said that only a handful of people knew about what had happened to Katz but that among them was Paul Vario, the Lucchese captain who was Burke's boss.

According to Valenti, Burke eventually bought the house with the body in the basement through a straw purchaser, a man who owned a dress factory adjacent to Robert's Lounge. FBI agents said that the property was actually registered to the wife of the factory owner, a man by the name of Jerry Vitta, who was the straw buyer Valenti referred to. For years, the secret burial went undisturbed. But in the 1980s while he was in jail Burke began to feel uncomfortable with a corpse buried in one of his homes. It seemed he was getting paranoid about someone revealing the burial site, so Asaro had another job for Valenti: to dig up the body at the house. Armed with a sledgehammer and a shovel, Valenti and Asaro's son visited the basement grave and dug up the remains.

What was left of Katz's corpse was folded in the grave, just the way his body had been left. The exhumation must have been strange and macabre as Valenti said that he told Jerome nothing about the identity of the body they were removing. Valenti said that he and Jerome took the bones and bits of corduroy and put them in some cardboard boxes. The floor was then re-cemented. (As the FBI discovered years later during the agency's own exhumation in 2013, there were enough of the bones still in the pit that they could be identified by DNA analysis as those of Katz.) Jerome took the bones and placed them in paint cans, which were filled with cement, and took them to a hunting lodge he owned in upstate New York, recalled Valenti.

Later on in the case, forensic anthropologist Brad Adams would go into more detail and reveal how the remains in the basement were indeed those of Katz. But just by describing how Katz's body was buried and then disinterred, Valenti had put some compelling testimony before the jury. If the jury believed Valenti, Asaro would be in some serious trouble.

Valenti's cooperation had fleshed out for investigators what had happened to Katz on the day he disappeared in 1969. But in the intervening years, Delores Katz, her children and even Katz's sister Joyce would try in vain to find out what had happened to the young hijacker. The women visited Robert's Lounge and fished around for leads. Someone suggested that Katz was in the witness protection program and yet another, a cop, reported that he had been murdered and buried in the Bronx.

In the 1970s, according to law-enforcement records, some investigators began to suspect that a police leak about Katz had led to his death. Allegations surfaced from an FBI informant that ex-cop Santa had even paid $25,000 to police officers to get Katz's name from the police and then personally killed him. Joey Allegro, the man who reportedly called Katz and saw him the day he disappeared, was also suspected of being the killer. The information about Allegro surfaced in police records during an interview of his associate Albert Wilkins who told cops in April 1974 that Allegro confided to him about tricking Katz to come out of his house and then putting a "dog choke" around his neck, killing him. Allegro then said he delivered Katz's body and that "they" disposed of him.

The stories about Allegro, who was part of Burke's circle of thieves, were consistent with what Valenti testified about what he knew about the method of Katz's demise, although there was no mention of Asaro's involvement in the actual murder. A hard drinker, drug user, and brawler, Allegro was killed on January 7, 1971, in an auto accident on Queens Boulevard after he left The Suite bar. Police suspected the brakes on Allegro's car had been tampered with.

Wilkins didn't fare any better. Police reports show he was murdered at a Queens motel in March 1975.

By the mid-1970s, special prosecutor Maurice Nadjari began to look into the Katz disappearance. The NYPD, records show, also conducted internal investigations into at least two detectives who Hill and others said were around Burke and the Robert's Lounge crowd. Because of civil-service rules at the time, the police department was unable to bring administrative charges against one of the officers before he retired. The other officer, according to police records, was found guilty in a department administrative trial of having leaked information about a criminal case to a defense attorney, information that was detrimental to the prosecution's case. The allegations raised by Hill that this officer might have been involved as an accomplice after the fact in the Katz murder were looked at by the NYPD in the late 1970s, but couldn't be substantiated to the satisfaction of the department, and the detective retired in 1980. No criminal cases were ever filed as a result.

Delores Katz dutifully talked to investigators for years, telling them essentially the same version of events surrounding her husband's disappearance. At one point Delores alleged that NYPD Det. Sal Petix had been seen by one of her daughters with her husband after he left the house the day he disappeared, something that flatly contradicted her previous recollection of events. Not long after her husband disappeared, Delores Katz moved upstate with her children to Sullivan County where she worked as a waitress. She died in 2001. Petix died in 2007.

With Katz dead, the Robert's Lounge crew continued its criminal ways. Valenti said that in the 1970s, he and Vincent did about one score a week, robbing gas stations, racetracks, a milk farm. Often Valenti was armed—he had learned the lesson about "coming dressed" for the crimes.

There was one episode at a catering hall inside a bowling alley that required Valenti to disguise himself as a woman. The strange get up—Valenti wore a red wig, a pair of burgundy boots and woman's coat—was to make it seem like he and another criminal named Joe Berger were just a girlfriend and boyfriend waiting for a bus on

101st Avenue in Ozone Park. In fact, the pair's plan was to wait for the catering-hall manager to take the business proceeds to a night bank deposit slot so they could rob him.

But while waiting around, some boys came by and noticing Valenti's beard and cross dressing started to harass him. To defend Valenti's honor, so to speak, Berger pulled out a gun and was ready to chase the boys away. Valenti told him to put the pistol away and not lose sight of the fact that they were there to grab the money. The manager eventually came by and the pair robbed him of a few thousand dollars, said Valenti. The proceeds were split with his uncle Jerome and Vincent.

There were other scores. Valenti said he also worked as a collector for Vincent's loansharking operation, which was funded by money from Burke. At local clubs, Vincent ran some big card games and Valenti sometimes ran the table. By 1977 or 1978, Vincent had a major change in his status. He became initiated into the Mafia, remembered Valenti. Usually, members become made men of a crime family in a ceremony at an apartment or other place that could be made secure from law enforcement surveillance. In Vincent's case, his ceremony took place in a cemetery mausoleum.

Once Vincent was a made man, he was placed under the crew of his uncle Michael Zaffarano. In turn, Valenti was under Vincent's wing as an associate and it was his cousin who would protect him and keep him earning money, the biggest haul of which was soon to come.

CHAPTER NINETEEN
"THIS IS IT!"

"JIMMY BURKE HAS A BIG SCORE COMING UP, and you're invited to go. Do you want to go?"

That was the simple invitation Gaspare Valenti remembered getting from Vincent Asaro to become part of what would be the biggest robbery at the time in American history. It was late 1978 and what Burke had it mind could be pretty big, maybe $2 million in cash inside Building 261 on Boundary Road at JFK.

Two million dollars. It was a lot of cash then and it was a lot of cash even now when Valenti described things on the witness stand. Valenti said he had no illusions about why Vincent wanted him in on the heist. It meant they would get two shares of the loot, which meant that Vincent would be able to claim a percentage of what Valenti got.

"He wanted to see me to earn, and he would also have a second income from the heist," said Valenti.

"Can you explain that?" asked Argentieri.

"Yeah. If they were eight people, we would get two ends instead of one end, which would be more money for Vinny," answered Valenti, referring to the way his cousin would have control over two shares of the loot—his own and Valenti's.

Throwing his lot in with the crew, Valenti went with Asaro to Robert's Lounge where the planning would take place. Burke was technically on a work-release program from prison, which meant that at the end of the day he had to report back to a special facility where he would spend the night. But the days were his own to ostensibly work at an approved job. At Robert's Lounge, Burke and his people started planning like it was the D-Day invasion coming up. They had schematic maps of the floor plan of the Lufthansa facility and did their own surveillance, checking out the airport and figuring out escape routes if things suddenly went bad. Burke had already learned from Werner's inside information that about as many as fourteen people might be working at the cargo area and congregating in a lunchroom.

Valenti said that the group involved in the skull sessions at Robert's Lounge numbered ten. There was Burke, Vincent Asaro, Valenti himself, Angelo Sepe, Tommy DeSimone, Danny Rizzo, Joseph Manri, Anthony Rodriguez, Marty Krugman, and Burke's own son Frank James. As Valenti remembered it, Burke had a way of naming his sons after famous robbers from the Wild West. Another son was named Jessie James and became a lawyer.

The plan was straightforward but not without risks.

"Six or seven would go in to the front of the building and capture them, hold them at bay with guns," remembered Valenti about how they would contain the Lufthansa workers. "And then the truck was to go around the back of the building, and wait until the bay doors were open, and then pull the truck in."

Henry Hill's job had been to bring the architectural plans from Krugman, but he had no role in the actual heist, recalled Valenti. (The plans had actually been initially provided by Werner.)

The night of the heist, Valenti said he and Asaro drove together to Burke's home in Howard Beach. It was going to be the coldest night of the young winter so far, with wind and temperatures getting into the teens. While driving, Asaro gave his cousin a pistol, remembered Valenti, and told him not to run away if anything went wrong.

Once at Burke's house, DeSimone took Valenti to a marshy area adjacent to the neighborhood to try out a silencer on a gun. Given DeSimone's reputation as a man who loved to kill for no reason at all, Valenti was nervous about walking in front of him into the reeds. DeSimone fired the weapon a few times just to check it out.

Jimmy Burke was the mastermind of the heist, but he knew he couldn't risk getting caught at the airport if things went wrong. If arrested it would be this third felony case, and that would put him away for a long time in prison. To keep his distance, Burke said he would sit in a crash car with Vincent, referring to a vehicle ready to interrupt and delay any pursuing cops.

After a final check, Valenti said he and some of the others drove from Burke's house in a black Ford van to a spot near the airport at 150th Street and Conduit. Inside the vehicle were "everybody except Jimmy and Vinny" although Valenti didn't precisely say who was included. But he did mention to Argentieri that Frank Burke drove and that Sepe and DeSimone were also in the van.

Once at the airport gate, Valenti said he got out and used a bolt cutter to cut the lock. Frank Burke drove to the cargo building, let out the robbery crew and then parked the van nearby as he and Valenti waited. They weren't wearing the ski masks like the other inside robbers were doing because they wanted to look inconspicuous. After about fifteen or twenty minutes, a man—this would have been Lufthansa employee Kerry Whalen—approached the van and Valenti decided he had to react.

"He must have surmised something was up," recalled Valenti. "He started running towards the door of the building and we chased him. As he starts to open the door of the building, I hit him with a pistol in the head, and he fell down, yelling 'help.'"

Frank Burke stuck a gun in Whalen's face while he was on the ground and told him to relax. Then, both Valenti and Burke picked up Whalen and put him in the back of the van. However, the commotion caught the attention of another man—this would have been Lufthansa employee Rolf Rebmann—who came over to find out what had happened. Valenti tried to say nothing was wrong and then pulled out a pistol, told the man to relax and sit in the van with Whalen.

Someone from the robbery crew then opened the door of the cargo hangar and Burke drove the van inside. Once in the building,

Valenti and Burke took Whalen and the other hostage upstairs to the lunch room where the other Lufthansa workers had been herded and were being watched over by Danny Rizzo. Valenti and Burke then went back down to the truck.

Lufthansa's high-value cargo vault had two doors that had to be opened one at a time. If both doors remained open at the same time, the alarm would go off and bring Port Authority police. As Valenti remembered it, he followed DeSimone into the vault. Before them were stacks of boxes and burlap sacks of what they later would find out was jewelry.

"Tommy took a box from the right-hand side, there on the shelf, and he threw it down on the floor," Valenti testified. Then DeSimone stomped on the box, which was cushioned with yellow Styrofoam pellets, which looked like popcorn and spilled out. Then DeSimone stuck his hand in the box and pulled out the money.

Money. Lots of it. There might be about $125,000 in American currency in each of what by Valenti's recollection was fifty boxes. Even an idiot could figure out that there was a fortune in that room. Burke had only expected a haul of $2 million in cash. Twenty of the boxes alone would hold $2.5 million. Forty boxes would contain $5 million, the official total used by police. Valenti's fifty box count was likely incorrect. In any case, this was big.

"This is it! This is it!" DeSimone screamed. He pulled down two more boxes, and they also had $125,000 in cash.

"Take all of these fifty boxes," DeSimone ordered. Take the burlap sacks of gold chains, the watches—in other words, take as much as we can. The crew opened some metal boxes. They held diamonds, emeralds, stones DeSimone couldn't even pronounce. Into the van they all went, and then the whole take was driven away.

But where would they go? As strange as it might seem for such an historic robbery, Burke and his crew hadn't even figured out where to go once they left the airport. They were lucky the cops never came. They didn't even have an escape plan.

"Bring it to my cousin's house," Vincent yelled, according to Valenti.

The van was driven to The Hole where Valenti was living with his wife and children, as well as his mother and sister, who were all asleep. Forming a human chain, Valenti and the others unloaded the van, and placed the stuff in the basement. Burke and DeSimone both had to be taken back to their respective prison halfway houses, so Vincent took them into Manhattan, said Valenti.

With Burke, DeSimone, and Vincent gone, Valenti said he and the others started separating out the jewelry and counting the money. The whole thing took about two hours. Gold chains. Platinum chains. Cartier watches. Diamonds. Rubies. Emeralds. Rings. Lots of gold. They also saw some German marks. They counted the cash and came up with $6.25 million, said Valenti.

Vincent was in a state of "euphoria" when he was told the value of the horde, remembered Valenti. But Vincent quickly tempered his joy with words of caution. After all, this was the Mafia where money was the goal of life. As Sal Vitale had always believed, only your friends could hurt you and with so much loot at stake friends could quickly become enemies.

"He said we got to be real careful now," Valenti remembered Vincent telling him. "He said they'll look to rob us, you know, look to kill us and take the stuff."

That was definitely a downer for Valenti, whose family was in the house with the stash. There were at least two crime families, the Bonanno and Lucchese families involved, and the Gambino borgata learned of it when Fat Andy Ruggiano was told. They could go into a feeding frenzy. Murder wouldn't be an impediment either. Then there was Jimmy Burke who would kill somebody if they looked at him the wrong way.

Immediately, the FBI got on to leads that the Robert's Lounge crew was involved, so the bar on Lefferts Boulevard became a place to avoid. Valenti stayed away and bought some Christmas trees to sell by his house. Why? He had to burn the evidence from the heist, the burlap, the boxes. When you sell Christmas trees on the street in Queens there was always a fire in a can for warmth. In this case everything burned except the Styrofoam so Valenti had to bag it up and take it a few blocks away to a sanitation dump.

The split for the heist came to $750,000 per person, said Valenti.

It was more money than any of them would ever see in a lifetime, assuming they lived to see it. But the money was also a curse. No one could spend it quickly or on anything that would show. If they did go on a spending spree, Burke would have them killed for being stupid. The FBI was watching everybody hanging around Robert's Lounge, and they would know if anybody started showing signs of having big money. Banks were also out of the question. Forget about brokerage accounts, stocks, bonds. They could all be traced.

So like generations of immigrants who never trusted the banks, Valenti was forced by necessity to hide his cash with friends in batches of $100,000 to $150,000. He also found spaces in door frames to secret the money. Valenti didn't get the money all at once, but when he did he said he made sure that some was kicked up to Paul Vario and his family: about $200,000. Porn king Michael Zaffarano, who was Vincent's captain in the Bonanno family, got $100,000 and Angelo Sepe took some up to upstate New York where someone in the family of Carmine Persico, the long-imprisoned boss of the Colombo family, had a home, said Valenti.

The jewelry was also dispersed. Some went to Massino, just as Vitale had said, for tribute. John Gotti, then an up-and-coming member of the Gambino family, got some watches, said Valenti, just as a way of keeping peace and making sure his crew didn't try to rob Burke's team. Some mob connected jewelers took some of the stuff. It was spread around.

It was up to Burke to dole out payments to both Valenti and Vincent, which he did in lots of $20,000 to $100,000 at times. Valenti gambled a lot of his money away, but he said Vincent eventually bought a home in Moriches on Long Island, cars and a boat. Yet, with other members of the heist going missing or dying, the other shares and whatever wasn't paid out in tribute seemed to remain with Burke, who must have had a personal stash amounting into the millions of dollars. Some of that money, investigators believed later, went to finance a drug deal Burke did in Florida involving Richard Eaton.

Valenti only met Eaton once, and that was on a Saturday night at the club Afters, a nicely appointed night spot near 86th Street and

Rockaway Boulevard. The place was owned by Burke, Vincent, and another man and its name Afters signified "after Lufthansa." It was a popular place, and while only opened for about a year attracted entertainers like the singing groups Blondie and Gladys Knight and The Pips, recalled Valenti. Burke introduced Valenti to Eaton, and the conversation over dinner revolved around a big drug deal Burke and Eaton had done in Florida. There was a lot of laughter, and Eaton was enjoying a dish of shrimp scampi. Nobody seemed to have a care in the world. Valenti noticed Eaton's dish because he himself was hungry.

The group closed After at about 3:00 A.M., and Valenti stopped by a White Castle and picked up some burgers to eat at home with his wife. You either liked White Castle burgers or loved them, and in Valenti's case, they were a good comfort food, even at such a strange hour. Then he went to sleep. During the night, Valenti was awakened by a tapping on the bedroom window. He looked out and saw Vincent's son Jerry. In the Mafia when your boss calls, you respond immediately, no questions asked.

"I went and let him in the hallway," Valenti remembered. "And he told me, 'My father sent me.' He said, 'We got to dig a hole.'"

Valenti said he knew that by digging a hole they were going to hide a body. But this was the dead of winter. The problem was that down in the area of The Hole, the neighborhood where Valenti lived, the ground and even the roads froze solid, often with thick sheets of ice because the drainage was so poor. To thaw the ground Valenti burned some kerosene but that didn't work. Burke showed up with his son Frank and Vincent but even they couldn't make any headway in digging.

They were stumped. There was a body to be buried yet it was impossible to dig in the cold ground. So, Valenti remembered that there was a trailer on some property his mother owned nearby. Someone figured that the body could be kept in the trailer overnight until Valenti had a friend use a backhoe to dig a hole, ostensibly for a new foundation. All they had to do was move the body into the trailer.

"Jerry and I walked down to the trailer, and Frankie Burke drove the car, backed it into the trailer, opened the trunk, and Jerry and Frankie lifted the body and put it in the trailer," said Valenti. It was then that he saw the face of the corpse. It was Richard Eaton, the man who only hours earlier had been enjoying an Italian repast.

But as luck would have it, things went terribly wrong as they often did at The Hole. The next morning a cop came by Valenti's house and said it looked like there had been a Mafia hit outside the trailer. Some kids who used the trailer as a playground discovered the body. Valenti convincingly feigned ignorance and concocted a story about having seen a car with two black men in the area the previous night. Valenti's lie deflected attention from himself and for that matter Asaro. But Burke would be dogged by the corpse years later when Henry Hill talked to the FBI about the way his comrade in crime had admitted killing Eaton. The result was Burke's indictment and conviction in 1985 for Eaton's murder.

There was one other trivial consequence from that horrible night for Valenti. He could never again even think about eating shrimp scampi.

CHAPTER TWENTY
ALL IN THE FAMILY

THE FIRST DAY OF GASPARE VALENTI'S TESTIMONY was riveting, to say the least. For the first time in the history of the Lufthansa heist someone who purported to be an insider, a criminal actually on the scene, gave sworn testimony about the fabled score. In many ways, what Valenti described tracked closely to what had already been revealed in the Werner trial, as well as the book *Wiseguy* and other retellings of the story.

But there were some key difference with Valenti, notably the specific number and identity of the people involved in the planning and his having done the beating of Lufthansa worker Kerry Whalen and not Angelo Sepe as previously claimed by law enforcement. There were also now more details laid out about how the loot was spread and who else in the mob got tribute.

As Asaro watched his cousin tell the stories of their criminal lives together, he seethed. Asaro may have been elderly, but his flinty eyes still seemed menacing and angry behind his glasses. Throughout the trial he would mutter to no one in particular or else badger his attorneys to be more aggressive. There was also someone else in court who found Valenti's appearance on the witness stand infuriating: his son Anthony.

An obese man, Anthony "Fat Sammy" Valenti showed up on the first day of his father's testimony and from the back of the courtroom seemed to glare at the witness stand. Mob aficionados had always remembered the scene from *The Godfather: Part II* in which the Sicilian brother of the mobster Frankie Pentangelie was brought to Washington to not so subtly intimidate his brother from giving incriminating testimony during a congressional hearing. Prosecutors would occasionally raise the issue of familial pressure during trials as a way of keeping some spectators out of a courtroom, even though a witness's freedom would depend on truthful testimony. But there was no evidence that the younger Valenti had any reason for showing up in court other than to see for himself his father's testimony. Confronted by a print journalist, Anthony Valenti would remark, "I have nothing to say," although when TV news reporter Mary Murphy caught up with him outside the courthouse he relented and admitted that it was distressing to see his father testify.

While Lufthansa and the Katz murder were the marquee acts in the case, Valenti described numerous other crimes from the witness stand that he and Vincent were involved in, sometimes together. The alleged crimes Valenti regurgitated on the stand went as far back as the 1960s and were as recent as 2010 and 2013. Under federal law, a racketeering conspiracy required proof of only two criminal acts over a ten-year period. But because of statute-of-limitation issues, the prosecutors had to try and link Vincent to the enterprise—in this case the Bonanno crime family—within *five years* of the date of his indictment in January 2014. If they were able to show such a recent connection, then Argentieri and company would be able to link Vincent with being part of a Bonanno crime-family enterprise, which went all the way back to the murder of Paul Katz in 1969 and Lufthansa in 1978.

So while he was on the witness stand for the government, Valenti talked about other allegations facing Vincent, which had nothing to do with Lufthansa. There were charges involving an arson in 1980 at the old Afters club location, which Valenti said was burned because it was going to become an African-American nightclub. Also spelled out by Valenti were abortive attempts to rob armored cars in 1984 and 1986, as well as the robbery of a FedEx truck carrying gold salts, which when put through a chemical process would have produced about $1 million in actual gold metal. Through the 1980s and 1990s, Valenti said there were numerous extortion attempts, illegal gambling, and in 2013 he and Asaro squeezed about $4,000 from a Bonanno crime family associate who was loansharking without permission. Such was the convoluted code of ethics of the Mafia. But the variety of crimes charged made for testimony that at times seemed confusing, disparate, and unconnected.

Yet it was Vincent's loansharking operation, said Valenti, that had direct ties back to the Lufthansa heist. Vincent's lending grew in terms of dollar amounts, which Valenti recalled stemmed from Lufthansa money. Through the 1970s and 80s, there were loans to a variety of borrowers ranging from local businessmen to Vincent's relatives, according to Valenti, who said it was his job to collect weekly from those who were in debt. Loansharking can be pernicious because not only are the interests exorbitant but payment of the so-called points charged did nothing to reduce the overall loan principle, which had to be paid separately.

Michael Zaffarano, the Times Square porn king, made a great deal of money from adult films and from his buildings along Broadway, which he leased to peep show operators, X-rated book stores, and bath houses. While his buildings were nothing to rave about, they churned out steady cash, and the properties were increasing in value as the prospect of urban renewal grew. Yet, even Zaffarano and his son John found that they had to borrow from Vincent, remembered Valenti. Both Zaffaranos paid back their loans but, according to Valenti, that didn't stop Vincent from pulling a bit of a scam with them, even if they were relatives.

When Michael Zaffarano died in February 1980, both Valenti and Vincent went to the funeral. While it might seem poor etiquette to talk business in such a setting, Vincent had no qualms about raising with Zaffarano's son John the subject of his father's old loan—which had already been paid.

"At Mickey Zaffarano's funeral, what, if any, discussion did you have about the loan?" Argentieri asked Valenti.

*   *   *

"Vinnie told his son, John Zaffarano, that his father owed us a hundred-thousand dollars," replied Valenti.

"Was that true?"

"No."

"Had Mickey Zaffarano already paid back that loan?"

"Yes."

Valenti went on to explain that the younger Zaffarano agreed to pay back his father's previously repaid loan again at two percent, or two points a week. But that wasn't the only financial hook Vincent had in the Zaffarano porn empire. John Zaffarano, administrator of his father's estate had to keep up the Times Square area property and continue to run the adult-film side of the business. For instance, the marquee on the façade of the well-known Pussycat Theater needed to be refurbished and for that, according to Valenti, John Zaffarano took out additional loans from Vincent. So, some of the Lufthansa loot appears to have gone to help publicize on the theater's marquee the exploits of the 1980s porn stars *de jour*.

With the elder Zaffarano's death, Vincent appeared to have become the major Mafia connection for the Times Square sex business of his old crime captain. Disputes would arise in the porn trade and for that Vincent was the man John Zaffarano turned to for help, said Valenti. One of the biggest female porn stars of that period dubbed by some the "Golden Age" was Marilyn Chambers, the blond former Ivory Soap model who went on to make her livelihood in films that the public clamored for. Her 1972 debut was in the movie *Behind the Green Door*, followed by other hard-core features, including the 1980 film *Insatiable*.

According to Valenti, Michael Zaffarano had a deal before he died that Chambers would make ten films although she was also working with other producers. In approximately 1982, a sit down was arranged between John Zaffarano and Valenti with two producers allegedly tied to the Gambino crime family who Chambers was working with in California. As a result of the meeting, Chambers was released to work with Zaffarano who ultimately had a change of heart and didn't use her in any films, said Valenti. For the trip, Valenti said he got nothing in terms of compensation but Vincent did. (After years of drug and alcohol abuse, Chambers crossed over into legitimate films but continued to work in porn. She died of a cerebral hemorrhage in April 2009 at the age of fifty-seven.)

By the mid-1980s, the porn industry was gravitating away from films in theaters to videotape. Consumers could get their pleasure by viewing cassettes in their own homes. This meant that at least some of the Zaffarano empire, the theaters, was heading to obsolescence. But to the rescue came the plans of New York State and New York City to turn the "Great Blight Way" around 42nd Street and its environs into something more upscale, family oriented and world-tourist friendly. This would turn out to be a gold mine for the Zaffarano family, not to mention some others in the mob.

The rush for development of Times Square and the surrounding neighborhood pushed property values higher and higher. By 1985, developers were ready to give the Zaffarano estate an enormous sum for the block of property the dead mobster had once owned. This was all business and it came at the right time. The city was ready for a big change, and the Pussycat Theater and sex shops were going to eventually give way to things like the Disney Store, Ghirardelli chocolate, and the Marriott Marquise.

With all of the competing interests, it took a great deal of finesse to make the deal work. One of the city's most experienced real estate brokers, Robert Shapiro, remembered working for months on the Zaffarano land parcels, a deal that was complicated by a number of pending commercial leases, including some housing businesses owed by Genovese crime family captain Matthew "Matty the Horse" Ianniello. Being a well-known gangster, Ianniello was constantly under scrutiny. His federal conviction in 1985 by the office of then-Manhattan federal prosecutor Rudolph Giuliani further complicated things because Ianniello wound up owing the federal government a great deal of money.

In interviews in 2015, Shapiro related to the author that eventually he was able to pull together a $18.5 million deal for the property. Included in it was the Pussycat, some gay steam baths, Ianniello's bar known as Mardi Gras, and some peep shows. Most of the money went to John Zaffarano and his mother, who were the beneficiaries of the estate. Ianniello's leases also had value, but since he owed $750,000 in forfeited funds to Giuliani, that money went directly to the federal government, Shapiro remembered.

Shapiro was certain that none of the money went to the mob and strictly speaking that was true: the purchase price poured directly to the Zaffarano estate or the federal government. But according to Valenti, his cousin Vincent had other plans, impelled by a sense of entitlement for the way he had helped out Zaffarano over the years. Resentful over what he had to fork over to Giuliani, Ianniello also felt that he should get something from the Zaffarano estate. As Valenti remembered things, Vincent and Ianniello started pressuring John Zaffarano for a cut of the real-estate deal.

"Being that John sold the business, Matty wanted a million dollars that he felt he would lose with John selling the properties. So he wanted a million dollars," recalled Valenti.

There was then the inevitable sitdown called and that led to be a big breach of mob protocol. Ianniello turned up at the Manhattan restaurant RSVP and was fully expecting Vincent Asaro to take part. Instead, Valenti showed up with another man, and Ianniello was peeved.

A big silver-haired man and a decorated World War Two veteran with a neck that seemed to merge directly with his head, Ianniello was not a man to be trifled with. Though facing various illnesses, he could be very intimidating, even as a senior citizen. Ianniello let Valenti and his associates have it.

"Get out. Leave," said Ianniello, who was on the verge of blowing his stack.

"He was really angry that Vinnie didn't show up. It was like disrespectful," said Valenti.

In the mob, a powerful captain like Ianniello was to be shown respect in a sitdown by the presence of another mobster of similar rank sitting across the table in the dispute. By not showing up, Vincent had slighted Ianniello, said Valenti.

With his tail between his legs, Valenti trooped back to Queens and told Vincent about what Ianniello said. At that point, Vincent said he would take care of it and did later on. Valenti said that in a meeting John Zaffarano was told he had to pay the million dollars to Ianniello. Zaffarano didn't want to fork that over but eventually did, said Valenti.

With his nephew flush with cash from the Times Square deal, Vincent saw some opportunity for himself. Harkening back to all he had done for the late Mickey Zaffarano businesses, Vincent told his son that he was also due a million dollars, remembered Valenti, adding that the young man thought it was a joke. But Vincent wasn't joking and Valenti said that his cousin sent him down to Florida where a now-relocated Zaffarano finally paid $400,000.

The demands for a cut of the Times Square real estate were painted by the government as attempts by Vincent to extort John Zaffarano, who was later called to the witness stand to testify for the government. Referring to Vincent as "My cousin Vinny," John Zaffarano was a reluctant witness and admitted he didn't want to testify. While contradicting Valenti on the amount of the payments, Zaffarano did say he forked over $750,000 to Ianniello and gave Vincent $400,000.

Zaffarano was fuzzy on some of the details, claiming that in the years of the property deals he had a substance-abuse problem and had trouble remembering things. He agreed that Vincent had helped him negotiate with Ianniello and said that he gave money to his entire family. He wasn't the most convincing witness for an extortion case, but Zaffarano's testimony in the grand jury had been enough to get Vincent indicted in the first place. Along with everything else being said on the witness stand, the cumulative effect might still prove to be trouble for cousin Vincent.

Valenti's testimony was proving to be a very important part of the government's case. But he also would be useful in explaining some of the hundreds of tape recordings he had made of Vincent and that Argentieri and company figured would be the coup de grâce to seal the defendant's fate. Valenti had been able to lull his cousin Vincent into a false sense of security so that they talked about anything and everything. From alleged crime in progress to nostalgia for the old days of the Mafia. There were hundreds of hours of tapes, and while not all of that would be played for the jury, the prosecution cherry picked what it thought was the best. Not only did the recordings seem incriminating, but they also made Asaro look bad in the eyes of some of his associates. He bad-mouthed people he was supposed to show respect for and bemoaned his miserable lot in life. Vincent Asaro may have hauled in hundreds of thousands of dollars—even millions of dollars—from a life of crime as described by Valenti. But in the end he portrayed himself in his own words as one step above a "brokester," a friendless gangster on the scrap heap.

"Where am I going to go? I got no place to go," said Asaro on one tape. It was a remark that he made years after fellow gangster James Tartaglione was overheard on another secret recording made in 2003 saying that Vincent might just be too poor to be in the Mafia life. Another day Asaro said on tape that he was an old man who had "good days, bad days," who stayed by himself and wasn't even aware of what was going on in the mob in his old neighborhood in Ozone Park.

Asaro also seemed like a vain man, fastidious about the way he dressed even if he was down on his luck. In a November 2011 conversation, he chided Valenti for wearing what looked like old sneakers. "I went through forty pairs of sneakers. You're still wearing those," said Asaro. "To me the way I look is very important."

But some of the most suggestive tapes indicated that Asaro was aware of what had gone on in the Lufthansa heist. Some of what he said skirted very close to an admission about being involved in robbery. At one point, Asaro related on a recording in January 2011 how one of the alleged heist participants, Danny Rizzo, was so broke that he had even asked for $200.

"He's still got money from . . ." said Valenti on the recording, referring to Lufthansa.

"No," answered Asaro, relating how Rizzo said he was cheated.

Then in a February 2011 recording, Asaro again bemoaned his pitiful existence, one far from the glory days of the old mob scene.

"It's life. We did it to ourselves. It is the curse of this fucking gambling," Asaro is heard to say.

Everybody on the street seemed to know of Asaro's compulsive gambling. Dollar bills flew out of his hands and toward the ponies as fast as he made them. If he earned a buck for every time he used an expletive as he recounted his bad fortune, Asaro would have had a healthy bankroll. On the tape, Asaro seemed wistful, taking stock of a life ill-spent and one in which he felt cheated.

"We never got our right money, what we were supposed to get," said Asaro. "We got fucked all around. That fucking Jimmy kept everything."

For those in the courtroom when the tapes were played, Asaro seemed in the latter recording to be admitting some involvement in the heist as he lamented getting shortchanged by Burke and being broke so many years later. "Asaro's Voice on Recordings Seem Damning," said the headline the next day on a story in *Newsday*.

Based on Valenti's testimony, Burke seemed to have kept his hands on about $3 million in heist proceeds for the simple reason that many of the participants were killed shortly after the robbery. While not part of the evidence in the case, former Bonanno crime family captain Dominick Cicale co-authored an e-book in 2015 in which he claimed that years after Burke's death, he and fellow Bonanno captain Vincent Basciano got their hands on money that Burke had secreted in a bank safe-deposit box. According to Cicale's account, which law-enforcement officials greeted with skepticism, he and Basciano, as well as Burke's son-in-law, mobster Anthony "Bruno" Indelicato, hatched the idea of getting the money over a December 2001 dinner at Rao's Restaurant in East Harlem. The idea was to use the money for a cartoon film about a ferret named "Ferretina," which was never made, said Cicale. Indelicato allegedly got access to the safe deposit box and took out hundreds of thousands of dollars in Lufthansa cash, claimed Cicale. But even if true that Burke left a cash-laden safe-deposit box, given his long history of crime, any funds could have been the proceeds of many other crimes.

                            *   *   *

Gaspare Valenti had been on and off the witness stand for over four days before Asaro's main defense attorney Elizabeth Macedonio was able to take a shot at him through cross-examination on October 26. For legal experts, a good cross-examination can not only bring out contradictory statements from a witness but also suggest a person's motives and prejudices for agreeing to testify—or cooperating with the prosecution. Valenti's direct examination had laid out the Lufthansa heist, details of the Katz burial, and other crimes ascribed to Asaro in seemingly convincing detail. It was not only Macedonio's job to cast doubt about Valenti's stories but also show something of his character and motivation for turning on his old friend.

Valenti had made no secret that he was cooperating because he was broke, dispirited, and in need of a meal ticket for himself and his family. He told Macedonio from the witness stand that the FBI had been giving him $3,000 a month for support, and since 2008, when he first started to help the government, he had collected $178,000 from the agency. For years, prosecutors had used paid cooperating witnesses, something that wasn't a secret to anybody. But in Valenti's case, he certainly saw money as the prime, and perhaps only, reason for turning on Asaro.

Macedonio's tactic was to question Valenti again about details of things he had first been asked by Argentieri: the Katz burial, the Lufthansa heist, the loansharking. The defense attorney indicated through her questions that Valenti had told the FBI different things about the heist, the burial, and the other crimes. But sometimes the questioning got bogged down in details, like whether it was a "post hole digger" or a "shovel" that Asaro and Burke had brought to dig the burial pit in the basement of the house on 102nd Road. They were both the same thing, with slight variations, explained Valenti.

On the Lufthansa heist, Macedonio raised the possibility that while Valenti had testified that Asaro was present at all the planning sessions for the robbery, he had told the FBI that his cousin wasn't present for at least one of the meetings. These were small points and for the most part Macedonio didn't ask Valenti to describe again in detail what Asaro allegedly did during the heist. But she did suggest that Valenti might be sculpting his testimony from what he read about the heist in the newspapers.

"The first individual that you came upon, did you learn his name?" asked Macedonio.

"Yes," answered Valenti.

"How did you learn his name?"

"He had a badge on, Kerry Whalen, and I took the badge off him, and I placed it on me."

"You didn't read about that in the newspaper?"

"Read about it? That was me. I didn't have to read about it."

"Certainly some time has passed since the Lufthansa heist?"

"I think my memory is pretty well."

But on one point, Valenti gave an answer to Macedonio, which conflicted with Sal Vitale's recollection about how he and Massino went to pick up the Lufthansa jewelry. Vitale had said he drove Massino to meet Asaro, who then gave the Bonanno gangster a briefcase filled with the gold chains, watches, and bracelets. However, under questioning by Macedonio, Valenti said Massino alone came to visit him and that he, not Asaro, passed him the case. There was no mention of Vitale being present. It was a contradiction and either Vitale or Valenti was mistaken—or perhaps lying.

Macedonio also tried to cast doubt over Valenti's story that after ripping off Lufthansa, the robbery crew went to his house on Blake Avenue to stash the loot and count it in the dead of night in a dwelling where thirteen lived, twelve of whom were asleep. There was also a dog named Beauty, a street dog Valenti had adopted and was protective about, even when questioned by the attorney.

"And Beauty was a barker, wasn't she?" Macedonio asked.

"No, she wasn't. She was a sickly dog," replied Valenti.

"She was always sickly?"

"Yes."

"What kind of dog was Beauty?"

"She was a street dog."

"A mutt?"

"That's cruel."

Much of Macedonio's cross-examination dug deeper into Valenti's checkered history, one filled with duplicity, cheating, lying to federal agents, and overall unreliability as a friend. He admitted that when he fled to Las Vegas around 1990 it was because he had cheated Bonanno mobster Anthony Spero out of around $25,000—money he was owed by Asaro—and then cooked up a crazy story about having given the cash to a man in a brown bomber jacket. At that point, Valenti had to get out of town and went west fast, leaving his wife and kids in the lurch. It was the start of a star-crossed fifteen years he would spend in the desert.

Once in Las Vegas, the hapless Valenti admitted that he started committing a series of other crimes with a man who was actually an FBI informant. He took up with another woman who sued him for money he supposedly stole. To make matters worse, Valenti fell under the control of an FBI undercover agent who plied him with stolen casino chips and got him involved in various fake invoicing and fraud schemes. Valenti couldn't have picked worse partners in crime, and in the end he was arrested and sentenced to eight months in prison. To add insult to his many indignations, when Valenti got out of prison he was arrested in Las Vegas for jay walking and went right back to jail for a short stint.

Another vignette brought out by Macedonio showed in the end how mercenary Valenti had been in the face of Asaro's own sentimentality and kindness. When Asaro's father Jerome died in 1977, his son took two of his prized cufflinks and had them made into rings. Asaro respected his father, as did Valenti, so a set of matching gold rings made from the cufflinks seemed appropriate. The ring didn't stay long with Valenti.

"So it was a gesture of love, fair to say?" asked Macedonio.

"Yes, it was," answered Valenti.

"And what did you do with your copy of the ring?"

"I hocked it."

So great was Valenti's need for cash that he said he also got rid of

Jerome Asaro's old car when it was given to him following the old man's death.

One of the last questions the attorney asked had to do with the weeks before his work as a secret informant came to an end just before the remains of Katz were found in the Ozone Park basement. For reasons that were never illuminated, Valenti felt the need on Father's Day to call Asaro. He wanted to tell him he loved him.

CHAPTER TWENTY-ONE
"WHAT IS THIS, WATERGATE?"

SITTING THROUGH DAYS OF TESTIMONY, including three involving his turncoat cousin, Vincent Asaro, never a guy to keep his emotions in check, was steaming. When Valenti was on the stand, Asaro made sure that he had a clear line of sight to the witness box to scowl at him and moved his seat or asked that a computer screen be moved so he could keep the witness in a withering stare. Asaro also knew that whatever was left of his life was in the balance and didn't like the way he saw the case unfolding in the courtroom. The testimony was damning and he knew it. Defense attorneys Macedonio and Ferrone did their best on cross-examination, but there wasn't much they could do to trip up government witnesses.

"He is fucking lying!" Asaro exclaimed more than once in a voice that could be heard by spectators—let alone the prosecutor, court personnel, and likely the jurors.

As Valenti testified, Asaro could be seen getting more animated with his attorneys and mouthing the word "liar." His family members in the courtroom could also be overheard by one reporter saying, "These are some fairy tales. . . . They gave him a book to memorize. . . . He should get an Academy Award."

Asaro would badger the attorneys so much that Ferrone finally had enough and moved her seat to a spot away from him to a place at the other end of the defense table. Argentieri also had enough of

Asaro's *sotto voce* remarks, and asked Ross to have the defense keep him muzzled.

The testimony didn't get any easier for Asaro to stomach as the case progressed. Peter Zuccaro was an old Gambino crime-family associate and admitted killer who turned government witness years earlier. Asaro didn't like him ever since Zuccaro killed a dog in self-defense, an act for which the canine-loving Asaro wanted to kill him in retaliation, according to Valenti. For his part, Zuccaro had his own standards, and once said he didn't care much for those in the mob who wanted to shoot people near a Catholic church. Asaro could only sit and stew as Zuccaro, who had the hard look of a Mafia operative, told the jury that Frank Burke admitted to him that he drove in the van with Valenti the night of the Lufthansa heist. This corroborated some of Valenti's testimony about the heist. Burke added that Valenti never did get his cut from the Lufthansa heist because it was taken by Asaro, according to Zuccaro.

"Frankie said that Vinny kept it and beat him for it," said Zuccaro, explaining how the real problem was with the way Burke's father was not paying people fast enough.

In a push to show the impact of the murder of Paul Katz on his family, the prosecution called the dead man's son Lawrence as a witness. Katz's wife Delores had died in 2001, and although she had given police lengthy statements about his last days, including some about her suspicions about police involvement in her spouse's death, there was no way to introduce them into evidence. Prosecutors hoped that Lawrence, who was only about five years old when his father disappeared, would humanize the murdered man and tug at the heart strings of the jury.

Asaro and his attorney could only watch as Larry Katz spoke haltingly about his father and how his father had gotten arrested in the weeks before he died. Katz seemed ill-at-ease on the stand, and his apparent discomfort just might make the jury feel more sympathetic to him. He didn't relish the idea of having to talk about his father's criminal record, his arrest, and the fact that it appeared he was dealing in stolen merchandise.

One incident from Katz's son's testimony stood out about the time of his father's arrest. After making bail, the elder Katz came home to the family apartment building in Lefrak City, an apartment complex near Corona. Spotting his father coming up the walk, Larry Katz ran up to him with a toy gun and handcuffs and jumped into his arms. Fresh out of jail, Paul Katz uncomfortably looked at the toys and said, "I've had enough of those for a while," the son remembered.

The stress in the Katz household was obvious, and Larry remembered his parents constantly fighting with his mother concerned about the characters her husband was involved with. To show that Paul Katz was talking with law enforcement, his son confirmed to Assistant U.S. Attorney Alicyn Cooley that an NYPD officer named Sal Petix called the apartment. As if to make the story poignant, Cooley had Larry Katz recall how his parents became mellow and peaceful when they talked about plans to move out of the city and escape upstate, into a house that his father drew a picture of for the children.

The day his father disappeared on December 6, 1969, Larry Katz remembered his parents arguing one last time. His father got a telephone call and told his wife he was going to go out to meet someone. The parents started one more verbal spat.

"They were arguing about him not leaving, and he said he had to go, and that my mom told him to take one of the kids," remembered Larry Katz. "He said, no. And she said, 'At least take the dog,' and he said no. And he grabbed his jacket, said, 'If I'm not back in a couple of hours, call the cops.'"

That was the last time Larry Katz ever saw his father. Fear seemed to pervade the Katz household for years. It was a sad story, and wisely Macedonio decided not to cross-examine him. Seasoned defense attorneys know that the questioning of a bereaved family member can backfire badly.

If Asaro didn't like sitting through the Katz testimony, he certainly didn't look forward to what FBI special agent Michael Byrnes and the famed forensic anthropologist Brad Adams had to say. They testified about the macabre dig in the basement of the Burke house on 102nd Road. Byrnes described everything from the breaking of the concrete, the methodical sifting of the soil and the discovery of the bones, the teeth and the hair in the pit. Adams fleshed things out, in a manner of speaking, by noting the various anatomical finds and the fact that the remains had been in the ground for over five years. This was the place where Katz's body was buried in 1969 and where, despite an earlier disinterment, some of his remains were left behind.

"We have portions representing the head. We have teeth from the head. We have bones from the neck. We have bones from the torso. We have bones from the chest, and we have bones from the hand," Adams told the jury. When necessary, Argentieri had him illustrate things by showing photographs of the pitiful bone fragments found in the basement.

It was then up to Frances Rue, a criminalist in the office of the New York City Chief Medical Examiner, to describe how the science of DNA put a name to the bones in the pit. Testimony about the intricacies of laboratory analysis, kinship studies, and placement of alleles on human chromosomes can be mind-numbing. But the bottom line was that Rue said with certainty that the bones in the pit were those of Paul Katz, father of Lawrence and Ilsa, his two children who had given samples of their genetic material for comparison. Rue's certainty was greater than 99.99 percent, carried forward by a few fractions of a decimal point—but never 100 percent. The bones were those of Paul Katz, no question, she said.

By November 3, 2015, the government's case had essentially wound down. The defense would bring in one witness—former Lufthansa worker Kerry Whalen who testified that he had seen a man identified as Angelo Sepe and Thomas DeSimone who accosted him outside the terminal and not Valenti. He also recounted the way he was forced into the van at the point of a gun.

"They threw me on my back. The driver stuck a pistol deep into my—into my brain, my left eye," remembered Whalen. "And with my right eye, I could see two bullets the size of submarine torpedoes. And I just thought they were going to kill me. I assumed I was dead then."

Whalen also described under questioning by the defense attorney how the Lufthansa ID he was wearing on his jacket was never taken by any of the robbers, a direct contradiction to what Valenti had said when he testified. On cross-examination, the government questions seemed aimed at painting Whalen as a crank who was angry at the way the FBI and previous prosecutors had treated him, to the extent that he even demonstrated with placards outside the courthouse. But Whalen essentially stuck to his story that he saw Sepe and DeSimone in the van and that his airline ID was never taken from his jacket—all points that directly contradicted Valenti.

There was one more defense witness, Carmine Muscarella, a relative of Valenti, who essentially testified that he gave Valenti a check for some money from the sale of property because he was family and not out of fear of Asaro. This was done to rebut the allegation that Muscarella was an extortion victim even though he admitted knowing about Asaro's reputation as a mobster.

"I was not afraid," Muscarella told the jury, adding that he made the payment to Valenti because he was being a proverbial pain in the ass about the $3,000. When asked by Macedonio why he later agreed to lend Asaro $2,500, Muscarella said that he felt sorry for him.

"Vincent Asaro is a very proud man, and for him to even come to me to ask to borrow money because he was in financial dire straits, I am sure was very humiliating to him, to actually come and ask me for money because he had been so down on his luck," said Muscarella

With Asaro's decision not to testify, the trial was on the final lap and from what had gone on for the past two weeks in Ross's courtroom, it looked and sounded like Vincent Asaro was in a great deal of trouble. Valenti wasn't shaken in his testimony, and other witnesses corroborated some of his story. However, there were some contradictions in the testimony and some of the extortion charges seemed weak, particularly that involving John Zaffarano and Muscarella, and all of the FBI agents who testified admitted they never saw Asaro commit a crime in all of the many hours of surveillance. It would be up to the prosecution and defense to try and make one final bid to convince the jurors about Asaro's guilt or innocence.

Summations are the final chance prosecutors and defense attorneys get to spin the case before the jury. They are bound by the facts, but the attorneys can appeal to the commonsense when trying to give their interpretation of the facts. The prosecution will tell how there is no other possible conclusion than guilt. The defense will hammer away at the presumption of innocence and show how the evidence is not so clear and that there is a reasonable doubt about guilt.

On Friday, November 6, 2015, it was Alicyn Cooley's job to pull together the various strands of the government's case to convict Asaro. The prosecution goes first on summations and with an indictment covering events over four and a half decades old what Cooley had to say wasn't going to be done in ten minutes. With the jury in the box and the press packed into the court, along with a goodly number of people from the U.S. Attorney's Office, Cooley began the long march to convince the jury that Asaro was guilty. For about six hours, Cooley spoke to the jurors. Six hours. Even the summation in the case against Joseph Massino went on for only about three hours. The danger in long summations is that jurors will tire and lose their focus. In this case, Cooley needed a long time to sketch out the evidence.

Asaro's forty-five years as a gangster was on trial in the case, Cooley reminded the jury. She branded him the "ultimate tough guy" who profited from years of criminal activity and killed people along the way.

Asaro, insisted Cooley, "lived by and enforced the Mafia's code—death before dishonor." Her summation was relentless. Cooley spent her time alternately reading from portions of the over 3,500-page trial transcript encompassing seventy witnesses. She played audio clips of the many tapes Valenti had made of Asaro, ones that showed how dissolute the life of an aging mobster had become. But the tapes also were solid proof that Asaro was involved in the Lufthansa heist and profited handsomely from it, said Cooley.

The prosecutor also reminded the jury that while Katz's murder may have taken place decades earlier, "justice can still be reached."

Of course, there were breaks in Cooley's summation. But such lengthy presentations had the added danger of making it appear that the prosecution wasn't sure of its evidence and whether it tied together well enough to convince the jury. Asaro was overheard to say of the summation: "It's absolutely ridiculous . . . a five-hour summation? What is this, Watergate?"

Macedonio had a Sisyphean task before her. The conventional wisdom around the courthouse was that Asaro would be convicted. Valenti seemed to be credible, and if the jury believed him, then Asaro would for the rest of his life be looking to the U.S. government for support in his old age—not from Social Security but from the hospitality of the Bureau of Prisons. So, it would be up to Macedonio in her summation to go deep into the evidence and show the jurors why they shouldn't believe Valenti—or any of the other Mafia turncoats—and why the government's case was so flimsy. She tried to do that by appealing to commonsense and using some inventive graphic techniques along the way.

There were photographs from forty-three years of surveillance of Asaro by police and the FBI, but not once did they catch him committing any crimes, said Macedonio. Instead, the images showed Asaro getting coffee, kissing people on the street, and sitting at curb side. Macedonio mocked the notion of Asaro being part of a secret society when she reminded the jurors of pictures showing he and his friends openly on the street. There was no crime of guilty by association in the United States, she stressed.

"All of these men are having a big secret meeting and there they are talking to each other, walking up and down the street, walking back and forth. That's the secret society. They came and went as they saw fit. Does any of that make sense to you? Macedonio asked.

There were a few pictures of what the government said was a Bonanno crime family meeting but even when that was shown, Asaro was not there, the lawyer noted. While the FBI watches Mafia funerals and weddings to glean intelligence, the findings were hardly surprising to the lawyer. Asaro did show up at his uncle Michael Zaffarano's funeral but then again that was his uncle. When Cathy Burke showed up at her father's funeral, well what would you expect, that was her father, said the defense attorney.

"The government claims these wakes were important Bonanno family and broader Mafia events. That's absurd. Surveillance photo after surveillance photo, trying to make it appear as if something nefarious was going on at a public wake," Macedonio said as if to mock the government surveillance.

Far from being a loyal mob member, Asaro was a free agent, a rogue who did what he pleased. When he wanted to, Asaro lived outside the roles of the Mafia, and if he associated with people the government said were in organized crime, so what, said Macedonio. It is not a crime to associate with someone the FBI doesn't like.

The lynchpin to the prosecution's case had been Valenti, and Macedonio had to neutralize his testimony. She attempted to do that by showing Valenti (and the other cooperators) were mercenary liars who, even if they had taken dozens of lives, can get a chance at a life outside a jail cell if they tell the government what it wants.

"In fact, the government has become the pension plan for organized-crime figures. When you're down and out, yes, the FBI will always take you and support you," argued Macedonio. "Here's Gaspare Valenti's motto in life: The more you tell them things, you make up stories, you know, they'll give you more money. That's pretty telling, isn't it?"

There were instances where Valenti admitted on the witness stand lying to the FBI to puff up his connections to the mob, and Macedonio reminded the jury about this. By doing so, she was planting the seed in the minds of jurors that even when he had an obligation to be truthful, Valenti could not be relied upon fully.

The defense attorney also underscored that many of the people Valenti had testified about—Jimmy Burke, Paul Vario, Thomas DeSimone, the elder Jerome Asaro, Michael Zaffarano—were all dead and not around to contradict him.

"So, is it any kind of stretch to think that Gaspare Valenti couldn't sit on that stand a couple of days and lie to you? No, not at all. He did it for years," Macedonio argued to the jurors, reminding them of the way he had defaulted on his debts, stolen money, and tried to escape his troubles and family by fleeing to Las Vegas.

Attacks on witness credibility are standard tactics for defense attorneys. But there was specific evidence, particularly about Lufthansa and the Katz murder, that Macedonio had to refute in her summation. Jurors might not like a witness or question motives but in the end, if the testimony was credible, well, the jury still might convict.

In the case of the Katz murder and burial, Macedonio stressed again that there was no one else alive who could verify Valenti's story. The only evidence that Asaro said he and Burke killed Katz came from the mouth of Valenti. But there was also evidence, from Katz's missing person's report, that on the day he disappeared that he went to see fellow criminal Joe Allegro, someone, Macedonio said, there was no evidence Asaro knew.

Picking apart Valenti's claim that he agreed to meet Asaro and Burke on a Sunday at one of his empty model townhouses, Macedonio said that didn't make sense because such a day is a busy day for showing homes to prospective buyers. The defense also pointed out contradictions in what Valenti said on the witness stand and to the FBI about driving with Asaro to get a truck after the burial of Katz's body, the moments when the defendant supposedly blurted out the name of the dead man. While Valenti testified that Asaro blurted out Katz's name and that he had killed him with Burke, notes of FBI agent Mininni indicated that Asaro was not in the vehicle.

"This is a major change because it's that ride that Gaspare . . . that Gaspare Valenti claims that Mr. Asaro told him that he had murdered someone. But that is not what he told the agents," said Macedonio.

The defense attorney also disputed the government's notion that the last conversation Asaro and Valenti had on June 17 indicated that the defendant suddenly knew his cousin was an informant. Instead, contended Macedonio, Asaro is actually telling Valenti that he was in big trouble and not to call him anymore.

Turning to Lufthansa, Macedonio noted how defense witness Kerry Whalen, who admittedly had antipathy toward the FBI, flatly contradicted Valenti about the incident in which Whalen was abducted outside the cargo terminal as the heist occurred. Valenti had testified that he and Frank Burke were in the van and abducted and struck Whalen with a handgun. But Whalen testified that he was certain he identified Sepe and DeSimone as the two men in the van. Whalen had no incentive to lie in the case, argued Macedonio.

She also attempted to make Valenti's claim that Asaro was waiting in a crash car one mile from the airport sound implausible. Since the night of the heist was in the era before cell phones and there was no evidence anyone had walkie-talkies, it seemed crazy that Asaro would have been somehow waiting incommunicado in an area filled with highways to act as a diversion for pursuing cops, said Macedonio.

"Does that make any sense?" the attorney asked.

Macedonio also challenged Valenti's story that some of the cash was hidden in door jambs inside his house. That, she said, didn't make any sense either. Each time he would have needed cash Valenti would have to do construction, something that would be noticed.

"Now, how does that make any sense?" Macedonio again asked.

But Valenti's selling point for the prosecution was that he knew a lot about Lufthansa. How would he know so much if he wasn't involved just like he said he was? Macedonio's answer was that he did know people like Angelo Sepe and Thomas DeSimone, two big players in the heist. It is possible Valenti was involved, she admitted. But the inconsistencies in his story about Asaro made him an unreliable indicator of his cousin's guilt or innocence, she argued.

Asaro did make some comments on tapes, which appear to be circumstantial evidence that he was involved, at least that is what the government argued. But the comments were proof of nothing, said Macedonio. The government also argued that by his silence at times on the recordings that Asaro was admitting complicity in whatever crime was being discussed. It was an argument Macedonio said the prosecution was making out of desperation.

"When the defendant says nothing, that's proof, that's proof he participated. Okay, so now silence is proof beyond a reasonable doubt," she added sarcastically.

The indictment contained numerous charges about loansharking and extortion, but none of the alleged victims, save for John Zaffarano, were called as witnesses, a glaring omission Macedonio pointed out. And when Zaffarano took the stand he didn't help the government's case.

"And what did he tell you? He told you he wasn't a victim of loansharking or extortion," said Macedonio.

"The bigger picture here, quite frankly, is that the government took anything that they could that had to do with money and through Gaspare Valenti, made it sound like Mr. Asaro was extorting everybody, but that's simply not the case," Macedonio argued.

In closing, Macedonio didn't back away from Asaro's prior cartheft-ring conviction, his ill-tempered remarks, and weird lifestyle. He marched to his own drummer and wasn't a loyal mob operative, she said. Sometimes the government gets it wrong. Take away Gaspare Valenti and Asaro wouldn't be found guilty of anything, the attorney said.

Macedonio's summation was only about two hours long, a welcomed change from the nearly full-day presentation made by Cooley. As is the practice, the government got a chance to offer a rebuttal and Argentieri spoke this time, arguing that indeed other witnesses did corroborate Valenti's version of the Lufthansa heist. She pointed out Vitale's recollection about taking Massino to pick up heist jewelry from Asaro and the testimony of Ruggiano, whose father admitted fencing some of the jewels through his Manhattan store.

Asaro may think he was a guy who marched to his own drum, but he was still part of the band—the Bonanno crime family, the prosecutor insisted.

It was after lunch that Ross charged the jury on the federal law that would control the deliberations. To the layman, sitting through a jury charge can be as tedious as watching paint dry. But a good charge is like a Rosetta Stone for jurors, guiding them through the deliberations by giving them the law that the facts have to fit when they weigh a defendant's fate. It only took Ross about ninety minutes to read the instructions, and then she had the jurors retire to begin their deliberations. They only had about an hour left for business on November 9, not enough time to decide anything important, before they went home.

CHAPTER TWENTY-TWO
"FREE!"

IT WAS ABOUT 2:55 P.M. ON NOVEMBER 12, 2015, that word began to spread like wildfire in the Brooklyn federal courthouse that a verdict had been reached in the case of Vincent Asaro. Reporters scurried to the eighth-floor courtroom of Judge Ross, followed quickly by the prosecution and defense teams. Not counting the one hour or so the jury had deliberated on November 9, the panel had been at work for about fifteen hours deliberating the case. That was not a very long time. In criminal cases, a quick verdict can mean either that evidence of guilt was overwhelming and easily decided or that the case didn't convince anyone about the defendant's guilt. It is hard to tell with a jury.

There was an indication that the jury was having trouble when the panel asked in a note if they could have copies of the summations. That is not allowed under the law but the fact that the jurors needed to hear all the closing arguments again suggested they were confused about how to sort out the evidence. But after that, things seem to settle down. Still, such a quick verdict in such a complicated case was puzzling.

After the courtroom filled up and Ross was on the bench, Asaro, wearing a charcoal gray sweater and dark slacks, was brought out from the holding cell. His face didn't betray any emotion, but he seemed resigned to hear his fate. He was rubbing his hands together as if he might have freshened up in the back cell with a hand sanitizer. Just before 2:58 P.M., the jury trooped into the courtroom. There were twelve of them, and it was impossible to detect in their faces and body language any hint about how they had decided. Macedonio glanced over at the prosecution table and she saw stress on Argentieri's face.

"Let me before I go any further just assure myself, is your verdict unanimous?" Ross asked.

"Yes," replied the jury foreman.

Ross was given the six-page verdict and read through it rather quickly, very quickly.

From the way Ross seemed to go fast through the six pages, which contained fourteen racketeering acts for the first count of the indictment including Lufthansa and the Katz murder, Macedonio believed that the defense didn't just win a few counts, it had won them all. Sometimes courtroom deputies ask the jurors to announce their verdict. But in this case, Ross herself asked the jury foreman the questions everyone wanted the answers to. She handed the pages back to the foreman. The courtroom was deadly quiet as Ross spoke.

"As to count one of the indictment, racketeering conspiracy under federal law, how do you find the defendant, guilty or not guilty?" Ross asked.

"Not guilty," the jury foreman answered.

There was a gasp from some in the audience. Did we hear that right? The acoustics in the courtroom weren't the greatest, but it sounded liked "not guilty." With an acquittal on the racketeering count, the jury didn't have to say if the separate racketeering acts— including Lufthansa, the Katz murder, the Zaffarano property extortion—had been proven or not proven. They were now all irrelevant. The big heist, the subject of so much media hype and attention, had been tossed out by the jury.

Ross then asked the jury about counts two and three, which involved an extortion conspiracy over the collection of a debt and the actual collection of that debt. The jury foreman had the same answer, erasing any doubt about what everyone had heard a moment earlier, "Not Guilty."

There was stunned silence in the courtroom. Asaro had a blank look on his face and started to look around. First left, then right. He was confused. Since the indictment contained so many racketeering acts, Asaro expected a much longer verdict reading. He didn't hear what had happened and didn't know he had won a rare victory. Finally, Asaro turned to his left and asked his paralegal Sam Tureff what the hell was going on. With a smile on his face, Tureff leaned closer to Asaro and told him. Asaro turned to Macedonio for confirmation, and she told him the same thing.

"That's it, not guilty, you are going home," she told him.

It was as if Asaro had a surge of electricity jolt through his body. His eyes suddenly shot wide open, and he slapped his hands with glee on the table in front of him. Jumping up out of his seat, saying "I can't fucking believe it!" Asaro embraced Macedonio and planted a kiss on her lips and then made as if he was going to walk right out of the courtroom until the federal marshals restrained him and had him sit down.

Ross said she didn't think it necessary to poll the jury panel and took the verdict sheet back, thanking the jurors for what she said had not been an easy trial. She then dismissed them, with the remark, "Have a nice rest of the week."

After Ross thanked and dismissed the panel, she had one more piece of business, to dismiss the alternate jurors who had been kept apart from the regular panel during the deliberations. She told Asaro and everyone else to sit down.

"Thank you very much!" Asaro exclaimed.

Over at the crestfallen prosecution table, Argentieri's stomach felt like it had dropped to the floor. She and her co-counsels, as well as FBI agents Ypelaar and Mininni, gathered up their files and walked out the courtroom door. They said nothing. Some of their colleagues seated in the public gallery and who were likely expecting a quick conviction in the year's biggest criminal trial looked like someone had just shot their pet dog.

With reporters tweeting the verdict back to their newsrooms, word of the acquittal shot around the world almost instantly. News camera crews had already been staking out the courthouse at Cadman Plaza East, but as word spread of Asaro's astonishing victory, more cameras rushed to the courthouse. It would take about a half hour for Asaro to be finally discharged by the marshals so he could walk out the door, a man who for the first time in seventeen months could sleep in his own bed. With Macedonio smiling to his right and Ferrone beaming to his left, Asaro looked at the gaggle of reporters and smiled.

"Free!" said an exuberant Asaro, holding his arms wide as if to signal a touchdown.

Stepping to a microphone stand set up by reporters, Asaro had each of his arms around his attorneys as he gave a short, celebratory statement.

"I want to thank my two lawyers. Without them I wouldn't be here now. I'd like to thank the U.S. Marshals Service for treating me great," said Asaro, referring to the people who specially arranged to drive him to court each morning.

"I can't say the same for the FBI," he added.

Anxious to get her client on his way, Macedonio told the reporters that Asaro wanted to go home and spend Thanksgiving with his family.

"I've got two years here, and I am dying to get home," added Asaro.

As he walked across Cadman Plaza Park, followed by a troop of reporters and cameras, Asaro admitted that "I was shocked, really shocked" at the verdict, an indication that he had been resigned to defeat.

"After two years it feels great, two years in here for nothing. I should have never got arrested," Asaro told the reporters who walked with him across the plaza.

A white sedan was waiting for Asaro and his lawyers at Cadman Plaza West. As Sam Tureff opened the trunk to place in some legal briefcases, Asaro couldn't resist a bit of strange, mob humor for the benefit of the press. It seemed his way of mocking the government for attempting to portray him as a homicidal monster.

"Hey Sam, make sure they don't see the body in the trunk!" quipped Asaro.

* * *

After the verdict, Asaro was driven to a daughter's home in Frank-
lin Square, Long Island, where a meal of spaghetti and clams awaited
him. It never tasted better. Meanwhile, Argentieri, Cooley, Gerdes
and the rest of the prosecution team repaired to the local O'Keefe's
Restaurant on Court Street in Brooklyn Heights to lick their wounds,
commiserate, and try to figure out what had happened in a case that
could have been a crowning moment in their careers if they had won.

The government lawyers weren't the only ones scratching their
heads over the acquittal. Since the jury was anonymous and elected
not to talk with reporters after the verdict, the true reasons for the
decision would likely remain unknown forever. But there were plenty
of theories, some more plausible than others and many revolving
around the way the case was constructed by the government.

On the street, according to one source familiar with the world of
organized crime, some in the Bonanno crime family speculated that
somehow Asaro must have compromised the jury. There had been a
case in the past with the late John Gotti where jurors were tampered
with. But with Asaro that theory is about as far-fetched as they
come. Even if he wanted to, Asaro didn't have the money or the
help to pay off anybody and the federal government had learned,
after the Gotti experience, to be extra careful and use anonymous
juries in mob cases.

The indictment against Asaro was a complicated one in that it involved, along with the Lufthansa heist and the Katz murder, various
extortion, arson, attempted murder, and other charges. The charges
spanned different periods of time, and, aside from claims that they
were all part of the racketeering activities of the Bonanno crime
family, they didn't seem to have any significant connection. The indictment seemed like a hodge-podge. Prosecutors like to bring in
enough charges to prove their case, but with Asaro it might have
been overkill. As the case was presented by the government, it may
have been just too confusing for the jury to keep straight and to accept that the allegations were all part of some big picture. It was
also telling, as Macedonio pointed out in her summation, that no al-

leged extortion victims apart from John Zaffarano were called as a prosecution witness.

Defense attorney Steven Zissou, who followed the trial closely after his client DiFiore pleaded guilty, believed that an earlier decision by Ross to sever Asaro's co-defendants from his case may have affected the courtroom dynamic, which worked in the elderly gangster's favor. At trial, the jury only saw Asaro, who with his spectacles, winter sweaters, and slender frame didn't seem to be a very threatening person—certainly not your stereotypical gangster type. But had some of Asaro's co-defendants been on trial with him, such as his son and the more physically imposing John Ragano, the jury might have had a different vibe, Zissou said.

The case largely rose or fell with Gaspare Valenti. The government likes cooperating witnesses because they were close to the action and could testify about their first-hand observations. Valenti was the key, and if he was believable, then his cousin was dead in the water. But the defense chipped away at his credibility in summation, planting the seed of reasonable doubt by bringing up inconsistencies and implausibility. Was it enough to finally sway the jury? Perhaps.

Valenti swore to tell the truth, something underscored by the fact that his agreement with the government and his future freedom largely turned on the fact that prosecutors had to be convinced that he never lied. But Valenti's rendition of the Lufthansa heist was unexpected by veteran lawyers and prosecutors who had followed the case. It has been said before but worth repeating that Asaro's name never came up in Henry Hill's public version of the heist and its participants, although in fact Hill was nowhere near the airport when it happened. Yet, Hill did tell investigators that Asaro was present during planning sessions at Robert's Lounge and claimed he was near the airport with Burke when the robbery took place. For legal reasons related to the rules of hearsay evidence, the jury never did learn during the trial of Hill's allegations about Asaro. Left only with Valenti's version of events—all the other heist participants were dead—the jury was unconvinced that he was telling the truth beyond a reasonable doubt.

The bigger problem with Valenti may have been his mercenary motive for deciding to cooperate. He received over $175,000 in living expenses, which to jurors who are working people just might have been offensive to their sensibilities. The other witnesses like Sal Vitale and Peter Zuccaro had a different kind of baggage. They had admitted to killing numerous people, sometimes in the most cold-blooded fashion. Where was the equity, jurors could ask themselves, in convicting a broke old man like Asaro while those killers walk around as free men? Those cooperators had been pretty bad as gangsters, and was this case then just an argument about whether old man Asaro was worse? He hardly had the body count to his credit to prove it. In fact, it seemed doubtful from the testimony that Asaro really did admit to Valenti that he actually killed Paul Katz, the one and only homicide alleged in the indictment.

This was not the first time prosecutors in Brooklyn federal court had lost a case against a mob figure despite having some impressive Mafia turncoats as witnesses. Over three years earlier, jurors acquitted reputed mob associate Francis "B.H." Guerra of double murder, extortion, and assault charges and then reputed Genovese crime family captain Anthony Romanello of extortion charges. In both those cases, the defense attorney was Gerald McMahon, who for a brief period represented Asaro early in his case. To McMahon's way of thinking, the jurors were getting tired of the way mob rats were getting deals to testify against others, and it was time for prosecutors to start thinking about how they use such cooperators. If true, this was a nuance that appears to have escaped the prosecution, which put its money on Valenti.

In American jurisprudence there is the concept of jury nullification. Essentially, nullification means that evidence and law be damned, the jury still won't find a defendant guilty. It may be that the jury doesn't like the law or it doesn't like the result that will occur if they follow the judge's instructions. Legal scholars point out that during Prohibition juries refused to enforce statutes controlling alcohol. One of the best-know nullification cases was that of John Peter Zenger, who was acquitted in 1733 of what amounted to criminal libel in Colonial New York.

Jurors in Vincent Asaro's trial were able to look at him for the four weeks he sat opposite them in the courtroom. They heard the evidence, listened to his sad-sack complaints on Valenti's recordings about how life had passed him by and how he didn't have two nickels to rub together. If Asaro was once a big gangster, the eighty-year-old in the courtroom on trial for a nearly forty-year-old crime, didn't seem like a threat to anybody. Why should he bear responsibility for Lufthansa when all those also involved—even more significantly involved—had escaped being held accountable? For all anybody knows, that could have been the thing that decided the case for the anonymous jurors.

EPILOGUE

THE FIRST THING I NOTICED as I walked up the front steps of the house in Ozone Park was the small patriotic sign visible in one of the windows of the door: "God Bless America." Given what the occupants of the house had gone through in recent months at the hands of the federal government, the sentiment was not one I had expected to see. I had tracked Vincent Asaro to this two-story frame house after going to his old address in Howard Beach and finding out he had moved from there some time ago.

It was an early July evening, and I had in my hand a one-page note I had typed. Through his attorney, Asaro had expressed the sentiment that he wanted to talk about his feelings, particularly as they related to Joseph Massino and Gaspare Valenti. But for reasons that he didn't want to explain, Asaro felt he couldn't talk to me. Nevertheless, I figured a visit might change his mind, even if only briefly.

Asaro lived in the three-bedroom home, built around 1935, with his girlfriend Michele. The dwelling was a detached structure that was typical for this middle-class area of Queens. The neighborhood was not far from Liberty Avenue and over the years had mirrored the ethnic changes in the borough, going from a mix of Italian, Irish, and German families to inclusion of more immigrants from the Caribbean and Latin America.

Michelle answered the door, and I asked for Vincent. She indicated he wasn't around so I told her I had a letter.

"I can take it," she said. Michele was a mature, well-groomed woman with short-cut blond hair. She had a slender face and friendly eyes, which looked at me with curiosity. I had recognized her from court, and I knew when she took the letter that I had the right house.

As she spoke, I heard the sounds of a man's voice coming from the enclosed area of the porch. She handed him the envelope. I moved and looked inside, and there was Vincent Asaro. He seemed taller than I remembered him being. He was dressed in a freshly pressed white short-sleeved shirt and blue Bermuda shorts—it was summertime after all. The day he was acquitted, he was all smiles and buoyant. But today, he seemed thinner, and his face was lined with concern. He seemed surprised to see me, but there was a flash of recognition, likely from the way I had shadowed him during his triumphant walk from the courthouse last November.

"How did you treat me?" he asked with a smile, referring to my news stories.

"I treated you fine," I responded, knowing that he must have seen my story reporting his courtroom victory.

I also reminded him that his attorney had told me of his declining to talk. The letter, I said, explained that I was respecting his decision and hoped he would reconsider. Asaro used his thin fingers to open the envelope. As Michele and I watched him, the only sound was the crinkling of the paper as he held it in his hands. I figured at his age and with the low light in the foyer that he might need my reading glasses. But Asaro had no trouble, and he read the note carefully for what seemed like an eternity. He folded the paper up carefully, placed it in the envelope, and looked at me.

"I'm sorry, I mean no disrespect, but I just can't talk," he said.

From years of experience as a reporter, I knew it was often a long shot to show up at someone's home to get them to talk. I already was told he didn't want to say anything. But sometimes in these situations a person, seeing a sympathetic face, might have a change of heart or at least say something. Asaro did not disappoint.

Gaspare Valenti's decision to become a turncoat hurt Asaro. My presence on the front steps brought back memories of his cousin's actions and seemed to enrage Asaro.

"I will say this," said Asaro. "He lied through his teeth."

As he spoke, Asaro's eyes flashed open with anger, and he was chomping at the bit, ready to explode. Along with the anger, I sensed a great deal of hurt with him. Gaspare had been his life-long friend, and in the gangster life they had once chosen together, becoming a rat was still a curse.

"They bought Gasper for $6,000 a month," Asaro continued.

He was referring to the money the government had paid for Valenti's subsistence during the eight years he had been cooperating with the FBI. The prosecution did admit to $3,000 a month, although security costs were extra. No matter what the amount, it was all blood money as far as Asaro was concerned.

Although he didn't name her, Asaro inveighed against Argentieri for going after him for an old state case in which he had paid his dues.

"She tried to frame me on a case I did five years on," opined Asaro, referring to the old state court auto-theft case involving Guy Gralto in which he was convicted and sent to state prison. One of the quirks in the federal law is that even though someone is convicted of a crime in state court, the FBI can use the old crimes to prosecute somebody for a conspiracy to commit that same offense, even roll it into a larger racketeering case. So, in effect, a person can be convicted for the same acts twice. While a permissible legal tactic, to Asaro the dredging up of the old crime he thought he paid his debt to society for was unconscionable. Only Asaro knows what he did or didn't do in his life. But in terms of his Lufthansa case, he has that six-page verdict sheet that he can show everybody and argue his innocence.

As Asaro spoke, Michele sensed his excitement, and she stretched out her hand and touched his chest. The action seemed as much to keep him from raising his blood pressure as it was to console him. Asaro already had heart issues. Her gesture was tender. Whatever their relationship, she seemed genuinely concerned about him.

"I have a lot on my mind," Asaro finally confessed as he quieted down. "My sister is sick."

Asaro glanced down as he spoke about her, although it wasn't clear how seriously she was ill. With all of his old friends either dead or having turned against him, Asaro's social circle had narrowed more and more. There was still Michele, his daughters, and his sister. But the loss of even one person now seemed too much for him to think about. As I looked at him, I saw the old man the jury had seen. Maybe it was right that they decided to let him have his freedom.

There was one more shot from Asaro. The government witnesses had all sorts of homicides to their credit. Sal Vitale. Andy Ruggiano. Peter Zuccaro. They were all admitted killers. Where is the fairness in that? Asaro asked as he clicked off their names.

It was time for me to go. Asaro asked me what the title of the book was and he smiled when I told him. I asked him what he had for that first dinner after his acquittal, and he told me about the spaghetti and clams. We all shook hands, and I watched Asaro go back into the house.

"I really can't talk," he repeated.

As I walked to my car, I realized that Asaro was living in what for him was the old neighborhood. To the south, about a mile away, was Jimmy Burke's old club. To the north, beyond Liberty Avenue by just a few blocks was John Gotti's old Bergin Hunt and Fish Club. On Valenti's recordings, Asaro lamented about the old street life, when Gotti reigned supreme on 101st Avenue, Jimmy Burke lorded over the crew at Robert's Lounge on Lefferts Boulevard, and the Bonanno crime family was the one borgata in the city the federal government couldn't touch. Times had changed. The city had changed. The mob had changed with its notion of *omertà* torn to shreds.

Vincent Asaro's world was now one where the people on the streets of Ozone Park were more likely to have come from the Punjab than Palermo, and the food served at Burke's old saloon was West Indian roti bread and not ravioli with marinara sauce. At least it was a world within which Asaro could walk around a free man. It was also his choice to accept the way things had become—or not—and daydream about the way life once was.

LUFTHANSA ROLL CALL

(as of July 1, 2016)

Nicole Argentieri (federal prosecutor) She became head of the public corruption unit of the Brooklyn U.S. Attorney's Office.

Jerome Asaro (Bonanno soldier and father of Vincent) He died in 1977. His place of interment is unknown.

Jerome Asaro (Bonanno captain and son of Vincent Asaro) He is currently serving a ninety-month sentence after pleading guilty to federal racketeering charges in 2014. He is serving his sentence in Schuylkill Federal Correctional Institution and is scheduled for release on August 6, 2020.

Vincent Asaro (Bonanno captain) He is living in the Ozone Park area after winning a verdict of acquittal in November 2015 in his federal trial on charges stemming from the Lufthansa heist, the murder of Paul Katz, and other crimes.

Vincent Basciano (Bonanno captain) He is serving a life sentence for a federal racketeering conviction in 2011 in which he was spared the death penalty. Basciano originally began serving his sentence in the high-security section of ADX Florence in Colorado. He is not eligible for parole but in 2015 was moved from the "Supermax" section of the prison to less-stringent living conditions, which allow him a cellmate and other privileges.

Janet Barbieri (girlfriend and government witness) She testified at the 1979 trial of her then-boyfriend Louis Werner for his complicity in the Lufthansa heist. Her whereabouts are unknown.

Catherine Burke (daughter of James Burke) She is living in Howard Beach and is married to imprisoned Bonanno captain Anthony "Bruno" Indelicato. She has never been charged with any crimes.

Francis Frank Burke (son of James Burke, Lufthansa participant, mob associate) He was killed in a drug dispute in 1987. He is buried next to his father.

James "Jimmy The Gent" Burke (gangster) The father of Catherine Burke and Francis Burke, he was never charged in connection with the Lufthansa heist but was convicted in 1984 on state charges for the killing of James Eaton. Burke was also convicted on federal charges in 1985 for the Boston College point-shaving scandal. Burke died in state prison in 1996 from cancer. He is buried in St. Charles Cemetery, East Farmingdale, New York. Burke's character, known as "Jimmy Conway," was played by Robert DeNiro in the film *GoodFfellas*.

Louis Cafora (mob associate) He was part of the planning and preparation for the Lufthansa heist. He and his wife Joanne went missing in March 1979 and are presumed dead.

Steve Carbone (FBI case agent) He was one of the lead investigating FBI agents on the heist investigation. He retired from the FBI and is living in Florida and New York.

Alicyn Cooley (prosecutor) She is a federal prosecutor in the Brooklyn U.S. Attorney's Office.

Thomas DeSimone (gangster and Lufthansa participant) He disappeared in January 1979 and is believed to have been murdered by the Lucchese crime family at the behest of the Gambino crime family in retaliation for his slaying of crime-family soldier William "Bill Batts" Benventa. DeSimone's character was played by Joe Pesce in the film *GoodFellas,* for which he won a 1991 Academy Award for best supporting actor. DeSimone's body has never been found.

Richard Eaton (mob associate) He was a member of Burke's crew of gangsters. After blowing over $300,000 in money Burke had earmarked for a drug deal, Eaton was killed by Burke and Sepe. His body was found frozen in a desolate area of Brooklyn.

Parnell "Stacks" Edwards (mob associate and Lufthansa heist accomplice) He was a part-time musician and thief who was shot dead around December 18, 1979, by DeSimone and Sepe after screwing up and not disposing of the getaway van used in the heist as well as shooting his mouth off about the heist. Cops found the van and started tracing evidence found with the vehicle. Actor Samuel L. Jackson played Edwards's character in the film *GoodFellas*.

Diane Ferrone (defense attorney) She maintains an active criminal defense practice in Manhattan.

William Fischetti (friend of Louis Werner) He cooperated with the government and testified as a government witness in the 1979 trial that led to Werner's conviction.

Lindsay Gerdes (prosecutor) She continues to handle organized-crime cases for the Brooklyn U.S. Attorney's Office.

Peter Gruenewald (airport worker and Lufthansa conspirator) He cooperated with the government and testified against Louis Werner in his 1979 federal trial for aiding in the Lufthansa heist. His whereabouts are unknown.

Henry Hill (drug dealer, hijacker, mob associate) He became a major government witness against Burke and others. He was the subject of Nicholas Pileggi's book *Wiseguys*. Hill died in 2012 before publication of the book about his role in the Lufthansa heist he co-authored with Daniel Simone. Actor Ray Liotta played Hill in the film *GoodFellas*.

Karen Hill (wife of Henry Hill) She and Hill divorced in 2002 and she reportedly uses her witness protection identity to shield herself. Karen Hill was played by Lorraine Bracco in the film *GoodFellas*.

Anthony "Bruno" Indelicato (Bonanno soldier) He is currently serving a twenty-year sentence after pleading guilty in 2008 to a count of racketeering, conspiracy to commit murder, and a charge of conspiracy to sell marijuana. He is scheduled for release in September 2023.

Martin Krugman (mob associate) He owned men's hair-piece retailer For Men Only and was also a bookmaker. Krugman disappeared in January 1979, a month after the Lufthansa heist. He served as the intermediary between Louis Werner and the Robert's Lounge crew, which pulled off the airport robbery. Krugman, who is believed to have been killed and dismembered by James Burke, was declared legally dead in 1986. His character, known as Morris Kessler in the film *GoodFellas*, was played by Chuck Low.

Stephen Laifer (defense attorney) He continued to practice criminal law in Brooklyn after defending Louis Werner. Laifer died in September 1979, a few months after the verdict in the Werner trial.

Paolo Licastri (Bonanno associate, Lufthansa heist participant) He was found murdered in a vacant lot in Brooklyn in June 1983.

Elizabeth Macedonio (defense attorney) She maintains an active criminal-defense practice in Manhattan.

Edward McDonald (prosecutor) He went on after the Lufthansa investigation to lead the Brooklyn Organized Crime Strike Force for the federal government. As a prosecutor, he secured a number of major convictions, including those of Bronx Congressman Mario Biaggi and Brooklyn Democratic Leader Meade Esposito, as well as that of New Jersey Senator Harrison Williams in the Abscam case. He left government service in 1989 and eventually became a partner at the Manhattan law firm of Dechert LLP. He was representing former Bonanno crime boss Joseph Massino at the time he decided to cooperate with the FBI. McDonald played himself in the film *GoodFellas*.

Robert "Frenchy" McMahon (mob associate) He took part in the Lufthansa heist and was found murdered in Brooklyn on May 16, 1979.

Joseph Manri (mob associate) He took part in the Lufthansa heist and was found murdered with McMahon on May 16, 1979.

Joseph Massino (former Bonanno crime family boss) He became a government witness in July 2004 following his federal racketeering conviction for among other things six gangland murders. Massino was released from prison in the summer of 2013 and is currently living in the federal witness protection program. While expected to be called as a witness in the Asaro trial, the government opted not to use him.

Frank Menna (businessman) He had occasionally gambled and introduced Louis Werner to Krugman who functioned as a bookmaker. Krugman eventually introduced Werner to Burke's Lufthansa gang. His whereabouts are unknown.

Adam Mininni (FBI agent) He is currently assigned to the FBI office in New York City.

Daniel Rizzo (Lucchese crime family member and heist participant) He was sentenced in 1999 to thirty months in federal prison and fined $5,000 for extortion in the New York garment district. He died shortly before Asaro's October 2015 trial where he was named in testimony by witness Gaspare Valenti as being one of the Lufthansa heist participants.

Vincent Santa (associate of James Burke) He was a former NYPD cop who left the department under a cloud. Santa was known on the street as "Jimmy Santos." He is said to have been a major link between Burke and corrupt cops who passed along law-enforcement information and the names of informants, allegedly for a price. Prosecutors said he died in the 1990s.

Angelo Sepe (Lufthansa heist participant) He was a member of Burke's crew and also is believed to have taken part in the murder of Richard Eaton. Sepe was found shot to death in the basement of an apartment in Brooklyn on July 18, 1984, along with girlfriend Joanne Lombardo, eighteen. His place of interment is unknown.

Gaspare Valenti (mob associate) He decided to turn his back on the mob life and became a government informant against his cousin Vincent Asaro. Valenti testified at Asaro's 2015 trial about his alleged involvement in the Lufthansa heist and the murder of mob associate Paul Katz. Valenti is now living in the witness security program and awaiting sentence for earlier federal crimes.

Paul Vario (Lucchese captain and consiglieri) He died in federal prison in May 1988 where he had been serving a sentence for racketeering. He is buried in St. John Cemetery in Middle Village, New

York. Actor Paul Sorvino played Vario's character, known as Paul Cicero, in the film *GoodFellas*.

Louis Werner (Lufthansa heist conspirator) He was the only person ever convicted of involvement in the Lufthansa heist for his role as an inside man who gave crucial information to the robbers. He was convicted in May 1979, sentenced to fifteen years in prison and then cooperated with the government, which relocated him. Werner married his girlfriend Janet Barbieri. He is reported to have died in 2007.

Robert Ypelaar (FBI agent) He remains a special agent with the Federal Bureau of Investigation.

John Zaffarano (son of Michael Zaffarano, cousin of Vincent Asaro) Along with his mother, he inherited his father's sizeable estate after his father died in 1980. He decided to sell his father's Times Square area real estate and related holdings for $18.5 million. He is now living in Florida and testified in the trial of Vincent Asaro.

Michael Zaffarano (Bonanno crime family captain) He was Asaro's uncle and a major mob player in the pornographic film business from the 1960s until his death of a heart attack during an FBI raid at his Times Square area office in 1980.

Peter Zuccaro (former Gambino associate) He was released in the summer of 2012 after serving a federal sentence of eight years and one day. He is currently in the witness relocation program and has testified in a number of major Mafia trials, including those of John A. Gotti, Charles Carneglia, and Dominick Pizzonia.

NOTES

Chapter One, The Message from the Bones

The bulk of the material for this chapter comes from the testimony of forensic anthropologist Bradley Adams in the trial of *U.S. v. Vincent Asaro*, 14-CR-26 (EDNY). In addition, Mr. Adams recounted in an interview with the author his experience in the June 2013 dig in the basement of the house on 102nd Road in Ozone Park, which uncovered the remains of Paul Katz. The author also examined crime-scene photos of the dig site showing, among other things, the bones as they were found.

Chapter Two, "The Feds Are All Over . . ."

Details of Gaspare Valenti's thoughts and actions are contained in his testimony in the trial of Vincent Asaro as well as that of FBI agents Robert Yeplaar and Adam Mininni. See trial record and case file in *U.S. v. Asaro* 14-CR-26 (EDNY). Author also interviewed attorney Scott Fenstermaker, who represented Valenti.

Chapter Three, A Goodfella's Lament

See case file in *U.S. v. Asaro* 14-CR-26 (EDNY). The early history of Vincent Asaro and his father Jerome Asaro can be seen in articles published about Jerome in *The Brooklyn Daily Eagle, The Brooklyn Eagle, The Long Island Star Journal*, and *The New York Times*. Vincent Asaro's earlier criminal record is contained in court filings in *U.S. v. Asaro*. Government and police documents detail the meetings of the Bonanno crime family in the 1990s, as well as reports of bodies buried in the basement of Robert's Lounge. Details of the arraignment of the defendants in the 2014 Lufthansa case are contained in the court transcript. The U.S. Attorney's Office for The Eastern District of New York published a news release about the arrests in the Asaro case. The post-arraignment comments of defense attorney Gerald McMahon are found in *The Daily News* and *New York Post*.

Chapter Four, "Super Thief"

Robert Cudak's testimony is contained in *Hearings Before the Permanent Subcommittee on Investigations of the Committee of Government Operations, Organized Crime: Stolen Securities, Part 1*, Ninety-Second Congress, First Session. June 8–10 and 16, 1971. Cudak's testimony was also reported in *The New York Times*, as was the testimony of Cosmos Cangiano. The history of John F. Kennedy International Airport is found in *The New York Times* and the website of The Port Authority of New York and New Jersey. The battle over whether the New York Waterfront Commission should take over policing of cargo activity at the airports was chronicled in *The New York Times* from 1968 to 1972.

Chapter Five, "We Will Get You"

Material for this chapter is found in the case file of *U.S. v. Thomas DeSimone*, 73-CR-336 (EDNY), *U.S. v. James Burke et. al.*, 74-CR-623 (EDNY). Also see *Wiseguy* by Nicholas Pileggi for Henry Hill's comments and observations.

Chapter Six, Tales of the Gold Bug

Attorney Joel Winograd, who represented Paul Vario for many years, provided perspective on his client's life in several interviews. Details about the ownership of Geffken's bar can be found in New York City property records. Vario's early criminal record and rape case was written about in detail in *The Long Island Daily Press* and *The Leader-Observer* (Queens) in the years 1937 to 1940. Former Brooklyn District Attorney Charles J. Hynes was interviewed by email about the genesis of the Gold Bug investigation. The Gold Bug case results, including the prosecution of certain NYPD police officers, was reported extensively in *The New York Times*, as well as in *Newsweek* and *Time* magazines.

Chapter Seven, "I Got a Couple of Million"

Information in this chapter comes from the case file and testimony in *U.S. v. Louis Werner, 79 US 89* (EDNY).

Chapter Eight, The Ring

Information in this chapter comes from the trial record of *U.S. v. Werner*. In addition, it comes from Hill's recollections in the books *Wiseguy* by Pileggi and *The Great Lufthansa Heist*, which Hill co-authored with Dan Simone. The author also had access to previously undisclosed NYPD and other law-enforcement files.

Chapter Nine, "My God, You Lost Millions"

The recollections of witnesses to events surrounding and during the heist are contained in the trial transcripts of *U.S. v. Werner*. DeSimone's excited statement about finding the cash is found in the trial transcript of *U.S. v. Asaro*. Kerry Whalen's account of his actions and life story are contained in his book, *Inside the Lufthansa Hei$t: The FBI Lied*. Contemporary news accounts of the heist are found in *The New York Times*, *The Daily News*, *Newsday*, and the *New York Post*.

Chapter Ten, The Friends Who Hurt You

Details of the approach of Paul Vario by the FBI were provided by his attorney Joel Winograd. Other persons who were interviewed and provided information for this chapter were Steve Carbone and Edward McDonald. Court records consulted were those in the case file of *U.S. v. Werner*. NYPD files made available to the author contain details of some of the murders of the Lufthansa participants. Details of the incident where Gruenewald and Werner confronted each other in the Brooklyn Strike Force offices are contained in Pileggi's book *Wiseguy*. Newspapers consulted for this chapter were the *The New York Times* and *Newsday*.

Chapter Eleven, "See, Big Mouth"

Most of the information for this chapter came from the case file of *U.S. v. Werner*. Additional information was found in summaries of debriefings of Henry Hill in NYPD and other law-enforcement files.

Chapter Twelve, Dead Fellas . . . and Gals

Information for this chapter came from the case file of *U.S. v. Asaro* and the docket sheet of *U.S. v. Salvatore Santoro, 85-CR-100 (EDNY)*. Also consulted was the case file of *People v. Burke*, Indictment 395-84, Brooklyn State Supreme Court. Additional matter was found in Pileggi's *Wiseguy*, *The New York Times* and *Newsday*. *The New York Times* was relied upon for information about the Boston College basketball point shaving case. Those interviewed were Ed McDonald and Steve Carbone. Information about Vario's and Burke's interments can be found on the website for FindaGrave.

Chapter Thirteen, The Shakedown Guy

Details of the state criminal case against Vincent Asaro are found in a November 19, 1998, news release about his conviction from the Queens County district attorney's office; articles about the trial in *The New York Times* and New York *Daily News*; Guy Gralto's experiences with the stolen car and chop-shop business is contained in testimony contained in *U.S. v. Trucchio* 03-CR-60267 (SDFL) as well as testimony in *U.S. v. Asaro*. A law-enforcement official provided additional details about Gralto's activities and about Asaro's conviction. Information about Paul Castellano's involvement in a different car-theft ring can be found in *The New York Times*; the author covered part of the trial involving Castellano's co-defendants in 1986.

Chapter Fourteen, "We're in Trouble"

Details of the arrest of Joseph Massino and events following it in January 2003 can be found in the author's book *King of the God-fathers: "Big Joey" Massino and the Fall of the Bonanno Crime Family*. Details of the infamous rape and assault case at the Sea Crest Diner can be found in *The New York Times* and *Newsday*. Information about the organization of the Bonanno crime family in the early 1990s and the transcripts of taped conversations related in this chapter were prepared in the cases of *U.S. v. Massino* and *U.S. v. Basciano* and made available to the author. Government documents concerning the statements of various government witnesses were also made available to the author.

Chapter Fifteen, Never Say Never

Much of the information contained in this chapter can be found in the documents filed in *U.S. v. Asaro*. Defense attorney Steven Zissou gave the author a number of interviews and related details of defense strategy. Details of the sentencing of Jerome Asaro can be found in the case file for *U.S. v. Asaro* and stories in the *Daily News*.

Chapter Sixteen, Dead Men Told No Tales

See case file and related documents in *U.S. v. Asaro*. Elizabeth Macedonio also was interviewed on a number of occasions by the author.

Chapter Seventeen, "Score of Scores"

Biographical information about Judge Allyne Ross is found in her official biography found at www.edny7.uscourts.gov and at www.wikipedia.com; biographical information about Nicole Argentieri, Alicyn Cooley, Leslie Gerges, Elizabeth Macedonio, and Diane Ferrone is found in the attorney directory of the New York State Office of Court Administration, www.linkedin.com, www.google.com, www.wikipedia.com, and the websites of the private attorneys. Diane Ferrone also was interviewed by the author. The opening statements are found in the trial transcript of *U.S. v. Asaro*.

Chapter Eighteen, "Come Dressed"

Information about Valenti's testimony is found in the trial transcript of *U.S. v. Asaro*. Intelligence information about the death of Paul Katz, the way James Burke paid his way out of an arrest and investigations into allegations of police corruption and misconduct related to the Katz case is found in law-enforcement files reviewed by the author.

Chapter Nineteen, "This Is It"

See trial transcript of Valenti's testimony in *U.S. v. Asaro*.

Chapter Twenty, All in the Family

See trial transcript of Valenti's testimony in *U.S. v. Asaro*. Information about Anthony Valenti was provided by stories in *The Daily News* and a video clip found at www.youtube.com. The author's story in *Newsday* about the property deals surrounding the estate of Michael Zaffarano detailed the negotiations and money raised in the transactions. See trial transcript of the testimony of Kerry Whalen and Carmine Muscarella in *U.S. v. Asaro*.

Chapter Twenty-one, "What Is This, Watergate?"

See trial transcript of testimony and summations in *U.S. v. Asaro*. News reports in the *Daily News* highlighted Asaro's exasperation and comments about the testimony.

Chapter Twenty-two, "Free!"

See trial transcript of verdict in *U.S. v. Asaro*. The author was also present in the courtroom and outside the courthouse when the verdict of acquittal was taken. The scene outside the courthouse and news reports from the day of the acquittal are also found at www.youtube. com.

BIBLIOGRAPHY

Books

Blumenthal, Ralph. *The Last Days of the Sicilians: At War with The Mafia—The FBI Assault on The Pizza Connection.* New York: Times Books, 1988.

Bonavolonta, Jules, and Brian Duffy. *The Good Guys: How We Turned the FBI 'Round—and Finally Broke the Mob.* New York: Simon & Schuster, 1996.

Carlo, Philip. *Gaspipe: Confessions of a Mafia Boss.* New York: Harper, 2009.

DeStefano, Anthony. *Gangland New York: The Faces and Places of Mob History.* Guilford, Conn.: Lyons Press, 2015.

———. *King of The Godfathers: "Big Joey" Massino and the Fall of The Bonanno Crime Family.* New York: Citadel Press, 2006.

Hill, Henry. *A Goodfellas Guide to New York: Your Personal Tour Through the Mob's Notorious Haunts, Hair-Raising Crime Scenes, and Infamous Hot Spots.* New York: Random House, 2003.

———, and Daniel Simone. *The Lufthansa Heist: Behind the Six-Million-Dollar Cash Haul That Shook the World.* Guilford, Conn: Lyons Press, 2015.

Lance, Peter. *Deal with the Devil: The FBI's Secret Thirty-Year Relationship with a Mafia Killer.* New York: HarperCollins, 2013.

Newton, Michael. *The Encyclopedia of Gangsters: A Worldwide Guide to Organized Crime.* New York: Thunder's Mouth, 2007.

Pileggi, Nicholas. *Wiseguy.* New York: Pocket Books. 1985.

Raab, Selwyn: *The Five Families: The Rise, Decline and Resurgence of America's Most Powerful Mafia Empires.* New York: Thomas Dunne Books, 2005.

Volkman, Ernest, and John Cummings. *The Heist: How a Gang Stole $8 Million at Kennedy Airport and Lived to Regret It.* Franklin Watts: New York, 1986.

Whalen, Kerry: *Inside The Lufthansa Hei$t: The FBI Lied,* e-book: New York, 2013.

Court Documents and Cases

James Burke v. Mann, 93-CV-5017, United States District Court for the Eastern District of New York.

People of The State of New York v. Vincent Asaro, et.al., Indictment 6007-94, Queens State Supreme Court.

People of The State of New York v. James Burke, Indictment 395-84, Brooklyn State Supreme Court.

U.S. v. Vincent Asaro, 14-CR-26, United States District Court for the Eastern District of New York.

U.S. v. Salvatore Santoro, et.al., 85-CR-100, United States District Court for the Eastern District of New York.

U.S. v. Paul Vario, 72-CR-424, United States District Court for the Eastern District of New York.

U.S. v. Paul Vario, 83-CR-289, United States District Court for the Eastern District of New York.

U.S. v. Louis Werner, 79-CR-89, United States District Court for the Eastern District of New York.

Government Publications

New York State Joint Legislative Committee on Crime, Its Cause, Control and Effect on Society. Report for 1970, September 1970.

Organized Crime Involvement in California Pornography Operations. California Department of Justice, Division of Law Enforcement. July, 1976.

Hearings Before the Permanent Subcommittee on Investigations of the Committee of Government Operations, Organized Crime: Stolen Securities, Part 1, Ninety-Second Congress, First Session. June 8–10 and 16, 1971.

Newspapers and Periodicals

Daily News (N.Y.)

Long Island Daily Press

Long Island Star Journal

Newsday (Long Island)

New York Magazine

New York Newsday

Newsweek

Rome Daily Sentinel (Rome, N.Y.)

The Brooklyn Daily Eagle

The Leader-Observer (Queens, N.Y.)

The New York Times

Time

Websites

www.biography.com

www.bop.gov

www.findagrave.com

www.fultonhistory.com

www.ganglandnews.com

www.infamousnewyork.com

www.loc.gov

www.nexis.com

www.usinflationcalculator.com

www.wikipedia.com

www.youtube.com

ACKNOWLEDGMENTS

For a book covering so many decades of organized crime history, I received a great deal of help from people I can acknowledge and some I can't publicly but who nevertheless have my gratitude. They know who they are.

I did attempt to interview Gaspare Valenti, the cousin who turned against Vincent Asaro and helped the FBI and federal prosecutors get the 2014 indictment that provided much of the material for this book. However, Valenti's attorney Scott Fenstermaker said his client wasn't going to talk unless he got paid, so that ended that discussion.

Vincent Asaro was a different story. He did want to talk with me, particularly about Massino and Valenti but for reasons that were never clear didn't feel he could do so. But one July evening I took a chance and drove out to Queens where he came to the door and gave me the courtesy of an impromptu interview at his home in Ozone Park. The story of that meeting is detailed in the Epilogue. He wanted nothing in return.

One person who gets a big thanks is Nicholas Pileggi. Over the several months I worked on this book, Nick proved helpful in many ways. It was his recommendation to take the story big, setting the scene with what the Mafia was like in New York City during the 1960s through the 1980s. This helped give the story a grander historical scope. His *Wiseguy* is cited in a number of places in *The Big Heist* and to my mind remains an iconic Mob story.

From the law-enforcement side, I received help in securing public records and trial exhibits from assistant U.S. attorneys Nicole Argentieri, Lindsay Gerdes, and their trial paralegal Teri Carby. At the NYPD, deputy commissioner Stephen Davis and Lt. Eugene Whyte of the public information office provided assistance and historical perspective. Former Brooklyn District Attorney Charles Hynes also provided me with perspective about the "Gold Bug" investigation. At Brooklyn federal court, Dennis LaSalle, courtroom deputy to Judge Allyne Ross, also helped in tracking down court exhibits, namely the whereabouts of the scale model of the Lufthansa terminal used in Asaro's trial.

The National Archives is a font of information for researchers, and in doing this book I used the organization's branch in Manhattan where Kevin Reilly helped me requisition many old federal criminal case files from archive repositories. Such files are national treasures of American legal history and the archives has very exacting standards for making sure the materials are used with care.

In terms of the criminal defense bar, Asaro's two trial attorneys Elizabeth Macedonio and Diane Ferrone were interviewed and provided much useful information. I also want to thank defense paralegal Sam Tureff, investigator Ron Dwyer, and James Macedonio, Elizabeth's son who worked as a paralegal.

Noted defense attorney Joel Winograd, one of those extremely knowledgeable lawyers with an encyclopedic memory about the history of organized crime, gets a special nod of thanks for regaling me with stories about Paul Vario and other characters in the history of La Cosa Nostra. Joel knows so much because, as a skillful attorney, he represented many reputed mobsters over the years. We had one of our interviews on the very day he appeared in court for the last time in 2016 before retiring as an active attorney, capping a career that began in 1967. Barry Levin and Steven Zissou, two defense attorneys I have known well over the years, also provided me with assistance.

Former Brooklyn federal prosecutor Edward McDonald left government service in 1989 and has gone on to a successful career as a defense attorney. But busy as he was, Ed would talk unceasingly about his investigation and prosecution of the early Lufthansa case with defendant Louis Werner as if it all happened yesterday.

I have often had the need as a journalist to speak with the Office of The Chief Medical Examiner in Manhattan and for this book had the assistance of Brad Adams and the office's chief spokesperson Julie Bolcer. Jerry Schmetterer, former spokesman for the Brooklyn District Attorney's Office under Hynes, also gets thanks.

Two retired law-enforcement officials provided help in telling the tale of the gang of Jimmy Burke and the Lufthansa Heist. One was retired FBI agent Steve Carbone, who was involved in the investigation of the heist and helped Ed McDonald put together the case against Louis Werner and tried to bring other suspects to justice. The other was Ed Vitty who, as a detective with the Port Authority of New York and New Jersey police, had investigated a number of people in Burke's crew and had many useful recollections.

In an effort to get information beyond Burke's criminal life, I sent letters to his daughter Catherine Burke and her husband, imprisoned reputed Bonanno crime-family member Anthony "Bruno" Indelicato. I never received a reply. I also sent email and telephone messages to his son Jesse but got no response.

Journalists whose work I relied upon in crafting this book include: Selim Agar, John Annesse, Jerry Capeci, Matt Chayes, Stephanie Clifford, John Cummings, Cy Egan, Kareem Fahim, William Federici, Chris Francescani, Martin Gottlieb, Robert Greene (*Newsday*), Pete Hamill, Edward Hershey, Edward Kirkman, Edward Kulik, Chau Lam, Leslie Maitland, Joseph Martin, John Marzulli, Owen Moritz, Alexandra K. Mosca, Nicholas Pileggi, Tom Renner, John Riley, Ray Sanchez, Corky Siemasko, Daniel Simone, Robin Topping, Ernest Volkmann.

Over at *Newsday*, I have to thank assistant managing editor Maryann Skinner who made the Newsday approval process for this book painless. My news editors Tim Drachlis and Monica Quintanilla helped me juggle my daily work load and the time off needed to produce the manuscript. Cathy Mahon, *Newsday*'s permissions coordinator, hunted down two photographs, which I was able to use.

My agent, Jill Marsal, gets special thanks for getting me through the negotiation process at a time when I was juggling two book proposals. Finally, I must thank my editor at Kensington, Gary Goldstein, for his perseverance in jumping on the project as soon as the verdict in the Asaro case was known. This had to be the fastest proposal I ever put together, and Gary made sure it resulted in this book, which is coming out in plenty of time for the thirty-ninth anniversary of the Lufthansa heist.

INDEX